BLACK and WHITE and BLUE

Adult Cinema from the Victorian Age to the VCR

Dave Thompson

ECW Press

Published by ECW PRESS
2120 Queen Street East, Suite 200, Toronto, Ontario, Canada M4E 1E2

LIBRARY AND ARCHIVES CANADA CATALOGUING IN PUBLICATION

Thompson, Dave, 1960 January 3–
Black and white and blue: adult cinema from the Victorian age to
the VCR/Dave Thompson.

Includes index.
ISBN 978-1-55022-791-8

1. Erotic films — History.   2. Sex in motion pictures — History.   I.Title.

PN1995.9.S45T56 2007   791.43'6538   C2007-902588-9

Developing editor: Jennifer Hale
Cover design: David Gee
Text design: Tania Craan
Typesetting: Gail Nina
Printed by Webcom

DISTRIBUTION

CANADA: Jaguar Book Group, 100 Armstrong Avenue, Georgetown, ON, L7G 5S4
UNITED STATES: Independent Publishers Group, 814 North Franklin Street,
Chicago, Illinois 60610

PRINTED AND BOUND IN CANADA

ECW PRESS
ecwpress.com

Table of Contents

To Ella.
Miss you, Princess.

And Snarkeyyowl,
the cat who got the beans.

Foreword

In Praise of The Dirty Picture House

By Chrissie Bentley

It is said that a stereotype is only truly offensive (and stereotypical) if it is true. In which case, memories of a certain Adults Only theater, in a medium-sized East Coast city in the early 1970s, are very offensive indeed.

Even from the outside, the building stood out like a dirty nail on a manicured hand, an off-white pile that was erected in the thirties as the latest in contemporary architecture and had neither been painted nor refurbished since then. Once it had been a proud and beautiful theater, but the mainstream movies had long ago stopped playing there.

Instead, a proprietor, who looked as seedy as his establishment, specialized in what the low-key marquee insisted were Continental and Scandinavian features, all of which starred the same blowsily made-up cartoon blonde, scantily clad and long since defaced beneath precisely the kind of graffiti you'd expect to find in such a place — ink-scrawled cocks and balls that assailed her from every direction, ribald commentaries that blossomed in speech bubbles and enough jets of Magic Markered semen to sink a battleship.

The place never closed. Early morning, late into the evening, and at any hour in between, one of two or three bored-looking youths would be seated in the ticket booth, and occasionally you'd see an actual customer shuffling in or out of the main door, and he'd be as clichéd as the establishment itself. He really would look furtive, he really would be wearing a raincoat and, nine times out of ten, he really would be wearing a flat cap, which he'd pull down over his eyes the moment he saw someone else on the street outside.

But there was one aspect of the experience that was not a stereotype. It was, in fact, so bizarre that even those of us who were aware of it were scarcely able to voice it out loud, for fear that the very act of open discussion might end the enchantment there and then. Every Thursday afternoon (but *only* Thursday afternoons), sometime before we turned out of class, the emergency exit at the back of the building would be mysteriously unbolted and would remain that way all evening.

The first few weeks after we discovered this magical portal, we four girls simply stood by the opening, squinting into the darkness on the other side, listening to the soundtrack that crackled off the screen: groans, gasps, cries and crescendos, all set to a kind of pulsing neo-rock music, played exclusively, it seemed, through a wah-wah pedal.

Occasionally a snatch of dialogue would emerge amid the grunting; occasionally the actual meaning of the words might be comprehended by one or other of us. So, when one of our number — I think it was Wanda — suggested we actually pass through the door and watch, instead of merely listening to the movies, it wasn't a difficult decision.

We were no strangers to sneaking into the movies for free. Every movie house in town had its weak point, be it a back door, a bathroom window or simply a turn-a-blind-eye commissioner, through which a stealthy form could slip and thrill to those quaintly X-rated flicks that no one at that time would ever have dreamed an impressionable teen should witness: *Straw Dogs*, *Soldier Blue*, *The Night Porter*, *The Exorcist*. If the marquee mandated patrons be twenty-one and over, we were in there, and it was astonishing just how discriminating we became, able within ten minutes or so of knowing whether the movie was worth watching (bush, blood, tits and terror) or if we should up and march out and do something interesting instead.

This experience was different, though. In through the out door, down a smokily unlit passageway and into an auditorium scarcely the size of a classroom, with a screen no bigger than a bedsheet. The room seemed darker than the usual theater and the audience more restless. Rustling sounds, mostly, interspersed with heavy breathing. "Someone," Lisa whispered in my ear, "is having a quiet jerk-off."

Only it wasn't so quiet. And it wasn't just some*one*. Judging from the rustling sounds, half the men in the room were at it.

A movie was already playing, a scratchy-looking black-and-white opus, whose plot — so far as we could distinguish one — was how far could a cock slide up a fat woman's asshole before it bumped tips with the one that was sliding down her throat? And that, we quickly learned, was one of the more erudite efforts. But to four girls who had only ever seen sex in a Hollywood production, where its camera work and angles give the scene its sensation, even the crudest coupling was fascinating stuff.

By the time they hit their late teens, most girls are at least theoretically aware of the mechanics of sex. They know where "it" is meant to go, they've heard of the other places it *can* go and they've already thought of one or two more where they'd like to think it could go. In an age where Internet porn, prime-time smut and cable-special in-between were utterly unimaginable, popular culture had already built sufficient hints and clues into its makeup that a well-developed imagination could join up most of the dots. And if there's one thing about a teenaged girl that is well-developed, it's her imagination.

What was taking place on that screen, however, went beyond anything we had ever thought up. The titles of the films themselves are, for the most part, long forgotten. So are their "plots." But the *impression* they left, the wonder they aroused, the excitement they provoked and the sheer sense of injustice they left behind — *why doesn't that ever happen to me?* — would remain long after we left the building that evening, through the never-ending week that followed, and probably well into adulthood.

Had I ever seen an erect penis before? Never. Had I ever watched a guy ejaculate? Never. Staring at the screen that first afternoon, I realized that everything — every single thing — I had ever read, heard, seen or been told about sex wasn't simply wrong, it was ridiculous. There was no romance here, no handholding and no eyes meeting across a darkened room while electricity flashed between their souls. It was hunger, it was greed, it was naked animal passion. It was cocks and cunts and juices and jizz. Love didn't even enter into it.

And it was quick. The main movie — *Deep Throat, Pamela Mann, Behind the Green Door, Misty Beethoven*, whatever — was "full-length" (an hour, maybe even ninety minutes) and there'd be plot and dialogue around the frenzied fucking. For me, though, the real meat was the supporting program, anything up to two hours' worth of shorts that could have been shot at any time since my granny was a girl and which made no attempt at being anything other than pure sexuality.

These shorts were rarely longer than nine or ten minutes. "That's because ten minutes is the length of the average jerk-off," disclosed Wanda, whose knowledge of such things was rarely questioned (alone among us, she had an older brother, you see). But they didn't need to be any longer than that, because there was more "action" crammed into one ten-minute dirty than you'd catch in a lifetime of watching Hollywood blockbusters.

I remembered reading a review of *Last Tango in Paris*, of how realistic the sex scenes were meant to be, and when I saw it, I agreed. They were realistic. But realistic isn't *real*, and no amount of fancy lighting will ever be a substitute for a close-up of a hard, thick dick slamming into a gaping wet pussy. So why even bother faking it? Especially when your audience could just walk down the road a few blocks and settle down to *Satan's Children*. I know that's what we did.

A black-and-white 1960s feature that was probably the theater owner's best shot at grasping the coattails of the post-*Exorcist* boom in supernatural chillers, *Satan's Children* was typical (I have since learned) of an entire school of British stag. But the girls were pretty, the action was astounding and, as the final feature of a dozen or so otherwise mundane oldies, it was the best advertisement Satanism could ever hope for.

It was also the last movie we ever saw at that shabby old movie house with the mysteriously unlocked door. The last truly great one, anyway. Other people learned the secret of that rear entranceway, including some who might otherwise have paid for their membership, and others who didn't believe such establishments had any right to exist in the first place.

One balmy Thursday the following spring, we arrived at the back door, at the same time as always, to find two uniformed policemen lurking in the shadows within.

We ran, they stayed, and the next time we passed by, the building was empty, the doors were chained, the marquee had been stripped bare. Only the cartoon blonde remained, and she'd had a poster slapped over her mouth. Even at our age, that seemed strangely symbolic.

Chrissie Bentley is the author of several dozen erotic short stories, published online by Ruthie's Place, Eroticstories.com and Literotica.com. Her first novella, What I Did on My Summer Vacation (*Mardi Gras Books*) *is now available.*

Introduction

Attempting to piece together the story of the stag movie can be compared to channel-surfing in a foreign hotel room. Books about the movies in general are almost as old as the movies themselves; books about erotic movies only marginally less so. The earliest volume in most collections to treat the subject, German author Curt Moreck's *Sittengeschichte des Kinos* (*History of Cinema Customs*), was published in 1926 and remains so highly regarded that its DNA can be traced in almost every subsequent history of the big screen ever printed.

But Moreck treats stag films in just one disdainful chapter, an approach echoed by the French-language publications by Ado Kyrou and Lo Duca that followed in the late 1950s and early 1960s. Neither is the English language any more forthcoming. With the barely deserved exception of a rash of exploitation paperbacks published in the late 1960s and early 1970s (*The Stag Film Report, Girls Who Do Stag Movies, Stag Films '69*), just one book — Al Di Lauro and Gerald Rabkin's *Dirty Movies: An Illustrated History of the Stag Film, 1915-1970* — can claim to offer an authoritative discussion of the field.

Prior to that, one needed to locate a single issue of *Playboy*, from November 1967, to learn anything on the subject, and the bare facts laid out by Part 17 of Arthur Knight and Hollis Alpert's mammoth serialized article *The History of Sex in Cinema* remain largely the same today as they were back then.

With but a handful of exceptions from the late 1960s (by which time the landscape had so shifted that stags already seemed old-fashioned), the people who made these films left no footprints. We do not know the names of the filmmakers nor, for the most part, of their stars or distributors. We do not know when or where the films were shot. We cannot even say with any certainty precisely who they were made for.

Inevitably, urban legend has filled in many of those gaps. Throughout the time I spent researching and writing this book, I lost count of the number of occasions upon which I was informed, in grandly disapproving tones, that my subject matter was synonymous with organized crime, a world in which hapless junkies, hookers and street people were coerced into acting out some other sicko's most degenerate fantasies for the price of a fix and, maybe, one less black eye than usual. And how did they know this?

"Oh, I read it somewhere."

Which they very likely did. Throughout the 1950s and early 1960s, an entire generation of pulp magazines grew up around a world of super sensationalized "true-life" adventures, with war, crime and sex at the top of the pile. Stags were a natural component of this universe, a seamless combination of two of those talismans (all but two American states, Illinois and North Carolina, declared it illegal to even own a stag film until 1968) and a faithful standby for those months when the editors ran out of harrowing escapes from piranha-filled Nazi death cages and the like. Plus, because nobody seemed to know who was making the films, nobody knew who *wasn't*.

Enter the sadistic crime boss and his nymphomaniac moll, and a white slave trade that journeyed directly from the heart of Middle America to a soiled mattress in a tenement slum. There, evil-eyed mobsters lurked behind scorching lights and the unblinking camera stared with pitiless evil, while syphilitic studs pounded their diseased seed into pure and innocent writhing flesh. Et cetera.

In fact, beyond the speculations of such publications, there is no evidence — written or otherwise — to suggest that organized crime was even aware of stag films prior to the late 1960s. The case for coercion is harder to prove or disprove, although the evidence of one's own eyes, watching the faces in the films, leads one to disagree with it, simply by turning one of the stag films' most publicized and, in this instance, accurate faults — the actors' absolute inability to act — on its head.

If they weren't taking part of their own free will, and enjoying every minute of it, you could read it in their eyes. Every other emotion, from ecstasy to impatience, from shock to shyness, is lit up like a neon sign. But one can count on two hands the number of films where fear, terror or dread can be registered. And why is that? Because stag films were made for stag audiences — loud and boisterous gatherings of predominantly (if not exclusively) male viewers, ordinary Joes who wanted to see ordinary people having ordinary sex. No kinky stuff, no whips and chains, no kids and no fear.

That promptly dismantles another popular misconception — that the stags subjected their stars to all manner of hideous sexual degradation. In fact, the vast majority of movies — certainly American ones — shot before those watershed late 1960s were almost homely in their convention.

Sex was generally between two people — one male, one female. Coitus was compulsory and oral sex was popular, but even here there were boundaries that make a mockery of the oft-heard complaint that women were the denigrated victims of a brutal male power trip.

Humor wasn't simply rife among many of the actors, it was contagious. A 1940s film, *The Director*, focuses on the making of a stag movie under the aegis of an astonishingly flamboyant director. Forever coaxing his cast to ever-greater lengths, he prances and cavorts across the screen, a display so hilarious that the woman is barely able to hold her costar's penis in her mouth, so heartily is she laughing. Doubtless the audience (minus mouthfuls) reacted in a similar fashion.

This innocence is, of course, comparative. A "dirty film" — that is, one that showed full penetration and orgasm — in 1916 would still be dirty in 2006, and the oldest stag film ever made could not be shown on network (or even cable) television today, no matter how tame it might seem when screened alongside the full-length epics of the last few years. In the world of erotic film, after all, it is not the content that has changed, but the presentation of that content. The human body remains the same as it ever was, and those souls who advocate an end to all forms of explicit sexuality would be as offended by the contents of the sex films of their great-grandfather's generation, as they are by the hottest new release.

Technical considerations notwithstanding, the stigma that surrounds stag films, then, is less a product of the films' own environment than a developing product of our own — one reason why these otherwise reviled little movies are, contrarily, much beloved by sociologists (and social historians — both street scenes and indoor sets capture a way of life that has long since vanished). More than any other medium, it is said in such circles, the stag film allows the inquiring mind to chart the evolution of our own cultural attitudes not only toward sex, but also toward one another.

Such ruminations are not an integral component of this book, beyond acknowledging astonishment at how stags can still inflame opinions — more so, even, than modern erotic movies. Wading through Internet discussions where such topics are raised, there is inevitably at least one thread discussing the genre's demeaning of women, and how such and such a film was designed solely to appeal to man's baser instincts. The problem with so much learned analysis of filmed erotica, however, is that there are as many opinions as there are sexual expressions, which suggests that most writers are either reflecting their own preferences or else attacking those that hang in stark opposition.

To cut away all the analysis and babble, let us agree that people enjoy looking at sex films for the same reason they enjoy looking at flowers or landscapes or cloud formations or precious stones. Because they find them appealing, because they are attractive, because there is a beauty in what they are witnessing that cannot be found elsewhere. And just as we do not analyze why people like to look at those other things, there is no need to analyze why people like to look at pictures of other people having sex.

Yes, there is a degree of avarice involved, jealousy perhaps, longing maybe. But do those same emotions not occur when one looks at an especially appealing museum exhibit? Or when a painter sets out to portray a sunset (for what is art, after all, if not an attempt to capture that which is otherwise ephemeral or at least immovable?) A man walking past a car showroom and gazing at the luxury he can never afford is experiencing the same basic emotional (and sometimes physical) sensations as if he was watching a sex film. The brain processes those sensations in a different manner to be sure, but if emotion could be bottled, the difference would be negligible.

Among the other topics this book will not tackle are the ever-shifting definitions of "obscenity" and "pornography," and the laws that governed those definitions, beyond an observation that censorship is rarely applied in anything approaching the commonsense manner that the majority of people would wish it to be. One needs only remember America Online's attempt to clean up its service in 1996 by creating a filter that would reject any "obscene" combination of letters from the system. Authors of spam e-mail got around this by adding a superfluous X or asterisk to the word in question. Residents of the English city of Scunthorpe, however, did not have that option.

Besides, how can you censor a film in which all but the opening few minutes (and not always that) could not legally be shown *un*censored in any conceivable public forum? In 1977, the New York cable show *Midnight Blue* attempted to air portions of a stag film, *The Personal Touch*, which purportedly starred Barbra Streisand. By the time the network's owners had finished masking the "objectionable" scenes, the movie was condensed to a single thin strip of indefinable movement on an otherwise blank, black screen.

If one thing can be said for certain about stag films, then, it is that, under any reasonable interpretation of the law as it stands (and not as we wish it was, or think it ought to be), they were unequivocal in their refusal to brush even the gray areas with which other erotic art forms coquettishly flirted. They were, by the standards of the day, shamelessly "obscene." They were, according to most popularly held definitions of the word, unerringly "pornographic" (or, at least, "flagitious," the term preferred by 1920s policy-makers). And, from the minute production began until the moment the movie ended, they were 100 percent illegal. In every conceivable arena, where the law ended, the stags began.

In 1921, Indiana politician Will H. Hays was selected to oversee the morality of the motion-picture industry, heading up the newly founded Motion Picture Producers and Distributors of America Inc. Effectively a heavily empowered watchdog, the Hays office essentially spent its first eight or nine years studying both the movie industry and its supposed (or potential) effect upon society at large, before drawing up a set of inviolable guidelines for the industry to follow. The results of this process would define the output of American cinema for the next fifty years:

Excessive and lustful kissing, lustful embraces, suggestive postures and gestures, are not to be shown.

Complete nudity is never permitted. This includes nudity in fact or in silhouette, or any lecherous or licentious notice thereof by any other character in the picture.

No picture shall be produced which will lower the moral standards of those who see it.

White slavery shall not be treated.

And so forth. A similar code for the stag-makers would have reversed those prohibitions altogether: Excessive and lustful kissing *must* be shown. Complete nudity is *always* permitted. *Every* picture should lower the viewer's moral standards. And white slavery is fine, especially if you can't think of anything else.

The Flesh That Flickers

The Babysitter

Stag films. Blue movies. Smokers. Beavers. Coochie reels. Dirty pictures. Between about 1900 and the late 1960s, if you wanted to see a film of other people having wild and uninhibited sex, those were the phrases you kept your ears open for, in the hope that sometime, somewhere, in the course of your normal day, you might over-hear somebody — a workmate, a chance acquaintance, a face in the bar or a man at the barbershop — mention that a few of the guys were getting together that night to watch a few.

The very mention of such things was loaded with a host of little triggers.

Men in masks and women in wigs — *The Three Masketeers*, as one 1930s movie punned appallingly. Fearful of being recognized by family or friends (which does make one wonder what sort of family and friends they had), the casts of these films frequently employed entire wardrobes full of disguises. Some donned a pair of sunglasses; others wore peculiar hats. Some went the Groucho Marx route, with spectacles, a false nose and mustache. Some picked up masquerade masks or even pulled ladies' stockings over their heads. And, in one memorable movie, the lovers — a woman at her ironing board, a middle-aged man who was as stiff as one — spend so much time trying to keep their camouflage in place, it's a wonder they accomplish anything else at all.

And black socks. Why did the men in these films so rarely take their socks off? And why were those socks so often black that their very mention quickly became another euphemism for a sexy film? Someone would tell you they were off to see some "black socks," and you knew they weren't talking about a baseball scandal.

The films were usually in black and white. And silent. A few hardy entrepreneurs toyed with color and sound, but it didn't really make a difference, any more than 3-D made a difference. The average onlookers were seldom searching for a master class in the latest movie techniques, and half of them didn't particularly care if the film was even in focus. Just so long as there was plenty of wriggling, oodles of close-ups and a lot of shots of moist, yielding flesh, the audience was happy. More than happy — it was boisterous, and often boastful as well, because there was always one guy in the room who'd done it all and was only too happy to tell everyone else about it. Very loudly.

It was a communal experience, after all — a room full of guys stoked on alcohol and adrenaline, the air thick with smoke and heavy with voices. Some people called the films "smokers," because that's what a lot of men did while they were watching them, until the fog was so all-pervading that the screen was barely visible. Others called them "stags," because that's where a lot of them were shown, at the no-holds-barred, men-only parties thrown to bid goodbye to a friend on the eve of his marriage.

But they could as easily have been called "frat films" or "dare-date films" or "retirement-bash movies" or even "auto-plant Christmas party entertainments," for any occasion that brought a group of guys (and sometimes girls) together was an excuse to hire in some fellow and his 8mm reels, and then hoot and holler all night long — or at least until you told the wife you'd be home.

And still we haven't touched upon all the names these little films have been known to travel under. "Blue movies," because that color has been associated with the loudly ribald and obnoxiously obscene ever since it was first hijacked from the New England Puritan lexicon, where it contrarily denoted rigid moral and religious observance.

"Beavers" and "coochie reels," because those words had slang connotations that could not be mistaken. In London in the 1940s the films were often referred to as "Charlie flicks," a term derived from the same ingenious double rhyming slang that gives us the English *Masterpiece Theatre*-esque insults "a right Charlie" and "a proper Berk." Charlie Smirk was a jockey who rode for the Berkshire Hunt. Smirk rhymes with Berk, and Hunt, of course, rhymes with coochie.

Whatever one chose to call them, viewing such movies was a rite of passage, a young apprentice's opportunity to prove to workmates that he knew which end of a woman was up, a college boy's chance to boast to his buddies about the gals back home who did all that and more.

But such get-togethers were more than simply meeting places for teenaged hormones and middle-aged testosterone. Today, when guys want to hang out together and shout and drink and act like kids, they order in a cable sports channel and do it at home. But what did they do in the years before cable, or if there wasn't a game being broadcast that night? They went out to where the other guys were — the bar, the Elks, the VA club, wherever. And when the talking ran out, or they just fancied a change — "Hey, how about we call up that feller with the films we had last Christmas and see if he'll put on another show for us?"

When Fred Flintstone hooked up with his Water Buffalo buddies, when Ralph Kramden and Ed Norton headed over to the Raccoons for the night, when the Moose moved together and the Oddfellows closed their doors, it wasn't all funny handshakes and secret whistles at the door. They had a lot of fun as well, which is why a conservative estimate claims that, by the 1950s, "one-third of all adult males over age nineteen were members"[1] of fraternal orders in America.

Neither is it any coincidence that, when the fraternal societies started to fade from everyday life, sometime around the late 1960s, the world in which their favorite films flourished commenced a similar decline. The forces that caused the end of one were much the same as those that killed another — expanding options, broader alternatives, competing attractions. Society was shifting, and its components shifted with it.

For the Elks and their ilk, that shift was the start of a long, slow and ultimately near-fatal decline, in prominence if not importance. For the stags, on the other hand, it was the signal for a complete rebirth, out of the clubhouse and, via the peep-show arcades, into the theaters, out of the gutter and into the mainstream.

I was sixteen when I first learned that such movies existed, although the discovery stirred little more than a vague curiosity in my mind. Only with the benefit of hindsight does it now seem a most serendipitous introduction.

It was 1976, summertime, and the London streets were just beginning to blaze to the sounds of the barely emergent punk rock. And just as stag movies, the often clumsy, frequently flawed, but never less than fearless clatterings of so many cinematic do-it-your-selfers, had once been proclaimed the very antithesis of everything that Hollywood held precious, so punk — equally amateurish, similarly sloppy — was swiftly lowered to a likewise leprous standing in the music business.

If ever sound and vision were born to be together, punk rock and stag movies were the happy couple. That's why Sex Pistols manager Malcolm McLaren's boutique on the King's Road in London's Chelsea district specialized in the fetish wear that, in turn, costumed a slew of late-1970s British sex movies. That's why many of the Pistols' earliest live shows took place in a Soho strip club. And that's why, when the Pistols came to make a movie (1979's *The Great Rock'n'Roll Swindle*), it co-starred Mary Millington, an actress who got her own cinematic start in a series of still-spectacular late-1960s English stags.

There were other points of linkage, both musical and sociological. Punk portrayed real life, as it was lived by real people. So, if one bypasses the one-dimensionality of their subject matter, did stag films. Punk was constructed around excitement, spontaneity, immediacy — if a song could not make its point in three minutes flat, it was dead. Stag films had around ten minutes, but the principle was the same.

Both were made, for the most part, by people with no more training and expertise than they could pick up from a library book. Punks, sniffed the serious musicians of the day, could barely play their instruments. Stag-makers, movie buffs still insist, scarcely knew one end of a camera from the other.

And they all reveled in a subterranean, almost subcultural outlaw status that so successfully defied polite society's attempts to rein them in that, today, punk rock is an integral part of the modern musical landscape, just as the erotic ("adult," in twenty-first-century terminology) film is the most profitable aspect of the modern movie business.

None of this was apparent at the time. Nor would it become so for some years to come. Rather, my introduction to the stag film, through the paradoxical auspices of the movie mainstream, remained the sum of my firsthand exposure for another two decades, not because I didn't seek out further information, but because I didn't even think to do so.

Director John Byrum's 1974 movie *Inserts* was my universe. At a time when movie sets were growing to absurdly behemothic proportions (burning skyscrapers, sinking liners, crumbling cities), *Inserts* reversed the trend by showing nothing more than the open-plan living room of a Hollywood hacienda, and then condensing that scenario even further by erecting its own miniature film set in one corner of the room. There, Boy Wonder (Richard Dreyfuss) — once a fabled silent-film director, but now a has-been hacked down by the arrival of the talkies — shoots stag movies with another fallen star, Harlene (Veronica Cartwright), and the up-and-coming Rex the Wonder Dog (Stephen Daves).

A visit from Boy Wonder's financier, an aspiring hamburger magnate named Big Mac (Bob Hoskins), ignites the movie. He has come to deliver the moviemakers' wages: cash for the boys and drugs for Harlene, who promptly overdoses and dies. Mac and Rex disappear to dispose of the body; Boy Wonder is left alone with Mac's girlfriend, Miss Cake (Jessica Harper), to contemplate the fate of the unfinished film. The main sequences were already in the can. All that remained to be shot were the inserts — the close-ups that distinguish the suggestion of sex from the full-bloodied actuality of it. And Miss Cake believes she can help.

Inserts wasn't the first movie to revolve around a stag film. *A Doppia Faccia (Double Face),* with Klaus Kinski, from 1969, and *Get Carter* two years later, with Michael Caine, both based their respective heroes' behavior around a glimpse of a familiar figure in a stag (Kinski's dead wife and Caine's missing niece respectively). But *Inserts* was the first to star two major American heartthrobs. *Inserts* was Dreyfuss's first motion picture since *American Graffiti,* while Harper was still the bewitching ingenue whose startling performance and startled-doe demeanor were the high spot of Brian De Palma's *Phantom of the Paradise.*

It was also one of those rare occasions when we Brits got to see something that the movie's domestic audience never did. At almost two hours in length, British prints of *Inserts* were some fifteen minutes longer than the heavily censored version released the previous year in the United States. So you knew it was going to be at least something approaching hot.

In truth, the film that Boy Wonder is shooting, a violent near-rape occasioned by Harlene laughing at the Wonder Dog's manhood, is scarcely typical of any period of American stag film. A number of movies did suggest the use of force, particularly during the 1940s and 1950s: *The Clown, Forced Entry,* the two-reel combination of *New Ways* and (the avowedly heterosexual) *Gay Times,* and others. There was even a lesbian gangster assault, captured in the 1930s-era *Love Affairs of Jane Winslow.*

But even the unequivocally titled *Rape,* a 1950s stag in which an escaped convict pounces upon a girl as she sits painting a landscape, loses its impact the moment it transpires that the woman is thoroughly enjoying herself. Boy Wonder's vision, however, did not allow for that eventuality. There would be no happy ending.

Neither is *Inserts'* characterization especially believable. For all the rumors, myths and urban legends that surround the involvement of "name" persona in these unnamed epics, only one example has ever been proven true, when B-movie legend Ed Wood turned his hand to anonymous hardcore in the late 1960s.

There were no Hollywood Boy Wonders in the story of stags, and no disgraced Griffiths showgirls, either. (Or, if there were, they have yet to be identified. Film historian H.C. Shelby suggests one of the women in the 1930s stag *Bare Interlude* was "quite probably . . . a professional actress during the early era of the Hollywood cinema,"[2] but he fails to explain why this should be, which means she equally probably wasn't.)

But *Inserts* rings true regardless. It is a film about obsession, insularity, desperation and, of course, sex — four terms that capture the essence of the stag film as well as any words can encapsulate a mood or an emotion.

Like the pioneering punk rockers of the mid-1970s, the majority of men and women who made stag films did not dream of fame, did not imagine that five minutes of frenzied fucking on a motel mattress was their passport to international superstardom. They did it because it was fun, because it was different, because it paid better than "real" work and because — without delving, unqualified, into the psychological swamps of exhibitionism — it scratched an itch that "nice people" would not even acknowledge existed.

Inserts celebrated all of this and, even today, it remains the most compelling study of stag *ethics* yet committed to screen. Not that it has much (if any) competition. Considering how many miles of documentary footage have been lavished upon every other aspect of movie history, and how closely linked they are to the modern world of adult entertainment, stags themselves remain outsiders, pariahs — the monstrous relative walled up in the attic. Film historians often speak of "orphans," movies that — through neglect, obscurity or simply bad luck — have been allowed to molder on uncaring shelves. Stag movies are the saddest orphans of all.

Why should this be?

Why is it that, again and again in the pages of movie history, the story of hardcore erotic film leaps almost unimpeded from Thomas Edison's *The Kiss* in 1896 to Russ Meyer's *The Immoral Mr. Teas* in 1959, yet neither feature anything even remotely approaching the vistas revealed by the average stag?

Why is it that, on the occasions stag films are mentioned in the course of such works, it is only so that they can be shrugged away with a haughty sniff?

And why is it, in an age in which the most insignificant piece of ancient footage is pored over by scholars, analyzed by experts, even memorialized by historical societies, the stag film is almost completely overlooked?

Writing in *The Moving Image* in 2005, Kentucky-based movie archivist Dwight Swanson recognized that, while "every general archival film collection of any significant size almost inevitably ends up with some pornographic films in its holdings, pornography, when it is kept, is often stashed away in dark recesses of collections, joked about, infrequently cataloged, and generally ignored."[3]

Swanson had been working at his own first archival job, with a historical society's photography collection, for almost two years before one of his colleagues apprised him of "a collection of hardcore pornographic pictures that was kept in a 'secret' folder in an obscure drawer in the stacks" — an all-too-common fate that not only skews the historic record, but is also a betrayal of "our roles as keepers of the totality of cinematic history."

Part of the reason is the sheer obscurity of the history and development of such films. In 1967, *Playboy* magazine noted that, "although everybody knows about stag films, nobody knows very much *about* stag films."[4]

Forty years later, that single sentence continues to encapsulate the subject, despite it representing a body of work that was produced consistently and copiously throughout the Western hemisphere (and beyond) for around seventy years, from the late nineteenth century until well inside the mid-twentieth. Even today, the life and times of the stag movie remains absorbed by an aura of such elusiveness that many studies would rather dismiss them out of hand than attempt to acknowledge how little is known of their story.

The situation is changing, though. In 2002 in Boston, the Association of Moving Image Archivists conference hosted its first ever "Dirty Movies" panel, in front of what author and historian Eric Schaefer described as "a standing-room-only audience . . . charged with a sense of both relief and excitement: relief that, finally, some of the dirty little secrets about moving image archives were coming out of cold storage."[5]

One cannot necessarily blame or even fault those earlier students' disdain. One does, however, object to the inaccuracies and generalizations that, by virtue of their authoritative tone, have become the accepted mantra of almost every subsequent author who has had cause to mention stags somewhere within his ruminations.

Lo Duc's *L'Érotisme au Cinéma* (*Eroticism in the Cinema*), one of the classic works on erotic European cinema, dismisses "*le film pornographique*" as "subjective eroticism, addressing itself to only a specialist plurality of perversions: fustigation for the sadists, sodomy for the homosexual,"[6] and so on.

The Greek-born French director and critic Ado Kyrou condemned the films: "they are not movies, but badly made documentaries and tedious surgical films."[7] Kenneth Turan and Stephen F. Zito, authors of the 1974 study *Sinema: American Pornographic Films and the People Who Make Them*, dismiss stags as "cheap stuff, made in someone's garage for a total cash outlay of $27.50," and shudder at the absolute dreariness of watching "the random copulations of two bored people." Stag movies, they declare, have no place in the world of erotic cinema. "[They] had no influence on the form or content of films for general release until the mid-1960s."[8]

Martin A. Grove and William S. Ruben, authors of 1971's *The Celluloid Love Feast*, agree: "The stags were usually pretty terrible. They did show intercourse, but they were so badly produced that viewers could easily wind up half-blind from looking! Stag films were over-exposed, badly edited, terribly lighted and silent. The actors and actresses were unbelievably inept, and the directors were anonymous. If you ever saw a stag movie, you won't have to ask why!"[9]

More damning still is the treatment meted out to stags by Legs McNeil and Jennifer Osborne's *The Other Hollywood: The*

Uncensored Oral History of the Porn Film Industry, probably the single most important account of the modern erotic movie trade currently in print. Stags do not even feature in the treatment, as the authors instead trace their subject's lineage no further back (or afield) than the nudist films and nudie-cuties of the 1950s and 1960s.

To these authors and authorities, and to so many other students of the erotic genre, the history of erotic film is told through the story of the mainstream studios, big and small, that spent cinema's infancy dodging the legal bullets fired by the authorities, and the self-censorial etiquettes laid down in Hollywood itself.

The development of celluloid sex is charted by the glimpse of nipple that brightened D.W. Griffith's *The Sorrows of Satan* (1926), Claudette Colbert's milky bath in *The Sign of the Cross* (1932), Cary Grant and Ingrid Bergman's bedroom scene in *Notorious* (1946), and so forth. Other accounts journey from the 1960s sexploitation flicks of David Friedman to the European art films that tossed nudity around like discarded underclothes; from the artful erotica of *Don't Look Now* and *Last Tango in Paris* to the garish grind-house shockers that made B-movies look artful; and so on back through the years, until they reach the pioneering flickers of Thomas Edison and the Lumière Brothers. Stag films simply don't enter into the equation.

Many of the criticisms leveled at stag films are true. They *are* inept, they *are* clumsy, they *are* absurdly amateurish and riddled with flaws. They *are* cheap. The length of a stag was dictated wholly by the length of the film reel it was being shot on, a limitation that very early on tied the genre to the ten-or-so-minute mark.

The typical stag can no more be compared to a "professional" film than Grandma Moses can be compared to Michelangelo (or the Sex Pistols to *Sgt. Pepper*). But that, as admirers of Grandma Moses (and the Sex Pistols) will know, is what makes them so important.

Unfettered by ambition, uncluttered by any boundaries beyond those that the filmmaker personally imposed, and certainly untainted by such notions as box office or commercial potential, stag films represent the first (and possibly sole) branch of the motion-picture industry that can be described as truly free; made by independent filmmakers in every sense of the phrase.

There were no rewards for the stag man. Even the most obscure experimental movie director can dream that his vision might one day reach a larger audience, if only to shock and horrify them. Even the tawdriest less-than-B-movie director could hope that someone might recognize his untapped potential and pay his way to Hollywood. But the stag-maker had no ambition beyond making his movie and collecting his dough; had no dreams of stardom or notoriety pinned to the coattails of his latest opus; would, in any case, have been horrified if he heard someone praise his technique or his use of subtle lighting. For, if anyone was able to notice those things, it meant they weren't watching what was actually taking place on the screen, which meant, in turn, that the movie was a failure.

Stag films are the cinema's folk art, if one halts that discipline's development sometime short of the point when the nouveau bohemians cottoned on to its appeal and every boutique in the land started selling it. Utterly unselfconscious, stag films were punk rock in its purest sense, films that were made not for the plaudits, not for the money and certainly not for the fame.

They were made because they could be made, and the only thing they had in common with the rest of the movie industry — "real films," as Jessica Harper calls them in *Inserts* — is that their creators believed they knew precisely what their audience required. And, unlike most of their peers, they were correct.

Dance the Coochee Coochee

The Goat

The title board, *A Les Culs d'Or* (*At the Golden Bottom*), dissolves to a view of a country inn, its white plaster walls weather-beaten and stained. A portly, middle-aged and waxed-mustachioed musketeer, clad in all the finery one would expect from that noble profession, stands outside, knocking on the door and hammering on an outdoor table. He has traveled far and is in need of sustenance.

The innkeeper, however, has no food. But, unwilling to disappoint so distinguished a customer, he instead ushers the visitor to a seat, then hastens to where one of his staff, a pretty, plump young girl, is cleaning glasses. They exchange some words, then she approaches their guest, leads him to another table, far more secluded than the first, pours him a drink and informs him what is really on the menu — herself.

With every scene ushered in by one more in a dizzying panoply of excruciating puns, each allying some form of physical intimacy with a foodstuff, the cavalier samples each "dish" in turn: the seafood *la crevette*, as he extracts one finger from between her legs and tastes it; *asperges en branches* (an asparagus dish) as he removes his own pants; *saucisse* (sausage), *moule* (mussel), the chicken and mushroom hors d'oeuvre *bouchées à la reine*; and so on, until the cavalier's climax marks the end of the first course, and the innkeeper serves up the dessert, a second naked girl, cross-legged on a serving platter. The trio fall upon one another with gusto, *sandwich à la gousse*, and there the reel — and the film — concludes.

A Les Culs d'Or is the oldest hardcore erotic film known to exist. It was shot in France in 1908 and, while it scarcely differs from any of the hundreds upon thousands of similarly minded movies that would be shot around the world over the next half-century-plus, this spry centurion must be applauded, not only for its survival, but also for its almost academic adhesion to every convention its genre demanded.

All the key ingredients are in place: a hungry man, a willing woman, and an eagerness to experiment in areas that other, watching, men might have experienced only in their fantasies.

Other elements, such as a storyline, a sense of humor and the unspoken understanding that audiences were sophisticated enough to appreciate both, would become less essential as time passed and were eventually deleted from the vast majority of scenarios. Nevertheless, a stag film shot in the 1900s would be instantly recognizable to the viewer of sixty years hence, and it is up to the individual to decide what that says for the medium itself.

Many commentators have complained that the genre was stagnant from the outset. Others prefer to think it found perfection from the first, and if it ain't broke, don't fix it. And others don't care either way. They just enjoy watching the things.

Regardless, the resultant corpus represents the single most important archive of twentieth-century sexuality bar none, the only major caveat being the fact that just a fraction of this archive exists today.

It has been estimated that no more than 1,500 to 1,700 genuine stag movies — that is, hardcore erotic movies shot prior to the late 1960s — are still in existence, although that figure applies only to the American contribution to the genre. Argentina, Brazil, Cuba, France, Germany, Great Britain, Hungary, Mexico, the Scandinavian nations and Australia all possessed very active sex-film industries at one time or another, and they were simply the leading producers. Other nations turned out smaller quantities, until it seems unlikely that there was any developed (or developing) nation that did not, at some point during the first half of the twentieth century, produce at least a handful of stag films. But their catalogs, too, have been destroyed, by the ravages of time, by expediency, by law and by simple decay.

It is only in recent years that society has become concerned with preserving every possible facet of its entertainment past, no matter how worthless or sordid it may once have seemed. As late as the 1970s, the major studios and networks parsimoniously wiped television shows and musical recordings immediately following broadcast, so that the tapes could be reused. Likewise, old movies were thrown into storage facilities that might as well have been graveyards once the films' usefulness (as in profitability) was perceived to be over. Nobody foresaw a time when audiences might again clamor to see a sitcom that had gone off the boil three seasons before; nobody could conceive of such windfalls as the home video market or DVD boxed sets. And if that is how the giants of the entertainment industry treated their heritage, what could one expect from the minnows?

In the decades prior to the emergence of the VHS tape as a saleable, rentable commodity in the early 1980s, a film — any film, erotic or otherwise — would circulate until its audience had had enough, and then it would be discarded. Beyond the output of the Hollywood majors (and not always then), few films were duplicated in any appreciable quantities, and many existed in mere handfuls, only a fraction of which would have survived intact.

Erotica, in particular, suffered. Favorite scenes would be surreptitiously cut out by unscrupulous hands; beer would be spilled, frames would be scratched; simple wear and tear would take its toll. Some prints, the lucky ones, disappeared into private collections. Others, however, might be confiscated by the law, and then destroyed once their value as evidence had been met; others still would simply be thrown away. The remainder would be left on a shelf, or lost in the attic, to either rot into oblivion or go out in one last literal blaze of glory.

The earliest films were shot on highly perishable and highly flammable nitrate stock. Even after cellulose "safety film" was introduced in 1912, simple economics ensured that most shoestring operatives continued working with the earlier, cheaper stock. One still hears today of precious one-of-a-kind reels from the infancy of moviemaking undergoing spontaneous combustion, despite all the conservation techniques the modern world can throw at the problem. In earlier decades, with neither scientific technology nor human inclination to safeguard these fragile fragments, the carnage was horrific.

The most commonly circulating print of *A Les Culs d'Or* bears testament to another fate that awaited many movies. No matter when they were created, few retained their "original" title throughout all the years they were circulated. Enterprising exhibitors not only retitled old films in the hopes of convincing an audience that they were seeing something new, some spliced scenes from other films into the action. Prints of *A Free Ride*, the best known of all American stag movies, exist under the titles *A Grass Sandwich*, *Pee for Two* and *The Roaring Twenties*, as subsequent exhibitors either repaired or retooled earlier prints.

The goal was not always outright deception. The first few inches of a film reel are incredibly fragile, easily broken or damaged, and frequently required repair. Opening sequences, including the title boards, were especially prone to loss, and could only be fully repaired if the exhibitor remembered (or even knew) the film's original title in the first place. If he didn't, he'd come up with another. *A Les Culs d'Or* was long ago retitled *Mousquetaire au Restaurante* (*Musketeer at the Restaurant*), and it is under this title that it appears in many filmographies, with an approximate date in the late 1920s. It was an ignominious fate for so historic a movie, but at least it remains available. One cannot even imagine how many other stags, equally entertaining, equally well-made, have been lost forever.

Certainly that was the fate awaiting another of the movies known to have existed at the same time as *A Les Culs d'Or*. Also a French production, *Le Voyeur* (*The Voyeur*) was shot, according to movie historian Lo Duca, a year earlier, in 1907, and one can safely presume from its title that at least a measure of its thrill derived from a clandestine viewing of another couple's less-than-surreptitious lovemaking — in a park, perhaps, or some similar public space.

One is also safe to assume that, in the spirit of smoke and fire, where there were two stag movies, there were plenty more as well. History, unfortunately, has not recorded the names of those others, but one thing is certain: no sooner had the motion-picture camera been perfected than somebody was making motion pictures with it; and, if nudity and sexuality were not among the very first things to pass through the lens, then that *would* be a first — the first time in the history of the creative arts that erotic imagery has not sensed the possibilities that a new technology offers, long before most people have heard of the technology itself.

The early history of the motion pictures, traced through the endeavors of such pioneers as Eadweard Muybridge, Thomas Edison and the brothers Lumière, is alive with the potential for film to capture the most intimate aspects of human relations.

Muybridge, a researcher at the University of Pennsylvania during the early 1880s, utilized a series of still cameras, each triggered a moment or two after the last, to create the illusion of a moving picture. A sequence depicting a galloping horse is Muybridge's best-known creation, but when Edison began purchasing sequential-action photographic plates from him in the late 1880s, he was astonished to discover the man's researches went far beyond the trotting ponies and gamboling wildlife that other pioneers were so keen to depict.

From a selection of 733 plates, Edison discovered no less than 448 nudes or partial nudes — 205 men, 243 women, including cricketers, boxers, wrestlers and baseball players. There were large-breasted women going about their daily chores, nude women bathing together and an all but naked mother being handed a bouquet of flowers by her similarly unclothed daughter.

Edison himself was no prude. Charles Musser, professor of Film and American Studies at Yale, once described the inventor's ethic as "the more sex and violence the better,"[1] and surviving footage certainly supports that claim.

Edison's own moving-picture machine, the Kinetoscope, was unveiled in 1889. Similar in appearance to the peep-show machines of later renown, the original Kinetoscope was fed with short films of just fifteen seconds (fifty feet) in duration. Yet still it caused an immediate stir. When the first Kinetoscope Parlor opened in New York's Union Square on April 14, 1894, the curious queued around the block to drop a nickel into one of the ten available machines and watch the pictures come to life. Across its first day of business, the parlor grossed $155.70 from the ten machines — equivalent to 3,114 separate viewings.

Within months, further "Nickelodeons" — so named for the price of entry — had opened throughout the Northeast. Within a year, they were a nationwide phenomenon, and period diaries and manuscripts capture the excitement they aroused, abounding with references to queuing for exhibitions that offered no more remarkable a sight than a traveling vehicle, a shuffling crowd, a flying bird. If it moved, it would be filmed, and if it was filmed, people would flock to see it and pronounce it even better than watching the real thing. The power of technology.

By mid-1894, Edison was working flat out to keep up with the demand for product. Under the supervision of W.K.L. Dickson and William Heise (who actually made the films and designed the equipment — Edison himself was merely the money man), Edison's Black Maria studio in West Orange simply cranked out the product. The oldest surviving Edison film (*Record of a Sneeze*) dates only from January 1894, although that is more an indictment of the perishable stock, and a period disregard for preservation, than a comment on the studio's output.

Black Maria was more than a workshop, however. It also offered a secure environment wherein the team could work without fear of the prying eyes that might otherwise have objected to the extremes Edison went to in search of salable subjects for his films.

Boxing, for example, was illegal in the United States at that time. The Black Maria hosted a boxing match regardless, and the ensuing kinetograph was a massive hit. So were the studio's depictions of another forbidden sport, cockfighting. But Edison's most popular and, by extension, inflammatory efforts were his dancing girls.

In summer 1894, just three months after the Kinetoscope made its public debut, the New Jersey resort of Atlantic City became the scene of the first ever "bust" of an "obscene movie," when local authorities forcibly removed the kinetograph *Dolorita's Passion Dance* from circulation, on the grounds that the dancer's very movements served to inflame passion.

It certainly took the authorities some time to cotton on, however. By the time the prohibition was issued, *Dolorita's Passion Dance* was the most viewed kinetograph the parlor had ever hosted, while its notoriety was assured as early as May, when a Mr. W.D. Standifer of Butte, Montana, approached one of Edison's East Coast distributors to ask whether the company had any material that might appeal to the clientele of that rough 'n' ready copper mining town.

Back came the reply: "We are confident that the *Dolorita Passion Dance* would be as exciting as you desire. In fact, we will not show it in our parlor. You speak of the class of trade which want something of this character. We think this will certainly answer your purposes. A man in Buffalo has one of these films and informs us that he frequently has forty or fifty men waiting in line to see it."[2] Dolorita, incidentally, remained clothed throughout her performance.

Censorship moved in. Edison kinetographs featuring such late Victorian beauties as Anabelle Whitford and Amy Muller have only survived with thick black bars obscuring the dancer's upper and lower body.

Sometimes, the very titles and cast of these films were capable of raising societal hackles. *Fatima's Coochie Coochie Dance* (1896) not only boasted a knuckle-whiteningly bawdy title (then as now, "coochie" was common slang for vagina), it also starred an Egyptian belly dancer whose appearance at the 1893 Columbus Exposition in Chicago was still the subject of condemnation and complaint, three years on. Her performance, one observer fumed, "is not dancing. It is walking about the stage to alleged music with peculiar swaying and jerking of the body, such as tends to excite passion."[3]

There was a degree of truth to such denunciations. No matter that nobody had yet dared venture beyond the sight of women dancing. The authorities knew that no good could come of this latest licentiousness and reacted accordingly, with local bans and furious editorials. By the standards of the time, an age in which the merest glimpse of female flesh was considered sufficient to reduce any man to a slavering lust hound, these short films were profoundly arousing, a point that was succinctly made in *A Country Stud Horse*, a stag movie dating from the 1920s. Here we see a man avidly watching just such a film on an old-fashioned Mutoscope (a peep-show contemporary of the Kinetoscope in which a series of tumbling snapshots fulfilled the illusion of movement) and vigorously masturbating while he does so.

Whether in his own imagination, or in reality, the film he is watching heats up as he toils, at which point a prostitute (introduced as Mary by an accompanying caption) stops to "pick up some business. . . ."

This is not a far-fetched scenario, especially if we place the Mutoscope in an area where women such as Mary might well be touting for trade. Brothels and bawdy houses had a long tradition of employing dancers and actresses to entertain their waiting room; in the second half of the nineteenth century, the better-appointed establishments built up vast collections of erotic daguerreotypes and photographs, for the amusement (and, ultimately, stimulation) of their patrons.

To the entrepreneurs of the late nineteenth century, a moving picture show was simply the logical next step, all the more so since the novelty of the medium might well have enticed some clients to visit even more regularly than they otherwise would have, simply to watch the films — a phenomenon that contributed to the early growth and popularity of the movies. According to Charles Musser, "the Edison staff often filmed coochee coochee dancers. Significantly, few of these films were ever listed in Edison catalogues, and then only long after their production. This suggests that a body of Edison films were circulated more or less clandestinely."[4]

But official attempts to suppress the potential evils of the motion picture were in vain and, again in 1896, Edison shattered all societal taboos with the production of *The Kiss*.

Earlier in the year, actors May Irwin and John Rice staged the first ever live kiss on Broadway during the play *Widow Jones*, and that, fumed Chicago journalist Herbert Stone, was "beastly." How he raged, scant months later, when that same imagery became available for all to see on the silver screen: "Manifested to gargantuan proportions and repeated three times over, it is absolutely disgusting. Such things call for police interference."[5]

No matter that the kiss itself was little more than a series of pecks. From the moment it was first screened, on April 23 at Koster and Bials Music Hall in Herald Square, New York, *The Kiss* became the most talked-about sensation in show business, creating such excitement that Rice ignited a whole new career, offering kissing lessons and demonstrations on the vaudeville circuit. Herbert Stone was not alone in his opprobrium, however. The establishment howled down *The Kiss*; there was talk of banning or, at the very least, censoring it. But *The Kiss* survived, and soon it was not just kisses that the camera was catching.

At the same time Irwin and Rice were outraging decent America, elsewhere around the world, other pioneers were rushing to offer similar entertainment to their own domestic audiences. In 1896, just a year after the Parisian brothers Auguste and Louis Lumière perfected their cinematograph, French society was gripped by *Le Bain* (*The Bathroom*) in which actress Louise Willy stripped herself naked. In 1897, Georges Méliès produced *Après le Bal – le Tub* (*After The Ball – The Bath*), in which a similarly unclothed woman is tenderly bathed by her maid; and, in 1898, the German film pioneer Oskar Messter began marketing brief films of young ladies indulging in such pursuits as exercising, bathing and, again, undressing.

Filmmakers across the Western world took their lead from such movies; either that, or they dreamed up similar scenarios in their own right, and all grew more daring as the physical boundaries of film increased. By the turn of the century, single films of one or even two minutes in length were commonplace and, in 1900, Edison exercised these new parameters when he returned to *The Kiss*, this time to capture a veritable cornucopia of hugs, pecks and kisses.

The following year brought the infamous *Trapeze Disrobing Act*, in which a young woman indeed disrobes (at least as far as her foundation garments) while perched upon a trapeze, and throws her discarded clothes to an excited gentleman seated in a nearby theater box. And in 1903, Edison delivered *What Happened in the Tunnel*, in which a young lothario (G.M. Anderson, the future Bronco Billy) pounces upon the young lady who's been avoiding his attentions all journey long. The darkness of the tunnel precludes any glimpse of what then transpires, but when the train returns to daylight, the smile on the face of the lady's black maid (with whom she craftily switched seats), and the contrarily horrified look on Anderson's, says as much for the possibilities of the incident as it does for prevailing racial attitudes.

Countless films of this nature were produced during the first decade or so of film and, as audiences grew more sophisticated and the technology further advanced, so the moviemakers galloped to remain ahead of the public's expectations.

Popular vaudeville and music-hall acts were a popular attraction, although the absence of sound necessarily ensured it was the more visual performers (jugglers, fireeaters, magicians) that appealed. Rudimentary newsreels, recreating major stories of the age, began to appear, together with the first stabs at cinematic comedies, slapstick incidents that, depending upon the target audience, could very much err on the side of "cheeky," if the maker saw fit.

Making Love in a Hammock, Jack the Kisser, Old Man's Darling, Beware My Husband Comes, Parissiene's Bedtime. Like *What Happened in the Tunnel*, titles such as these undoubtedly promised a lot more than they delivered. For moviegoers, however, the thrill was no less powerful because of that. Again, we must recall an age of such innocence that tablecloths still touched the ground, so as to cover up the furniture's sinful legs, and even the lightest suggestion of forbidden fruit was the height of daring. But that age of comparative innocence was about to come to an end.

CHAPTER THREE

The Lure of the Secret Cinema

Suor Vaseline

The precise chronology of the commercial hardcore erotic film will never be pinned down. Carl Bennett, editor of the excellent Silent Era Web site, reflects that "finding reliable information on the erotic film productions of the silent era is problematic at best. Often the only information that passes down through the years is through word of mouth, since people did not take erotic productions seriously."[1]

Historian Curt Moreck traces the physical origins of the genre to turn-of-the-century France and the introduction of our old friend the Mutoscope. This was followed by the Stereoscope, a viewer that gave a similar impression of movement and whose most popular attraction was a monthly series of female nudes, *Le Stereo Nu*, which were sold for 1.50 francs apiece.

For the most part, however, the art of the moving nude had scarcely been perfected beyond those optical illusions that any half-decent artist of the age was able to create. The Mutoscope and Stereoscope were remarkable gadgets to be sure. But in terms of actual realism, they offered little more than any of the other tricks being sold on the street corners of the day. These included harmless-looking maps that revealed the form of copulating figures when folded and manipulated in a certain fashion, and "flick books," in which figures were drawn in slightly different poses on every successive page, and then viewed in action by flicking through the pages.

It took film to truly bring these imaginings to life. According to Ado Kyrou, when Shah Muzaffar-ed-Din of Persia became the first private individual ever to purchase a full movie setup for his personal use in 1900, the first thing he asked his cameraman to shoot was a couple having sex.

Nevertheless, filmmaking was not an easy pursuit to follow during the first decades of the twentieth century. Early movie cameras were cumbersome, heavy, hand-cranked affairs, and projectors were equally unwieldy. Users also had to be wary of the dangers inherent in the hobby from the outset — such as the explosive nature of the nitrate-based film stock.

It was also a very expensive pursuit. A complete professional-style setup was priced firmly out of reach of all but the wealthiest patrons, but even cheaper rigs were largely prohibitive, and that despite a number of manufacturers attempting to remedy the situation.

A turn-of-the-century German 35mm "home movie" setup was the first to combine camera and projector into one, lowering the price, but only adding to the size and weight of the actual device. Another innovation sought to cut down on film costs. Unveiled in 1895, the Englishman Birt Acres' Birtac camera was the first of several to utilize 17.5mm film (that is, half the width of the then-standard 35 mm.); it too served as a projector and could also print the films it shot.

Other devices launched during this period included the French company Reulos, Goudeau & Co.'s Mirograph, which employed a 21mm film, and Gaumont's 15mm Pocket-Chrono. There was the Kammatograph, an ingenious contraption that utilized circular glass plates, similar to the LP record, which fit 600 frames onto a twelve-inch disc. Or you could splurge on the Kinora, a machine whose pictures could then be assembled into reels, for use in a special viewer. Each of these innovations was trumpeted as the latest cost-cutting innovation, designed to bring the pleasures of filmmaking into the home, but they were still prohibitively expensive. Even the Birtac cost over $50, or around one month's pay for the average American worker.

Clearly, then, home-movie production was not a pursuit open to everybody, a restriction that quickly gave rise to the still-popular stereotype of the hobby being confined to the wealthy indolent alone.

It would be the 1920s before moviemaking became an affordable pursuit to the average consumer, one reason why films dating from earlier decades are so scarce. Another reason is the ready deterioration of the film stock. And a third is the simple fact that very few people shooting films for their own purposes would have dreamed of making even one extra copy, let alone multiple duplicates. The survival of any non-commercial film from this period, then, must certainly be ascribed to sheer good fortune, and uncommonly careful storage.

Then as now, most home movies were shot for viewing in the home alone, and this is doubtless true of many of the sexual adventures that may have been committed to film during these formative years. But not all of them, for there was one market that was more than ready for such titillating fare and that pounced upon it the moment the technology was available. Having rushed to snap up the movie-viewing machines of the day, the brothels of Western Europe, Latin America and the United States were now investing in on the means to make the movies themselves.

In the United States and Canada, logging camps and mining towns very early on provided a voracious environment wherein the moving picture would find an avid audience, and the more revealing, the better. And, no more than five or six years after Butte, Montana, was offered the delights of *Dolorita's Passion Dance*, the first movie camera arrived in another western mining town. Or, as an anonymous correspondent declared to me in an e-mail, "my grandfather used to make blue movies in Cripple Creek, Colorado, in the early 1900s."[2]

Around the same time as producer William Selig was restaging the Colorado landscape in the California desert for such silent classics as *A Lynching at Cripple Creek* and *The Hold-up of the Leadville Stage*, Cripple Creek itself boasted its own aspiring moviemaker.

A miner whose interest in photography allowed him to appropriate a movie camera from one of his bosses, this fast-thinking gentleman "was friendly with some of the girls that worked on Myers Avenue [the city's notorious red-light district], and he used to film them playing with each other. Then he'd put on shows for the other mine workers, who would then head for the bordellos to try and find the girls from the films."

Like so much of Cripple Creek's illustrious history, these films were lost long ago. But if one entrepreneur had the idea in that city, then it would certainly have been shared in others. Soon erotic cinema was flourishing in most major American cities. So were its opponents.

In November 1907, the City of Chicago introduced the country's first municipal censorship board, expressly to stem the explosive tide of lewdness and prurience perceived to be flooding out of the moving picture houses.

The following year, New York mayor George McClellan dealt with the same fears by physically closing down all of the city's movie houses, an iron fist that saw no need to differentiate between "clean" movies and "dirty" ones, and which was vindicated when McClellan's enforcers discovered theater after theater screening erotic films to their most select patrons, playing the movies on a screen positioned behind a false wall, into which a row of surreptitious peep holes had been drilled. No record has survived of precisely what these movies entailed, but it is unlikely, more than a decade after Dolorita shocked the boardwalk, that the customers were content with dancing girls alone.

The United States were not alone in their fascinations. Writer Tom Dewe Mathews has described how the first Edison camera ever to reach Brazilian shores, in the mid-1890s, was promptly press-ganged into erotic action, encouraged every step of the way by the absence of any legal prohibition against such enterprise.

28

Argentina, too, moved swiftly to the forefront of the excitement. Growing fat on its booming meat and wheat export industry, and benefiting from a boom in western European immigration that raised the standard of living to unparalleled heights, Argentina entered the twentieth century as one of the most prosperous and cultivated nations on earth.

The first Kinetoscope was up and running in Buenos Aires before the end of 1894 and, by 1896, at least one local enthusiast was experimenting with his own variation on the technology. The following year, an ex-pat Frenchman living in Argentina imported the country's first camera and shot *La Bandera Argentina* (*The Argentine Flag*), a short motion picture of, indeed, the flying of the Argentinean flag. By 1898, Dr. Alejandro Posadas, a surgeon in Buenos Aires, was filming his own operations and, in 1900, the first movie theaters were screening filmed news reports.

Argentinean movie historian Ariel Testori has suggested that such well-known institutions as Pathé and Gaumont, pioneers of the cinematograph, were responsible for introducing erotic moviemaking to the country, taking advantage of its distance from European laws and moralities to hire local residents to shoot erotic films for export elsewhere.

As in so many other distant lands, Argentina's expat community was certainly hallmarked by its disregard for the prohibitions of their homelands, and lived life as a near-perpetual party. The Argentinean stag trade was thus overseen by a German immigrant whose European contacts enabled the local product to travel as far afield as Russia, France, the Balkan states, South Africa, Germany and England. This same unnamed merchant should also be remembered for devising a most ingenious courier system. According to German historian Curt Moreck, "in order to remain undetected by the customs authorities, the films often made their way hidden in the underwear of international prostitutes."[3]

The recipients of these exquisitely smuggled gems paid heavily for the privilege, although they were all but guaranteed a near unique return for their riches. Individual movies were made to order; a customer communicated his wishes, and an appropriate movie would be forthcoming. Even allowing for a sudden run on one particular theme, however, the customer base was so small that Moreck estimates no more than five prints were ever taken from any one negative, while the time and expense involved in shuttling movies across the oceans was such that any monopoly Argentina might once have claimed was soon to be cut down by local, European-based suppliers.

In Italy, though the shadow of papal disapproval hung over almost any remotely enjoyable experience, an erotic-film industry was in place long before the production of the country's oldest surviving stag film, *Suor Vaseline (Sister Vaseline)* — shot around 1913 and devoted to the transgressions of a nun, a friar and a bisexual peasant named Andre.

Hungary hosted a thriving market and is generally believed to have produced her first stags around 1910, while an indication of the sheer profit involved can be gauged from a report from London, around the same time, when a movie entitled *The Baking Fish* "excited [such] a secret sensation . . . [that when] shown in clubs and closed societies, it brought in 153,000 German Marks"[4] — more than $36,420, at the then-current exchange rate.

France and Germany were the most active stag producers of the early 1900s, the former by virtue of its long-established position at the head of world carnality; the latter as a result of the erotic blossoming fed, on the one hand, by the proximity of Sigmund Freud's warnings against sexual repression, and, on the other, by a burgeoning fascination with sundry so-called mystical variants on the healthy living creed of eugenics.

German film historian Gertrude Koch has written that stag films were in "full bloom" in her homeland as early as 1904, while Moreck pinpoints Berlin and Dresden as the primary centers of production, particularly in those years before the local authorities truly comprehended the dangers that motion pictures presented: "The bloom time extended until 1908. There was no danger from surveillance, and no censorship difficulties to obstruct international traffic."[5]

Am Abend (In the Evening), a German production that has been dated to around 1910, blueprints what subsequently became one of the genre's most time-honored plot devices, the Peeping Tom who watches through a keyhole as a woman masturbates alone in her bedroom, then enters the room to have full sex.

German journalist Kurt Tucholski, a fervent supporter of the belief that "low" forms of entertainment should be granted as much coverage and appreciation as the higher arts, recalled several further titles and plots from this period in his account written for the Berlin theatrical magazine *Die Schaubühne* (*The Stage*) in September 1913.

The screening that Tucholski attended was packed, but silent as showtime approached: "No one spoke aloud. But then the wall became white . . . [and] it began. And everybody laughed. I laughed."[6] The audience had been expecting something "outrageous, excessive." Instead, they were treated to footage of a puppy and a kitten romping across the wall.

"Perhaps," Tucholski mused, "the exporter had included that, in order to deceive the police — who knows?" Whatever the reason, he felt sorely disappointed. "I had come in order to see something quite indecent." Instead, "the film rattled monotonously on without music, an uncanny and not very pleasant experience."

Finally, the main attraction got underway. *Szene im Harem* (*Scenes in the Harem*), a slow-moving effort in which a dancer strips naked for a watching sultan, was so dull that Tucholski instead found himself contemplating the distinctly un-harem-like set where the movie was shot. It reminded him, he said, of the tiny rented rooms available in Berlin's working-class Schlesisches Tor neighborhood — "the wallpaper pattern of the small room was completely like that, and also the curtains and the carpet."

One movie ended, the next began; first *Klostergeheimnisse* (*Monastery Secrets*), and then the girls-only *Anna's Nebenberuf* (*Anna's Other Occupation*). Finally the room began to heat up — audience members called out encouragement and comments at the screen, and Tucholski offers up the first recorded formal identification of a stag actress: "it is Emmy Raschke, laughing constantly as she wonders nervously what she has got herself into." (Unfortunately, Ms. Raschke appears to vanish from the historical record thereafter.)

So far, the movies had lasted just a matter of minutes. Many of the earliest stags, particularly those that dispensed with any kind of storyline, wrapped up within two or three minutes. *Die Frau des Haupmanns* (*The Wife of the Corporal*), however, was a lot longer, maybe as many as ten minutes and, judging from Tucholski's description, the military ménage could easily have been a dry run for the tabloid revelations of on-base wife-swapping that transfixed the American media some forty years later.

All told, Tucholski described perhaps an hour's worth of ribald entertainment, and all so "viceful" that, once the audience had vacated the screening room and passed into an adjoining restaurant, it was to discover that the landlord had recruited no less than twenty prostitutes to administer to their needs!

Tucholski called the venue where the screening took place a "secret cinema," one of an informal network of such establishments that spread not only across Germany, but throughout Europe and beyond.

They were well-named. Few secret cinemas operated from the same premises more than once. Like modern raves, their locations were fiercely guarded secrets until as close to screening time as possible. In Germany, details of upcoming events were entrusted to the same barbers and coffeehouse waiters who were already directing likely customers to the local brothels. In Moscow, enthusiasts passed around the information via cleverly disguised invitation maps, inscribed in pidgin French. In Cairo, where the majority of secret cinemas catered exclusively to American tourists, events were promoted by hotel staff and tour guides. Paris was riddled with such places, with admission prices as high as 100 francs.

Argentina also boasted its own circuit of secret cinemas, as revealed by Luxembourgian novelist Norbert Jacques, the future creator of Dr. Mabuse. Traveling the world, he arrived in Buenos Aires around 1909 and was exploring the tangle of industrial buildings, dockyards and tumbledown slums that comprised the riverside Barracas district, when he was accosted by a man in a small rowboat and invited, in a broad, but unmistakable lingua franca, to witness "cinematográfico, Nina, Deutsch, Francés, Englishman, amor, Schwäneräen-Cinematográfico."[7]

Jacques leaped aboard the boat and was transported to the mid-harbor Isla Maciel, where a huge arc light hung over a large hall and a sign read Cinematográfico Para Hombres Solo (Movies for Single Men). Policemen stood at the door, searching the patrons as they entered the building, confiscating knives, knuckle dusters and weaponry, and then the films began, a kaleidoscope of intercourse, fellatio, sodomy, coprophilia and lesbianism — and all displayed, Jacques realized, to drum up customers for the brothel next door. Interestingly, Jacques declared all the films to be of German origin.

Jacques was not the only future literary figure to experience the joys of Barracas, as playwright Eugene O'Neill revealed in spring 1914. That season, he wrote what he later described as his first play of any substance, the one-act *Bound East for Cardiff*.

Twenty-six at the time, O'Neill had already lived a very full life. Expelled from Princeton in 1907, he tried his hand at gold prospecting in Spanish Honduras, toured America as the assistant manager of a theatrical company, acted in vaudeville, joined the staff of a small-town newspaper and spent six months in a tuberculosis sanatorium. *Bound East for Cardiff*, however, drew on his experiences as a merchant seaman around 1910-11, during which period Argentina impressed herself very firmly on his memory.

Yank, mortally wounded in a fall, is reminding his buddy Driscoll of happier days. "D'yuh remember the time we had in Buenos Aires? The moving pictures in Barracas? Some class to them, d'yuh remember?"

"I do that," replies Driscoll, "and so does the piany player. He'll not be forgettin' the black eye I gave him in a hurry."

Later in life, O'Neill reflected on those moving pictures in even greater detail: "Those pictures were mighty rough stuff. Nothing was left to the imagination. Every form of perversity was enacted and, of course, the sailors flocked to them."[8]

New York City became the scene of America's first recorded bust of a secret cinema, on January 8, 1912. The police, reported the *New York Times* the following Friday, had been aware "for several months . . . that moving-picture shows of a questionable nature were being given, but evidence sufficient to justify an application for a bench warrant was not forthcoming. This industry, which has sprung into existence within a few months, furnishes amusement at so-called 'stags' and smokers given by private clubs or individuals to which admission is by 'invitation.' Owing to the fact that the[se] invitations . . . were limited to a select list, the police were powerless to get the needed evidence."[9]

This particular Monday evening, however, two detectives attached to the Sixth Inspection District "were sauntering along West 116th Street when they were accosted by a shabbily dressed man, who asked them if they wanted to see 'something rich.'

"'What is it?' queried one of the sleuths.

"'A ripe motion picture show — something good — hot stuff,' was the response.

"The detectives expressed their willingness to witness 'hot stuff' of any description, and were directed to the Lenox Casino [now the Malcolm Shabazz Mosque], at Lenox Avenue and 118th Street, a dance hall. . . ."

The local lockup was very busy that night.

For all the mystique with which time and history have imbibed the concept of the secret cinema, sharp operators were not necessarily above duping their own customers, by arranging screenings, collecting the entrance fee and then vanishing into the night, leaving behind a roomful of increasingly restive would-be viewers. Indeed, so effective was this particular scam that, into the 1960s, a similar trick was still being played out on the streets of London's Soho district.

Armed with nothing spicier than a pocketful of explicit postcards and standing in front of a doorway, such characters would latch on to passersby, usually obvious tourists and out-of-towners, and invite them inside to watch a certain kind of movie — the postcards would suggest the nature of the film itself, while the salesman's patter would fill in any gaps.

A sum of money would change hands, and the visitor would be ushered into the building and directed to wait in an upstairs room — the higher up the better. The salesman would then move on to the next derelict or abandoned building and await the next sucker, while the last one could sit there till doomsday for all the good it would do him. This so-called blue film racket eventually grew so prevalent that, in June 1966, with London expecting a flood of visitors for the World Cup soccer competition, the police all but shut down Soho entirely. But it was up and running regardless, and was still a thriving business well into the late 1970s.

In Praise of Unnatural Acts

A Free Ride

The first golden age of European stag films ended in 1914, with the outbreak of the Great War. One by one, as more nations were drawn into the conflict, and more and more young men were lured onto the vast killing fields of the western front, so all attempts to echo normal, prewar life and recreation slipped away.

Across the ocean, of course, life continued as before. The United States did not enter into the war until 1917; prior to that, the country simply watched from afar as Europe consumed itself, and brightly stepped into any business breaches that the continent's preoccupation had suddenly rendered vacant.

It is, therefore, no coincidence that what is generally regarded as the oldest American stag movie in existence, *A Free Ride*, has been dated (by the Kinsey Institute) to 1915, less than a year after the cameras went out in Berlin, Paris, London and Budapest. American businessmen had already assumed Europe's prewar preeminence in such disparate worlds as fashion, confectionary and legitimate film. Why not dirty movies as well?

In fact, this scenario is extremely misleading. Although European imports certainly constituted a sizable proportion of the films available in the States, America was no slower in both manufacturing and marketing erotic movies than any other nation; it was just a lot less careful about preserving them. *A Free Ride* might well be the oldest surviving American stag movie, but, as the oral evidence from Cripple Creek and New York makes clear, it was by no means the first.

Neither is it at all certain that the movie was even shot in that year — or even that decade. Although the vast majority of printed sources continue to date *A Free Ride* to 1915, historian Kevin Brownlow believes (and other specialists concur) that "judging by the fashions, [it] was actually made around 1923."[1]

That said, the most frequently cited evidence for this later date, the curly blonde Mary Pickford wig sported by one of the two women in the film, is itself somewhat misleading. The young Pickford's characteristic hairstyle was attracting attention from the very dawn of her career, and a 1914 *Photoplay* interview finds her complaining how "tired" she was of "letters asking me if I wore a wig, or if part of my hair was mine, or if it was naturally curly, or if I had to curl it on an iron."

Hairdressers labored to recreate Pickford's tresses on their customers from the moment the actress first appeared on the screen, while actual Pickford wigs hit the market sometime after 1918, when they were launched by New York's Follender Wig Company. They remained in vogue at least until the mid-1920s — former first lady Nancy Reagan, born in 1921, recalled a Pickford wig among her most treasured childhood possessions.

Besides, who can say for certain that the girl in *A Free Ride* is actually wearing a wig?

In many respects, the precise age of *A Free Ride* is irrelevant. If it is not the *earliest* surviving American stag, it is certainly one of them, while the standards it set for production and direction offer a remarkable one-stop distillation of twentieth-century U.S. erotica, from the coarse humor of the obtuse opening credits ("Directed by A. Wise Guy; photographed by Will B. Hard; titles by Will She"), through to the action itself.

It is this professionalism that led Buffalo State University professor Frank A. Hoffman to point out that "the relative smoothness of production shows clearly that experiments in the genre must have been carried out for some years before that time."[2]

It also gave rise to some remarkably inventive theories regarding the film's origin, including one that describes it ("unfairly," writes Brownlow) as one of D.W. Griffith's early works. It isn't, although the notion is extraordinarily entertaining. From *The Birth of a Nation* to the birth of an industry, in two easy steps. (The notoriety of *A Free Ride* can still be felt today — in 2004, it was even remade by New York director Lisa Oppenheim. Incredibly, the film features no actors. In her version, it is the landscape and trees that converse and cavort!)

Filmed entirely out of doors, *A Free Ride* is set, according to its opening caption, "in the wide open spaces, where men are men and girls will be girls, [and] the hills are full of romance and adventure." A motorist picks up two female hitchhikers and, having established their character via a few crude advances, he excuses himself while he goes behind a tree to urinate. The girls follow to watch, and are clearly excited by what they see; then, when he returns, they venture into the woods for the same purpose, while he spies on them. One girl then accompanies the man into the woods for sex, with the second girl joining them a little later. Then all three go back to the car and, in just a shade under nine minutes, the viewer will have enjoyed a camera's-eye view of coitus, fellatio, troilism and urophilia.

If the film's makers disguised their true identities in the credits, its cast is equally mysterious. Although several silent film stars have, over the decades, been associated with early stag films, the trio that perform so gallantly in *A Free Ride* bear not even a passing resemblance to any recognizable star of the era, and they go to great lengths to ensure that remains the case. The man is clad in both a hat and an outsized false mustache; and when, a minute or so before the movie's end, the latter falls away, he raises one arm to hide his face, while the offending fur is reattached. So, no clues there, either.

So, who were they?

A common thread that runs through many casual histories of

early erotic film insists that the actors were drawn from the lowest end of the social spectrum — the homeless, the mentally ill, drug addicts, prostitutes, petty criminals and the like. But there is little documentary evidence for this claim. Indeed, there is much to suggest that the opposite was more likely, with the sheer novelty of the movies undoubtedly playing its part in the lure.

For a smooth-talking operator looking to cast his latest erotic opus, it might take nothing more than a few calming words, a few more of encouragement, a couple of drinks and a handful of lies ("I know for a fact that the guys over at MGM love my work"), and he'd get his leading lady. Particularly in those early decades when *everything* about the movies was magical, who needed whores and harridans when almost every girl (and a lot of guys) would do anything to appear on the silver screen? In fact, a French film dating from the 1920s offers a revealing glimpse into just how unsuspecting many people were when it came to photography.

Amanda et Jacki follows a young beauty to a portrait studio, where the photographer is clearly taking great pains to capture her charms as naturally as possible. Scurrying behind the camera, he studies her through the lens for a moment, and then reemerges to suggest she remove an item of clothing. First to go is her long dress. Her slip follows, then her corset, everything, in fact, but her hat . . . Oh no, there goes the hat as well, to be laid tastefully across her naked lap. And though she certainly looks surprised, she merely smiles because, after all, he's the professional. He knows what he's doing. Only when she sees the finished picture does she smell a rat: it's a head-and-shoulders shot.

Many of America's earliest stag stars were undoubtedly equally innocent. However, the rise of the American stag film did coincide almost seamlessly with the fall of another national institution, the officially tolerated (if not altogether sanctioned) red-light districts that had, since the end of the Civil War, been a feature of almost every major city in the land.

The dismantling of the brothels was a process that had begun in 1910, with the passage of the Mann — or White-Slave Traffic — Act, legislating against the interstate and international transport of women for immoral purposes. Over the next five years, virtually every state in the union had passed laws expressly aimed at prohibiting the keeping of brothels, or otherwise profiting from the earnings of prostitutes.

One of the first casualties of this new wind was also among the most famous. Chicago's Custom House Levee had, after all, entertained thousands of visitors during the six-month World's Fair in 1893. According to the reformist W.T. Stead, author of the tract *If Christ Came to Chicago*, this one district was home to no fewer than forty-six saloons, thirty-seven brothels, eleven pawnbrokers and an opium den. For many years, the area was so lawless that the police did not even enter it. By the end of 1912, however, all had been swept away.

Other, equally renowned neighborhoods fell in its wake: Boston's Scollay Square; Marcy Street in Portsmouth, New Hampshire; Seattle's Pioneer Square; and so on. Many of the closures were treated as major public spectacles in their own right; the outdoor revelries that accompanied the final evening of business in San Francisco's Barbary Coast red light district in 1913 were even filmed by director Sol Lesser and released just before Christmas as *The Last Night of the Barbary Coast*.

Such gaiety, however, barely camouflaged the forcefulness with which the new winds of intolerance swept the country and, by 1917, even New Orleans' Storyville, the most legendary of all American red light districts (not to mention the birthplace of jazz music), had effectively shut up shop.

Where did the whores go? Some simply took their chances with the law and carried on as before. Others may indeed have reformed. But there is a third possibility, one hinted at in early histories of Hollywood and which finds further credence in the police reports and the yellow press of the day.

Hollywood's rise to cinematic preeminence was a direct consequence of New York mayor McClellan's campaign against the picture houses in 1908. Immediately, the ten largest movie producers and distributors of the day (including Edison, Biograph, Pathé and Gaumont) banded together to form the Motion Picture Patents

Company, the industry's first concerted attempt to prove that it could be trusted not to corrupt the American people.

It was also a supremely self-serving cartel. The MPPC effectively controlled every aspect of the filmmaking business, from the patents applied to the necessary equipment, through the usages to which that equipment could be put, and on to the venues in which it could be utilized. Furthermore, it allowed non-members less than two months, until the end of January 1909, in which to comply with all of its regulations and demands.

Most of the larger filmmakers complied. Painfully aware of the direction in which the political winds were blowing, what choice did they have? Many smaller operators, however, opted not to heed their new master's voice. Foreshadowing the controversies that rage today around the policing and financing of the Internet, they saw the infant medium of film as a wide-open prairie, unfenced and ungoverned, and free for all to use as they saw fit — and they were determined it should remain that way.

It was a courageous stance. The penalties for disobeying the company's codes were rarely enforced by law, although that option was available. Rather, the MPPC preferred to employ hired muscle, dispatching bands of thugs to handle everything from breaking up "unsanctioned" movie showings to confiscating and destroying "unlicensed" equipment and film, and even blockading the theaters where such films were persistently on display.

The MPPC would not survive for long. In 1912, the U.S. government moved against the monopoly with a series of anti-trust charges that brought about its disbandment. But the damage — or otherwise — had already been done. New York City, the hub of American moviemaking since its birth, was finished. Led by Cecil B. DeMille, rebel after rebel fled instead to the West Coast, far out of reach of their tormentors' brutal enforcers.

There, amid the palm trees of Hollywood, on the fringe of Los Angeles, they established a new renegade community where movies could be made without fear of interference, and screened free of intimidation and violence. Within a decade, a sparsely populated patch of farmland had been transformed into a glittering dreamland whose very name was synonymous with the silver screen.

The area's population soared accordingly. In 1910, barely 500 people lived in Hollywood, religiously devout midwesterners for the most part. By 1930, the population had soared to over 120,000, and God scarcely got a look in any longer.

Many of the young women arrested for soliciting and prostitution in early-1920s Los Angeles (and beyond), when pressed to give their profession, proclaimed themselves actresses. Their logic was impeccable. Even the dimmest cop would have known that far more young women aspired to the silver screen than could ever actually fit onto it, and there were only so many ways of making ends meet while one awaited her lucky break.

A decade later, however, historian Lionel B. Hampton shed a new light on the subject when he claimed that the motion pictures themselves had rescued many young women from a life of prostitution, stating, in his 1931 *A History of Movies*, that, in the motion pictures, they found "amusement and recreation and a new outlook on life that propelled them away from the red-light districts and into homes of their own."

One can take that claim at face value (in which case it appears implausibly naive), or one can read it with the same eye for innuendo that many of Hampton's own readers would have developed from perusing the scandal sheets of the day, and conclude that for any young woman determined to continue making her living from her natural sexuality, the stags arrived at the most opportune moment imaginable.

There is no way of knowing how many prostitutes, "reformed" or otherwise, chose to enter the moviemaking business, just as there is no way of knowing how many of those arrested on the streets of Hollywood really were aspiring thespians. But let us not forget, the girls who made cheap stag films in the 1920s were no less actresses than those who perform in big-budget erotic movies today, and no less deserving of the viewer's admiration and respect. In fact, they may even have merited more, for today's stars are essentially rumpling sheets that have been rolled on for close to a century. The actresses of the 1910s and 1920s were looking at a freshly made bed.

If the closure of the brothels gifted enterprising filmmakers with a ready influx of willing, adventurous and well-experienced talent, it also presented them with a serious problem. As already noted, the brothels offered a ready-made and comparatively risk-free market for the stag-maker's wares. Even if a brothel were busted, the authorities would have far more pressing concerns than trying to deduce who supplied the half-time entertainment.

The market still existed, of course. The red light districts were gone, but the brothel trade itself never closed. It simply relocated around town and maybe scaled back on the staff a little. The men who frequented the brothels and bagnios of Edwardian America, too, were not about to disappear and would still be willing to pay handsomely to watch, if not actually participate in, the pleasures that had suddenly been forbidden them. All the filmmakers needed do was reconnect with them. That, however, was easier said than done.

Exhibiting erotic film was a venture fraught with great risk. The spirit of Puritanism that swept across the United States in the years following the Great War was not only more stringent than it had ever been, it was also more observant, requiring the merest hint of a tip-off to dispatch a phalange of lawmen to any establishment suspected of operating an illegal entertainment.

The arrival of Prohibition, in January 1920, only increased the surveillance. Prohibition itself undoubtedly did more to feed police corruption than any comparable piece of legislation in American history, but still there was a world of difference between a friendly officer turning a blind eye to a private drinking club (in exchange for a drink or two for himself, perhaps) and him adopting the same approach toward the bizarre perversions routinely playing out in the course of the average stag film. For let us not forget that sexual practices that the twenty-first century takes for granted — oral sex, for instance — were, considerably less than a century ago, "officially" regarded among the most unnatural activities it was possible to indulge in.

The problem was exacerbated by the brothels' own position on the frontlines of Prohibition. Historically, among the other attractions such establishments offered, the availability of a drink or two for waiting patrons was universally taken for granted. Prohibition did not necessarily alter that — alongside the illegal speakeasies, brothels were among the leading sources for good quality illicit alcohol. Indeed, many madames later reported that they made more money from selling booze during the Prohibition era than from their main line of business. And the police knew it.

Movies could still be screened in private, rented out to trusted citizens or shown after-hours in courageous theaters. The bordello-centric freedoms that exhibitors had once enjoyed, however, seemed long ago and lost. And then — as it so often does in this line of business — technology stepped in to lend a helping hand.

The early 1920s saw America in the grip of what the newspapers quickly dubbed "auto-mania," a flashflood of motor cars that erupted out of the showrooms to convey the ultimate status symbol upon all who could afford the monthly payments. It was nothing short of a phenomenon. One contemporary observer even compared the mobility of the modern motorist with the transience of the settlers who first trekked west. The only difference was, the trekkers never knew where they might end up. The automobile owner could be home in time for dinner, and the only question he might ask was, how many adventures would befall him in the meantime?

The stags worshipped the car. More than the knock on the door, more than the secretive glance across a crowded room, more than any other way of introducing two people, it was the motor car that allowed man and woman to be brought together in a never-ending succession of exotic (or otherwise) locations. *A Free Ride* could never have unfolded as it did had the girls not been picked up in a car; *The Pick-Up* would not have been half as amusing; and *A Smash-Up Romance*, a mid-1920s movie that blueprinted the naughty-nurse scenario so beloved of future efforts, could never have taken place had the hero, Bob, not first wrecked his automobile.

For the vast majority of owners, the motor car was a luxurious indulgence. They drove because they could, not because they had anywhere special to go. For some, however, it opened up business horizons never before available. In the past, traveling salesmen had been dependent wholly on the whim of the railroads. If the rails did not reach to a certain town or settlement, or if the timetable clashed with another appointment, that town would have to go without. Now, however, the world — or, at least, the nation — was in the enterprising salesman's grasp. And few salesmen were more enterprising than those who had some movies to show.

Nobody knows the name of the first man to bundle a few tenminute reels and a portable projector into his Model T and drive out into the wilderness in search of people to screen them for. More than likely, he was either the same person, or an associate of the same person, who made the films in the first place, stopping off at a bar on his way who-knew-where and casually mentioning to a new found acquaintance that he had some very interesting movies in his trunk. And if a few of the locals would care to make it worth his while, he'd be delighted to screen them.

Word of mouth took over. The next time our man passed through that town or one of the neighboring communities, he might find the local Shriners or Elks awaiting him, to ask if they could possibly rent his services for an evening. A college fraternity would hear the whispers and make their own arrangements, and then spread the news back to the students' hometowns.

Soon, our man could be making a comfortable living, charging up to $100 for the two or three hours he would spend running a dozen or so movies through his projector, with his only major expenses being gas and the need to maintain a plentiful supply of new films, for those occasions when he was called back by a group he'd already entertained. Because the consequences of disappointing his audience — a roomful of predominantly manual laborers or college jocks, high on testosterone and illicit booze — would certainly travel way beyond simply refunding the price of admission.

It was the success of the road shows (as these exhibitions were quickly christened) that ensured that very few stag movies ever stretched beyond a single reel. If a movie was spread over two, then audiences would expect to see them both, in sequential order. But, in a dark and smoky room, illuminated only by the screen and projector, the last thing an exhibitor needed to worry about was making certain his films were filed correctly! (As if to prove this point, several modern DVD collections include the 1930s stag *The Greek Cheater (Part One)*. But wherefore part two?)

Likewise, few operators even labeled their films, as a precaution against accidental discovery, and one could, if so inclined, now argue that the development of the stag movie was curtailed by the very men who ensured its popularity. But given the excesses to which erotic cinema traveled, once longer vistas were readily available, it might be more accurate to say the limitations ensured the stag's purity. If you only have ten minutes of film, you're less likely to waste a second of them.

Ingenuity was key to a successful road show. Several sources tell of enterprising projectionists who, at the end of the evening, would pull aside likely looking members of the audience and ask if they would be interested in making a film of their own. All they needed to do was supply a location and a girl. Sometimes, the audience itself would make the request.

As they were traveling, too, a good operator would keep a keen eye open for likely locations and/or participants. The 1930s *Highway Romance*, filmed atop Kentucky's Pinnacle Overlook and starring two purported tourists, might well have been created in this manner. So might the 1940s-era stag *The Hillbillies* (a.k.a. *Hillbillies Frolic*), a delightfully staged romp in which neither the cast members nor the rundown farm location are anything but the real thing, and both the sex and its aftermath, an object lesson in down-home sexual hygiene, have an honesty that likewise could not have been manufactured. (*The Hillbillies Frolic* might also be the only stag in which the woman is seen to insert a diaphragm prior to sex.)

By the early 1920s, road showing had overtaken both the brothels and the secret cinemas as *the* major means of distribution for stag films, with the traveling projectionists established as the absolute cultural successors to the carnival hucksters and holy rollers who rode horses and rails across the country in earlier times.

Neither was this new profession any less rife with cheating and corruption than their snake oil and salvation-hawking predecessors.

Some operators would not deliver the promised goods — and would indeed hit the road again before the deception was revealed.

On occasion without number, the revelers gathered for a so-called stag night would be regaled, not with the latest in all-action, all-fucking, cinematic sensation, but with any of the many legal alternatives; that is, nonstop glamour and striptease reels; shorts extolling the benefits of exercise and nudism; officially sponsored health films; military warnings on the dangers of venereal disease; and the like. One disgruntled customer even recalls attending a screening where the opening film was *The Story of Menstruation*, an educational cartoon coproduced in 1946 by Walt Disney and the personal products industry for the benefit of America's schoolgirls.

Not all these substitutes were necessarily a disappointment. Artistic modeling films, for example, were notoriously revealing, even within the confines of the law. Seldom exceeding two to three minutes in length, they comprised lingering vistas of one or more nude women stretching and posing, with their educational purpose flagged only by the opening explanation that "constructive figure drawing can be and is generally done from life, but models are not always available. It is for this reason we have made this movie." Others would caution, "this film has been produced solely for students of the Graphic Arts and Cinematography. It is not to be used for Public Exhibition." But, inevitably it would be, and 1941's *Lady Godiva* indicates just how near to the knuckle these films were prone to travel. Two young women are discussing the best way to lose weight, the cue for lots of shots of shapely legs and bared bosoms, before the exercises degenerate into horseplay, and one girl gives the other a mouthful of cream pie. Real cream pie, in this case, but the insinuation was clear regardless.

Other road shows, unwilling to pay for high quality prints of the films they required, would instead borrow (or otherwise temporarily obtain) copies and then run off their own poor quality bootlegs. Others would simply collect their fee ahead of time and then never show up.

Such iniquities were not confined to the erotic trade, just as stags were not the only movies being road shown at the time. Many film-makers, finding themselves unable (or unwilling) to break into the established cabal of movie distributors, chose instead to circumvent the financial and cultural inhibitions that dominated the "official" circuit and take their films on the road themselves. And road showing itself was not necessarily a disreputable occupation.

One doubts whether the average stag entrepreneur would have necessarily admitted to his granny the kind of movies he kept in his trunk. Vivid Entertainment head Steve Hirsch still remembers what his parents told him the day his father was offered a job retailing 8mm stag films for Reuben Sturman, the self-styled kingpin of the 1970s U.S. erotic industry: "The Hirsches warned Steve and his sister that if Daddy took the job, some parents might not let them come over to play."[3]

But what if Hirsch Senior had been peddling religious films? Or cautionary tales about crime and drugs?

One of the earliest movie road shows was organized by Louis Sonney, the sheriff of Centralia, Washington. In 1921, flush with the reward money he received for capturing the notorious and hitherto uncageable railroad bandit Roy Gardner, Sonney made a film about his accomplishment, *The Smiling Mail Bandit*, and then transported it around the country himself, screening it wherever he could, as the highlight of a lecture on the dangers of crime.

Actress Dorothy Davenport, too, became a road-show pioneer following the death of her husband, matinee idol and *Birth of a Nation* star Wallace Reid. In 1919, at the peak of his popularity, the so-called King of Paramount was injured in a train accident while filming *The Valley of the Giants* in Oregon. In hospital, he was given morphine to dull the pain and, upon his return to the film set, the studio was careful to ensure that his supply of the drug never ran out. Inevitably, Reid became addicted, and then compounded his problems by turning to alcohol. He voluntarily committed himself to several sanatoriums in search of a cure, but his condition continued to deteriorate, until his death in January 1923.

Heartbroken, Davenport immediately poured her savings into a movie that illustrated the horrors she had lived through. *Human Wreckage* emerged so brutal a study of the dangers of drugs that, even with the sympathetic support of the Hays Office, no reputable studio or distributor would touch the production. So she followed

Sonney onto the road and, like the sheriff, simply set up wherever she could draw a paying crowd.

Of course, there was one major difference between the likes of Sonney and Davenport, and the stag showmen. No matter how hard-hitting their films might have been, and no matter how salacious their preshow spiel insisted they were, Lou and Dot genuinely believed they were informing their audience, educating them, in the hope that anybody contemplating a life of degradation and disgrace might be given pause for thought and a clear path toward redemption. If there was anything objectionable in their films, it was in the eye of the beholder.

The stags, on the other hand, left nothing whatsoever to the imagination.

Lewdness and the Law

Keyhole Portraits

Throughout the first half of the twentieth century, the basis of the United States' prohibition on the distribution and ownership of sexual material in any form whatsoever was the Comstock Law of 1876, named for that most formidable of antismut crusaders, Postmaster General Anthony Comstock.

By far the most exhaustive of the twenty separate obscenity laws enacted by the Congress between 1842 and 1956, Comstock made it a federal misdemeanor to "sell . . . or offer to sell, or to lend, or to give away, or in any manner to exhibit, or . . . otherwise publish or offer to publish in any manner, or . . . have in his possession, for any such purpose or purposes, an obscene book, pamphlet, paper, writing, advertisement, circular, print, picture, drawing or other representation, figure, or image on or of paper or other material, or any cast instrument, or other article of an immoral nature . . . or [to] advertise the same for sale, or . . . write or print, or cause to be written or printed, any card, circular, book, pamphlet, advertisement, or notice of any kind, stating when, where, how, or of whom, or by what means, any of the articles in this section . . . can

51

be purchased or obtained, or . . . manufacture, draw, or print, or in any wise make any of such articles." Penalties for contravening these prohibitions ranged between six months and five years' hard labor and fines of between $100 and $2,000 for each offense.

Revisions to Comstock were few and far between. A provision relating to the distribution of condoms, for example, was not overturned until 1936, and the marvelously titled case of *United States v One Package of Japanese Pessaries*.

Other clauses in the law were loosened by such Supreme Court decisions as *One Book Called "Ulysses"* (1933), and Judge John M. Woolsey's determination that obscenity should be judged by the effect of the work *in its entirety*, as opposed to in part; in other words, one paragraph of explicit language could not be used as an excuse to outlaw an entire work. Should something be adjudged to have failed that particular test, however, there was no law in the land that could protect it.

It is convenient for historians of the years between the two World Wars to ally stag movies with those other expressions that were considered flagitious — risqué postcards and erotic photographs, suggestive movies and explicit comic books, certain art exhibitions and literature. All flaunted the general notion of spiritual cleanliness to which the authorities wished the entire country to cling. All were subject to the same hysterical distortions and insinuations by those who would eliminate them. And all faced the same implacable foes, both official and otherwise.

In New York City, the public face of the antismut crusade was John Sumner, the president of the New York Society for the Suppression of Vice. It was Sumner, in 1933, who prosecuted a New York lecturer, Timothy Murphy, for displaying obscene artworks at a Broadway gallery. When Murphy was able to prove that every one of the paintings he hung was a copy of an acknowledged old master, Sumner responded by claiming that the reproductions had purposefully been rendered "franker," and therefore more obscene, than the originals.

This particular case was thrown out, but Sumner remained a tireless avenger, sighting and confronting obscenity in every direction.

However, he sought not only justice (as he declared the suppression of vice to be). He also sought publicity for his cause, and proof that the obscenities he battled were a danger to society at large.

The locked and closeted world of the stag movie was not beneath his gaze. Any number of suspected distributors and exhibitors were prosecuted as vigorously as any so-called booklegger or smuthound. But he did not pursue the movie trade with the same vigor and enthusiasm with which he persecuted publishers, for the simple reason that few of the movies he turned up even merited their day in court. Films were seized and their owners or distributors would be punished. But there were no headlines to be gained or plaudits to be awarded from busting a dirty movie. The best legal mind in the world could not argue in its favor; the most liberal interpretation of the Constitution could not be bent to accommodate a stag film. For all the landmark (and otherwise) decisions made regarding obscenity, not one ever suggested that the public exhibition of a film showing two (or more) people having abandoned and explicit sex was protected by any constitutional doctrine whatsoever. In fact, it was not until the tail end of the 1960s that the very ownership of such material was granted any form of legal protection.

The law of the land at this time was implicit in its insistence that it was the individual states' right to determine what was and was not obscene, and to pass whatever legislation they saw fit to regulate it. Thus, while two states, North Carolina and Illinois, held that the exhibition of stag films *to personal associates, not for gain* and *not in front of children* was legal, the remainder of the union firmly and specifically legislated against the manufacture, sale, exhibition and possession of any "obscene" material whatsoever.

In 1968, Atlanta police launched an investigation into the activities of Robert Eli Stanley, a suspected bookmaker. A search warrant was procured, and the police proceeded to seek out the evidence they required. In fact, they found nothing whatsoever to tie Stanley with the original charges. Instead, they turned up three reels of 8mm film, apparently hidden beneath Stanley's bed, and a projector and screen in an upstairs living room.

The films were run and declared obscene. With the authorities having ascertained that the bedroom in which they were found was indeed Stanley's, the bookmaking was forgotten and he was charged and indicted on possession of obscene material.

Stanley launched a series of appeals, a long and laborious process that finally wound up in the Supreme Court in April 1969. There, the court transcripts noted, "the requirement that warrants shall particularly describe the things to be seized makes general searches under them impossible and prevents the seizure of one thing under a warrant describing another. The agents were acting within the authority of the warrant when they proceeded to the appellant's upstairs bedroom and pulled open the drawers of his desk. But when they found . . . not gambling material, but moving picture films, the warrant gave them no authority to seize the films."

More importantly, however, the justices declared that the "mere categorization of these films as 'obscene' is insufficient justification for such a drastic invasion of personal liberties guaranteed by the First and Fourteenth Amendments. Whatever may be the justifications for other statutes regulating obscenity, we do not think they reach into the privacy of one's own home. If the First Amendment means anything, it means that a State has no business telling a man, sitting alone in his own house, what books he may read or what films he may watch. Our whole constitutional heritage rebels at the thought of giving government the power to control men's minds."

What the ruling did not address was what actually constituted obscenity. That remained the decision of the individual states. But the boundaries were beginning to blur, and the first steps toward the modern state of affairs, where the obscenity laws tend (with certain exceptions) to end once you close your own front door, had finally been taken.

In many ways Stanley's case was an anomaly. Private possession of obscene material was seldom pursued into the courts, the authorities sensibly understanding that it was the makers, not the viewers, of obscene matter that posed the greatest threat to their own vision of puritanical utopia. Many more obscenity charges were leveled against the book, magazine and photographic trades than film, not only because the opportunities for printed matter to stray into the wrong hands were far greater, but because the "guilty men" were frequently a lot easier to trace.

Stag audiences could be rounded up as often as the local police department deemed necessary. But they were often all that would be caught. The road-show operators would have run the moment the first nightstick came through the door and, although the police would promptly impound any film equipment he might have left behind, there would be little hard evidence to be garnered from that, although an almost-certainly apocryphal tale does credit one rural police chief with issuing an arrest warrant for the actors Dick Hard and Lotte Jizz, names he noted at the end of one particular stag.

Likewise, the entrepreneurs who warehoused stag films were frequently gainfully employed in retail professions that were nominally above suspicion. Many companies catering toward conventions and private parties would have a secret stash of stags on hand, should their customers require something spicier than the usual fireworks, decorations and novelty hats. The popular notion (and more recent reality) of erotic film being available from the same sources as erotic literature was certainly not the case throughout the first half of this century — indeed, with only the handful of exceptions that every generalization must necessarily admit, the book and movie trades were very separate indeed.

So were their audiences. The printed page is a solitary preoccupation. Books and pictures might be passed around from one reader to another, but outside of the lecture room, the public reading or the book club, there are few social gatherings at which the study of a book — *any* book — is regarded a communal event.

Stag movies, on the other hand, were intended to be viewed by as large an audience as could be gathered into one place. And while there were those collectors and connoisseurs who might prefer to view their acquisitions in private, for the most part the stag's natural habitat was a smoke-filled room, crammed with boisterous males, all loudly applauding and remarking upon the action on the screen. No less than a football game, a strip show or a boxing match, stags were the focal point of a night out with the boys. And the boys themselves couldn't see anything wrong with that.

Prostitutes and publishers, photographers and procurers, back-street abortionists and alleyway booksellers, all conducted their business in the shadow of the Comstock Law. But filmmakers, once they had actually made their film, were more or less out of the woods. Provided they did nothing stupid, the further the film traveled from its creator, the less chance there was of discovery.

There might have been another reason for the authorities' reluctance to pursue stag films. Quite simply, the majority of people had no idea that such a thing even existed, or if they did, they had no way of actually seeing one. In 1926, movie historian Curt Moreck opened his discussion of the subject by remarking, "The general public knows nothing about *pornographischen* films, and is surprised to discover that such a thing even exists."[1]

Any publicity for such films, then, could only broaden the public's awareness of and interest in them, and even the dullest bureaucrat understood the laws of supply and demand. When the newspapers talked of obscene movies, it talked of those Hollywood efforts that brushed the borders of the Hays Code, or the road-show exploitation flicks that shocked without showing anything.

When the Legion of Decency arose in 1934 to rid popular films of sex and vulgarity, the emphasis was on the word "popular," while an inventory of obscenities seized in New York by John Sumner's Society for the Suppression of Vice that same year included "18,000 pamphlets, 16,000 magazines, 3,281 postcards, 5,125 bound volumes, 222 business cards and a comparatively small assortment of so-called objectionable images . . . and other novelties."[2] There was not a film in sight.

In fact, on the occasions that a stag film did reach the authorities' attention, it was as likely that they were renting it themselves as attempting to suppress it. In 1969, author Donald H. Gilmore gleefully recalled how "a prominent publisher of erotic fiction recently received a telephone call from a ranking member of the local police force, asking for the loan of some stag films for a semi-official party. This same police department harasses the publisher regularly. The publisher . . . suggested the caller try the local office of the FBI."[3]

Likewise, in May of that same year, police in Silver Spring,

Maryland, received information that there was a screening of stag movies taking place in the heart of their jurisdiction. They rushed to round up the miscreants, but were surely shocked to find themselves raiding a local branch of the American Legion, an organization that traditionally campaigned vigorously for tighter moral standards. Fortuitously, they had also forgotten to secure a search warrant, and the case against the Legionnaires was dismissed.

No less than Gilmore's anecdote, this particular incident proved that stags had deeper roots in American male society than anybody cared to acknowledge and, within the context of an all-male environment, were scarcely even considered obscene. One man's lewdness is another's harmless entertainment, after all; or, to paraphrase Benjamin Franklin in Sherman Edwards' play *1776*, "pornography is completely harmless in the first person, when we are enjoying it. It is only in the third person, when someone else is watching it, that it becomes dangerous.

Ah! girls look at
that horrible thing

El Satario

Rudeness, Raunch and Revolution

While the United States was throwing legislation hard and fast at the perceived tidal
wave of filth that was threatening to engulf
the country, other nations were seeking their
own ways of repairing the moral fiber of
society in the years following the Great War.

In February 1920, just months after the
newly formed Weimar government took on
the task of rebuilding defeated Germany, members of the Württem-
berg state legislature, in the traditionally conservative south, convened to witness a screening of recently confiscated sex films,
courtesy of the local police force. It was, lamented the minister of
interior affairs, so shocking a display that the police refused outright
to permit any female parliamentarians to remain in the room while
the films were being shown. "Only the men had to suffer," the
wretched man mourned. "A worse poisoning of the mind than that
produced by such pictures is virtually impossible to invent."[1]

The legislature pronounced itself similarly and suitably shocked
by what they witnessed. Despite such opprobrium, however, the
national government did much to liberalize German concepts of

obscenity, albeit marred by some very peculiar dichotomies.

It was now no longer an offense for full nudity (or "beauty evenings," as they were known) to be presented on the cabaret stage. It was illegal, however, for that same nudity to be captured on either postcard or film, for fear that such items might wind up in the possession of "uneducated" youth and poor people, "who did not have the proper aesthetic training to view such [materials] in a 'disinterested,' that is, non-sexual manner."[2]

Aesthetic considerations, too, might sway the opinions of the lawmakers. A movie recording a performance of Cäcilie Funk's generally acclaimed nude ballet *Celly de Rheidt* was banned on the strength of the film medium itself. "The dances are impaired . . . by the flickering light, so that the movements are less gracious in the film. Furthermore, [it] utilizes only black and white. Through all of these defects . . . the pleasing aspects of the dance movement recede and the grossly sensual aspects of the presentation come that much more to the fore. The film produces an even more obscene impression than the dances of the ballet on the stage."[3]

Despite such regulations, stag movies continued to flourish in Weimar Germany, lending their own fission to the fast-developing aura of carefree decadence for which post–Great War, pre–Hitler Germany is now renowned, and flickering in back rooms of the clubs and cabarets that grew up in every city. In 1926, Curt Moreck not only marveled at the "vast" quantities of stags confiscated by the police in Berlin alone, he was also able to use the statistics against the growing tide of right-wing politicos who were then striving to place German morality on a higher plane than her neighbors. "A view into the annals of the police shows that such enterprises are no rarer here than elsewhere," he wrote.[4]

France, too, resumed production, not only reinitiating the symbiotic relationship between erotic film and the brothels, but also creating a system of virtual self-sufficiency, in that many of the movies shown in the higher-class brothels were filmed there as well.

The French authorities never really troubled themselves with either the presence or the growth of the brothels. Occasionally, the police might move against the so-called "slaughter houses" wherein a particularly brutal and degrading form of white slave trade lived on, preying on runaways and immigrants. At the other end of the social scale, however, *les maisons closes*, or "closed houses," weren't only legal, they were among the most opulent and luxurious venues in France, palatial, civilized establishments that many visitors, French and foreign alike, regarded as the ultimate symbol of Gallic taste, civility and sense.

Such venues as Le Chabanais (in Victorian times, a favored haunt for both the future King Edward VII of England and the Belgian King Leopold), Le Sphinx, Chez Suzy and The One Two Two were spoken of in the same tones of reverence and awe as the Opera House or the Moulin Rouge. And, like them, they became a magnet for the visiting rich and famous. Marlene Dietrich, Humphrey Bogart, Marcel Proust, Pablo Picasso and Ernest Hemingway, not to mention a steady parade of British and American dignitaries and officials, were frequent visitors to these establishments, happily paying as much as 100 francs (then equivalent to around $25 U.S.) simply to be admitted to the premises. Any other entertainments cost extra.

One of the most fascinating bodies of work to have survived from this postwar era is a collection of photographs and movies produced, for his own private use, by a wealthy French erotica collector whom posterity has named Monsieur X. According to French writer Alexandre Dupouy, who cataloged the collection following its sale to a Parisian bookseller in the mid-1970s, Mr. X pursued his photographic interests exclusively in the Parisian brothels (one photograph clearly shows the view out onto la Place Pigalle), where the girls would be paid their usual rate simply to pose for his camera.

Occasionally, Mr. X would be accompanied by a male friend, but neither man took part in the action that followed. The girls — whose names were frequently noted on the back of the photographs: FanFan, Gypsi, Nénette, Suzy and so on — were the sum of Mr. X's interest, "nude or scantily clad, in either academic or very licentious poses. There are no men" beyond the odd occasion when Mr. X's companion strayed into camera shot, or once, when the photographer himself is caught in a mirror's reflection.[5]

His subjects appreciated his visits. "What's nice is that with Mr.

X, we never have to do any of the oddish stuff we sometimes have to do with some of the others," wrote one of his subjects in her diary. "All he wants is to take pictures of us. Marie, Fanfan and I think maybe he's impotent, and it makes us laugh, but never in a mean way."[6]

Mr. X appears to have shot just two movies, neither of which display the artistry of his still photography. Utilizing a clockwork camera, *Scènes d'intérieur de Mr. X* (*Indoor Scenes by Mr. X*) was filmed, as its title suggests, inside the brothel, and revolves around short sequences of girls undressing, caressing and cavorting with one another; *Scènes d'extérieur de Mr. X* (*Outdoor Scenes*) repeats the same activities out of doors.

It is uncertain whether these films were ever granted a public airing. Presumably, Mr. X would have shown them to friends who shared his interests, in either photography or brothels, but the fact that he declared his prints to be the only copies ever made (his negatives, he told the buyer, were thrown into the Seine long ago) would suggest that their circulation was extremely limited.

Not so the work of certain of Mr. X's contemporaries. In fact, one filmmaker, Bernard Nathan, operated almost as legitimately as any conventional French director. He even advertised his wares in the newsstand magazines *Paris Plaiser* and *La Vie Parisiene*. There was no shame, no lawlessness, no obscenity. Nathan was a filmmaker. He made films. (And he is no relation to the contemporaneous Bernard Natan, despite many misidentifications elsewhere.)

"Bernard Nathan" was a pseudonym — the man's true identity is unknown. But as both director and, on many occasions, the leading man in a lengthy series of films made specifically for the 1920s French brothel trade, that distinction becomes irrelevant. Just as no one has ever described *Stardust Memories* as their favorite Allen Konigsberg movie, so few members of Nathan's audience would have lost any sleep wondering, who was that unmasked man? (Not so another of his leading men, the heavily disguised Henri D, whom Parisian gossip insisted was actually a well-known French opera singer. Unfortunately for posterity, however, nobody seems to have thought to record which one.)

Nathan's films were seldom less than ambitious. He prided himself on the sheer quality of his work; extravagant costuming, detailed sets and well-appointed locations were all hallmarks of a Nathan production, while his scenarios were audacious, to say the least.

One of his most complex productions, if only because it seems so simplistic, was *Je Verbalise* (*I Speak*), in which a succession of "ordinary people" — a farmer, a gardener, a laundress, a hunter and so on — demonstrate their preferred sexual positions. On other occasions, Nathan stepped into the realms of full-fledged drama. One early effort, 1920's *Les Filles de Loth* (*Lot's Daughters*), was a sexual retelling of the Biblical parable of Lot's daughters. He took on the historical character of Madame Pompadour in 1922's *Musique de Chambre* (*Chamber Music*) and toyed with the popularity of the operetta *The Mikado*, with *Le Songe de Butterfly* (*The Butterfly Song*), restaging popular elements of the Gilbert and Sullivan classic as a period-costume rampage through both hetero and homosexuality, masturbation, sodomy and fellatio.

Another Nathan classic investigated that most quintessentially prewar of sexual fantasies, the mystery of what lies beneath the Muslim woman's all-obscuring burkha. In *Nektoub, Fantaisie Arabe* (*Nektoub — An Arab Fantasy*), Dick the photographer is visiting the Sheikh D'Abd-El-Zob, when he finds himself alone with two veiled women. Naturally, he attempts to interest them in having their pictures taken and, putting aside their initial uncertainty, they first pose and then start to dance. Unsurprisingly, the dance quickly develops into a striptease and, from there. . . .

Dick's triumph is shortlived. With a cry of "Dog!" the Sheikh and his bodyguard burst onto the scene, and one cannot help but fear that Dick's dick, at least, is history. But his assailants are merciful, preferring merely to ravage him from both ends at once, before permitting him to take his photographs after all, of the pair of them making love with their womenfolk.

Nathan may also have been responsible for *Le Verrou* (*The Bolt*), a painstaking homage to the artist Jean-Honoré Fragonard (1732–1806). Titled for one of Fragonard's best-loved paintings, the opening scene of the film places the actor and actress in the exact same poses as the figures in the painting, the woman in her lover's arms, as they prepare to tumble onto a bed. The question that has exercised generations of subsequent art lovers as they gaze upon the canvas was — what happened next?

Sadly, as it transpires, not much. According to Nathan, the couple are suddenly disturbed by the woman's elderly husband. While her lover scrambles out of sight, she somehow convinces her suspicious spouse that she's feeling unwell and would prefer to be left alone. He leaves, she returns to the bed, her lover places his head on her lap and . . . *FIN*.

Perhaps the most bizarre of Nathan's films, however, is one that might almost be described as a follow-up to Edison's now-twenty-year-old *Trapeze Disrobing Act* — except on this occasion the woman is already disrobed and engaged in vigorous sex with one of her fellow circus performers. Seven decades before the first idle fingers typed the words "clown porn" into an Internet search machine (66,800 hits at the time of writing), Bernard Nathan had already demonstrated it.

Nathan was not the only "named" director working in France during the 1920s. Somewhat less flamboyant, but no less prolific, was the singularly named Dominique, whose work included a clutch of three-, four- and even more-somes, under such titles as *A la Cuisine* (*In the Kitchen*), *La Nouvelle Bonne à Tout Faire* (*Maid of all Work*), *Le Coiffeur* (*The Haircut*), *Le Prince et le Groom* (*The Prince and the Groom*) and *Les Modistes*.

Perhaps his best-known production, however, was *Pendant l'Entr'acte* (*During the Intermission*), in which the renowned American opera star "Sarah Barnum" returns to her dressing room following the first half of her performance, to discover a strange man lurking behind a screen. Joined by her maid, she promptly sets about undressing and ravaging the intruder, before reassembling her costume and heading out for the second half of her scheduled performance.

Bernard Nathan and Dominique are historically regarded as the masters of French stags, because theirs are the names that are known. However, a vast body of others' work both enlarges upon and departs from the stylistic nuances of their known peers. One popular theme among French directors was the relationship between the aristocracy and their staff, a subject well demonstrated by an untitled movie that opens with the lady of the house catching a manservant romping with a maid in her bedroom. The maid is sent from the room in disgrace, only for the lady to take her place in the manservant's arms. Unfortunately, the disgruntled maid heads directly to the master to inform him of what is transpiring. He rushes to the room but, rather than punish his unfaithful wife and the treacherous houseboy, he demands that they continue with what they were doing, while he submits both to his own sexual ministrations.

Another prewar specialty was voyeurism, especially when it could be made to appear unintentional. Many such films were almost touchingly innocent. Sadly viewed without its opening titles, one early French stag depicts an elderly couple rediscovering their sexual appetites while watching a younger couple spooning in the park. In the 1930s stag *Quand Vous Allex au Bois* (*When You Go to the Woods*), the camera simply focuses up a woman's skirt while she rows a boat across a lake. *La Sauvageonne*, meanwhile, accompanies a young man in delightedly watching a woman as she walks naked (for who knows what reason) through the woods, stopping occasionally to flick her nipples with a fern. On this occasion, the two are even permitted to come to grips with one another, although the movie ends before he does more than squeeze a breast and caress a leg.

Not all such sightings are accidental. *La Grand Bagarre* (*The Big Fight*) opens with two girls talking in a field, when they spy a strange man approaching. One of the girls hides, while her friend allows herself to be seduced, knowing her companion is watching from behind a bush and growing increasingly excited. It is this girl who then becomes the movie's focus, a series of close-ups contrasting her masturbatory paradise with the less than overwhelming pleasures her friend is being subjected to.

Finished with the one girl, the man gets up and promptly stumbles across the second. His interest is awakened, but so is his first conquest's ire. A catfight ensues, before the watching gent finally breaks it up. He forces the girls to kiss and make up, and then makes them the offer that the viewer has probably been expecting for the past five minutes. They can both have him — and they do, which turns out to have been their intention all along.

Hotel d'nudiste (*Nudist Bar*) also draws an initially hapless onlooker into the unfolding action, and emerges one of the most striking French films of the 1930s. Two young women enter a hotel bar, order drinks and then commence caressing one another. The barman affects to ignore them, until he realizes one of them is suddenly completely naked. His attempts to wrap her back in her cloak, however, merely prompt her to switch her amorous attentions to him.

Following some initial resistance, he succumbs, drawing her behind his bar, where he and the other girl take turns performing cunnilingus on her. This interlude ends when the still-clothed woman locates the contents of the barman's pants, after which *Nudist Bar* is disappointingly transformed into one of those all-too-common threesomes in which the third party —the girl whose nakedness started all this in the first place — becomes more or less extraneous to the action (although she is used as a pillow a one point).

If postwar France and Germany simply reclaimed their former dominance of the European stag market, the situation was very different in the Western hemisphere. Both Brazil and Argentina had undergone substantial social change during the war years. The foreign investment that fueled both nations' growth earlier in the century died out when the European guns commenced firing, and had yet to return. Any filmmakers working in those countries did so for local consumption, leaving the field wide-open for two comparatively new entrants.

The first, of course, was the United States (with the satellite nation of Cuba making its own distinctive contributions to that corpus); the other, perhaps surprisingly, was Mexico — "surprisingly" because, although Mexican filmmakers turned out some of the most starkly striking erotic imagery of the age, they did so not for sexual reasons so much as political.

It is a seldom-discussed etymological fact that the word "pornography," so gratuitously thrown around by the modern moral crusader, was never intended to address erotica (with which it is now synonymous), at least not exclusively. Rather, pornography emerged into European culture during the sixteenth century as a literary style, popular among those heretics and libertines who would use shock tactics not only as a means of testing societal boundaries, but also to criticize the political and religious establishment by highlighting its contradictions and hypocrisies, demonstrating it to be engaged in the very acts that it forbade — including, but again by no means limited to, rampant sexuality.

It was toward this original, unsullied meaning that Mexico's new leaders turned as they prepared to usher the country away from the revolutionary turbulence that had torn it apart through much of the 1910s and into a new era of comparative political enlightenment.

In 1917, following seven years of turmoil and violence, the newly elected President Venustiano Carranza set in motion a series of reforms that addressed every social ill the country had suffered, specifically targeting concerns that had hitherto been the preserve of the Catholic Church — education, landownership and so on. Indeed, for Mexico to have any hope of building upon the rocks of the revolution, the power of the Church needed to be diminished at every level, from its control of regional (and even national) politics, all the way to its hypnotic hold on the lives of the people themselves. What we would term stag films were one of the weapons with which this new war would be fought.

Few extant films have been unequivocally dated to this particular period; much as the modern historian might appreciate it, there are no naked men shouting, *"¡Vive la revolución!"* while waving their members in the air. Rather, Mexican stags of the 1920s slip unobtrusively into the long line of undated (and undatable) movies that filmographies note merely as "Latin."

One very likely candidate, however, is *El Satario* (*The Devil*), a movie that epitomizes the Mexican mood of the moment, while offering a case study of how difficult it can be to precisely date a stag movie.

Claiming it to date from Argentina, circa 1907, several historians have proclaimed *El Satario* to be the oldest stag film in existence today, although none have been able to explain how they arrived at this conclusion. Others, retaining the Argentinean angle, have tied the movie to the 1912 visit to Buenos Aires of Diaghilev's Ballet's Russes, because elements in the film echo Stravinsky's *L'aprés-midi d'un Faun* (*Afternoon of a Faun*), which formed a part of that season's repertoire.

Another school of thought, as cautious as its colleagues are extravagant, prefers to date *El Satario* to 1930s Cuba, the years during which America's rich and decadent regarded the island as their own tropical trough of sin. Splitting the difference between these extremes, however, other students place it firmly within the Mexican post-revolutionary period; and, within the context of those times, it would certainly feel most at home.

To the modern viewer, *El Satario* is little more than a dirty film with a dim view of society's religious devoutness. As it opens, six naked women are seen frolicking in a meadow, playing ball. They think they are alone, but suddenly a figure emerges from the undergrowth. It is the Devil, complete with tail, horns and thick whiskers. He watches for a moment, absorbing the scene before him, then leaps out to scatter the screaming girls. One, "the queen," stumbles and faints, and he pounces, carrying her off to a nearby thicket. She awakens to his caresses but, rather than attempt to flee, she decides to make the most of her predicament. Besides, it's only his head that is demonic; without his clothing, he's really quite buff and, by the time the other girls return to the scene, the pair are happily sleeping off their excesses.

Oh yes, just another dirty film.

But *El Satario* had a subtext that, though easy to overlook today, spoke loudly to audiences of the time. A girl enjoying consensual sex with the Devil; a nun being pleasured by a donkey; a priest being blown by a saint . . . these were images that stepped beyond the traditional values of blasphemy and into the realms of revelation — the revelation, that is, that the priests and nuns who preached celibacy and more, and who formed such a disapproving barrier against any possibility of their flock enjoying sex, were going at it like rabbits and having a wonderful time.

Perhaps the most heavy-handed, but unquestionably effective, commentary upon the papal rape of Mexico was delivered by *Viase de Bodas*. The film's opening scenes, of a young couple having sex, initially relegate it to the ranks of the most simpleminded stag. Their loving completed, however, the pair get dressed, donning full Mexican national regalia and assuming, therefore, the characters of Mexico herself.

The male has business elsewhere and leaves his lady in the care of the local priest, who promptly forces her to her knees and demands she fellate him. But when the boyfriend returns to collect her, she is clearly too scared to reveal what happened, and the three part as apparent friends.

Films such as these were not intended to promote sexual licentiousness. They were designed to harpoon the insidious hypocrisy that permeated the entire system and, though it is unclear whether the films were made by the authorities themselves or merely with their tacit approval, their intended effect upon all who saw them is unmistakable.

Crazy Cat House

Germany tolerated its erotic film industry, France encouraged it, and Mexico politicized it. Other countries simply swept the matter under the carpet. The United States, however, was unable to leave it alone, picking at the "problem" as though it were a stubborn scab, and never failing to be astonished at its failure to heal. Indeed, the infection only spread, carried abroad with such virulence that, as the 1920s and 1930s unfolded as the most violently lawless decades in American history, there could only be one explanation for the plague.

Organized crime was a hydra that invaded every walk of life. From bootlegging to bank jobs, from protection rackets to prostitution, the American dream was beset on every side by those who would turn democracy on its head if they thought there was a profit to be turned.

Yet, despite the efforts of law enforcement agencies the length and breadth of the country, not an iota of evidence ever surfaced to link the criminal kingpins with the trade in obscene movies.

It is true that the sex-movie business in 1940s Calumet City,

Illinois, was dominated by Jake Guzik, the son of Al Capone's former bagman. Guzik Junior regularly commuted to Phoenix, Arizona, to shoot "wild sex orgies . . . obscene soirees where every form of degeneracy was both taught and practiced."[1]

It is also true that a self-styled exposé of "the Stag Film Racket" published in the August 1957 issue of *Man's Exploits* magazine repeatedly indicted "the racketeers who 'produce' the present crop of pornographic pictures," and waxed eloquently on "a Syndicate-run central agency that gets the reels out to 'wholesalers' in various parts of the country. These wholesalers in turn feed out the films to the operators who rent them to the public."[2]

But even the 1970 President's Commission on Obscenity and Pornography was moved to accept that, "although many persons have alleged that organized crime works hand-in-glove with the distributors of adult materials, there is at present no concrete evidence to support these statements."[3]

This situation would change over the next decade, as the barriers that had hitherto blocked access to the cultural mainstream began to shift, and such films as *Deep Throat* demonstrated the sheer amount of profit available to the smart entrepreneur. According to the 1986 Attorney General's Commission on Pornography, *Deep Throat* itself "was produced by the Peraino brothers of the Columbo organized crime family for $25,000, and is reliably estimated to have grossed fifty million dollars as of 1982."

However, even at ground level, the authorities could find no conclusive links between organized crime and the sex trade prior to the late 1960s, with L.A. police chief Daryl F. Gates categorically informing the 1970 commission that it was not until 1969 that "organized crime infiltrated the pornography industry in Los Angeles."[4] (The 1972 erotic *Godfather* spoof *Blue Heat* entertainingly follows one filmmaker's attempts to refuse the Mob's offer of a merger.)

The Mafia moved into the New York trade around the same time, when John "Sonny" Franzese, an associate of the Perainos, began supplying 8mm stags to the Times Square peep-show trade. So yes, there was a definite connection. But the story of erotic film in America was already sixty years old by the time it was made.

If the evil tentacles of the Mob were not pulling the strings of rampant licentiousness in America, then what — or who — was? Ironically, it was precisely the same freedoms and prosperity that the reformers insisted were at risk from the onslaught of filth. The Great Depression might have laid waste to great swaths of the nation's fortune and confidence but, before it hit, the United States was in the thrall of the New Economic Prosperity, emerging triumphant from the trenches of the Great War to assuredly take her place at the forefront of the world.

From the flappers dancing the night away in the most chic hotels and nightspots, flashing their knickers at any man who tutted to see such shameless behavior, to Charles Lindbergh's epic transatlantic flight sounding the death knell for the age of the ocean liners; from the birth of jazz music to the property boom that changed the face of Florida, the boundless promise that America had always represented to the world was about to come to fruition.

Consumerism was king. In less than twenty years, the ultimate status symbol — the automobile — had transformed a way of life forever, but every day seemed to bring another gizmo, gadget or gewgaw into the average household, as rising wages brought about a revolution in people's spending habits. The radio, the phonograph . . . technological inventions that had once been the province of the fabulously wealthy alone were now in the reach of everyone. And when a slew of new home-movie cameras suddenly appeared on the market, economically priced and easy to use, that hobby, too, was suddenly available to anyone who wanted to try their hand.

The hand-cranked 9.5mm Pathé Baby, Eastman Kodak's 16mm Cine-Kodak camera and Bell & Howell's clockwork Filmo all debuted around 1923. Two years later saw the introduction of Kodak's clockwork Cine-Kodak Model B, a five-pound device that was destined to become one of the best-selling amateur cameras of all time. They were affordable as well. Within two years of its introduction, the retail price of a Cine-Kodak had fallen from around $150 to $100. A projector cost $60 and 100 feet of Cine-Kodak film, with processing, cost $6. Dealerships were popping up in every city in the land, processing labs on every corner.

The advantages offered by these new cameras were manifold. The dangers inherent in the old style nitrate-based film stock were a thing of the past, as the new cellulose safety film became the industry standard. The film itself was so-called "reversal film," which significantly reduced the cost of processing incurred by negative film, while the new small gauge lowered the price of the material, without sacrificing image quality.

As in earlier times, the vast majority of movies shot with these new devices were as innocent as the age itself is frequently remembered as being. But, just as there were exceptions to the first rule, so the second is not as clear-cut as it might be.

It is difficult to quantify sexuality in any past age. As in any other field of human nature, there are always those people whose appetites are exaggerated far beyond the accepted norm, just as there are those who go in the opposite direction entirely. But, if any one social movement characterized the 1920s, it was the empowerment of women, a wave that grew out of the prewar suffragette movement, only gathering speed once the conflict reached America and women found themselves employed in professions that had hitherto been solidly male preserves.

Prohibition was, at least in part, brought about by the demands of women, but if the Volstead Act put a dent in the American male's ability to drink himself into a stupor, it also increased his chances of meeting women instead. In the past, the booze- and violence-soaked atmosphere of bars and speakeasies had been out of bounds to all but a very certain kind of female. Now young ladies of every class flocked freely to such establishments, a social revolution that, in turn, fostered a sexual revolution at least as profound as that which swept American campuses during the 1960s.

Firmly at the forefront of this movement were the flappers — girls who proudly stood for every value that their mothers, even elder sisters, had regarded as a mortal sin. "A flapper is proud of her nerve," announced an anonymous "ex-Flapper" in the *New York Times*. "She is shameless, selfish and honest, but . . . she considers these attributes virtues. She takes a man's point of view as her mother never could."[5]

Sex was as crucial an element in this newfound freedom as any other attainment. "She will tell you where you stand in her catalog," ex-Flapper continued, "and, if she wants you badly enough, she will come out in the open and work for you with the same fresh and vigorous air that you would work to win her."

One of the keenest observers of the flapper phenomenon was Eleanor Rowland Wembridge, a contributor to *Survey*, a nominally philanthropic magazine published by the non-profit, non-partisan Survey Associates Inc., between 1912 and 1952, and dedicated to documenting the humanities in all their guises. "It is distinctly the *mores* of the time to be considered as ardently sought after, and as not too priggish to respond. As one girl said, 'I don't particularly care to be kissed by some of the fellows I know, but I'd let them do it anytime, rather than think I wouldn't dare.'"[6]

Another girl told Wembridge, "[Kissing] is terribly exciting. We get such a thrill. I think it is natural to want nice men to kiss you, so why not do what is natural?" Wembridge pointedly noted that "actual illicit relations between the petters was not advised nor countenanced . . . [but] they admitted . . . that it often did so lead."

The stags, naturally, were fascinated by the flapper phenomenon and the stereotypes therein; the movement's distinctive hairstyles and clothing were as ubiquitous in 1920s stags as hippies would be to their 1960s counterparts, and for many of the same reasons. The girls who followed the fashion represented a breed apart, particularly if one considers the opposing social strata from which the flappers (middle-class and beyond) and the stag audience (predominantly working class) were drawn. To watch a film that purported to show these fabulous creatures in their natural habitat — flat on their backs, with their legs wrapped around someone's waist — was to receive reinforcement for all of your own generation's class prejudices.

To the average auto worker and his ilk, flappers were the idle rich and semi-famous and, three decades before the first truly sensationalist gossip magazines arrived on the newsstands to scandalize his wife, Mr. Blue Collar was already well aware of how the wealthy frittered away their time.

In the mid-1920s, *The Adventures of Christine*, for example, a bright young thing decides to become an artist's model, answering an ad in the local newspaper. Much demur giggling ensues as she strips to pose, and even more follows once the artist lays his paintbrush down.

Tapping into the stags' tradition for coarse humor, meanwhile, *The Pick-Up* (1923) opens by asking if "you've heard about the girl who stepped out with a taxidermist, and then played dead? Well, our story is about that girl. . . ." Shot in the hills above L.A., the film details the adventures of Lizzy the Flapper, and Gus's attempts to win her affections. Three times he picks her up in his shiny car and drives her into the hills, ten miles from town the first time, then fifteen, and then twenty. And each time Lizzy rebuffs his advances and ends up walking home.

On their fourth journey, however, he drives fifty miles and this time finds Lizzy as compliant as he could wish. So he asks her — why did she make him wait so long? Well, she replies, "I don't mind walking ten, fifteen or twenty miles. But I'll be damned if I'll walk fifty miles, just to keep you from getting a dose of clap."

If these were the only building blocks that lay behind the emergence of the stag film as a cultural phenomenon — an explosion in home-moviemaking equipment, and a generation of girls who would rather do *anything* than risk being described as one who did nothing — then fortune would indeed have smiled upon the infant genre.

But there was more. The 1920s also saw many of America's historical fraternal orders launch aggressive recruitment drives (and relax their once-stringent admission standards), in a bid to combat a fall in membership that had been threatening their existence since the turn of the century, as younger men turned to such less-structured recreational clubs as the Rotary and Kiwanis.

Each of these organizations was forever seeking new ways of attracting and, more importantly, retaining their membership, and film shows had long since proven popular. As the novelty of the movies themselves wore off, however, that particular carrot became less and less alluring to the rank and file — unless the movie promised something that the local movie house could not provide.

Many road-show operators, both the proselytizing variety and the more sensationalist, naturally zeroed in on the lodges as a captive audience. Now, as that audience grew, both in size and hunger, so it became apparent that anybody with a mind to make stag movies had a ready outlet for their wares. The means, the manpower and the market were all in place.

An industry was under way, and so boldly confident was it of success that, in 1928, the National Committee for Study of Social Values in Motion Pictures revealed that no fewer than fifty independently produced movies had been made specifically for "the sex circuit" during 1927 alone — that is, for screening by road shows, for fraternities and clubs, and at the tiny picture houses that were beginning to spring up in the seedier corners of the big cities, ostensibly catering to transients and the homeless.

Extrapolating from that total, we can roughly estimate that 300 to 400 such films were produced in America alone during the 1920s, and though not every one would have offered what we would describe as a hardcore sexual experience (nudity, whether posing or dancing, was probably far more prevalent), still that figure offers some understanding of just how popular stag films had become.

Just a handful of 1920s vintage films are known to have survived into modern times, but one assumes from their content that even this small sampling is representative of the fare going the rounds during this period.

Titles such as *Easy Money*, *A Bare Interlude*, *The Chiropodist*, *Chinese Love Life* (a rare, early mixed-race offering), *Night in a Turkish Harem*, *An English Tragedy*, *A Hot Dog*, *The Ice Man*, *Mixed Relations* (a film that combines its sexual content with some wonderful glimpses of small-town America, circa 1921) and, naturally, *A Free Ride* did not enjoy anything approaching nationwide (or even statewide) distribution. Nevertheless, the premise of each would have been familiar to viewers everywhere, as they balanced the desire for at least a loose narrative thread with the need to get on with the action as quickly as possible.

Many modern discussions of stag films refer disparagingly to the limited number of scenarios that arise, a complaint already firmly established by the end of the 1920s. "The topics do not vary," complained Ado Kyrou. "One can find whole series of films employing the same plot. There is the theme of the convent gardener, on whom the nuns vent themselves; that of the highwayman who attacks and violates a solitary woman; that of the lavender fields which call a passer by; that of weddings, etc."[7]

Other themes include the amorous delivery boy/man who accepts sex in lieu of payment or gratuity (*Girl Next Door*, *Lady Pays Her Bills*, *The Butcher Boy*, *The Handyman*, *The Tax Collector*, *The Bill Collector*), the voyeur who gets more than he bargained for (*Peeping Tom* — one of several movies to bear that title), the desert-island castaway who discovers Man Friday might not actually be a man at all (*Robinson Crusoe*), and even a locksmith come to relieve a brunette of her chastity belt (*The Locksmith*).

Housebreakers and similar nocturnal intruders were regular characters, frequently winding up the hapless victims of a sleepless nymphomaniac. More than one masked man is seen breaking in on a naked sleeper, and the only variation is how she reacts when she discovers the intruder. She might remain sleeping throughout the entire performance, but then wink happily at the camera once the deed is done; she might awaken mid-coitus, to prove as willing a participant as her assailant; she might even have left her window unlocked and her covers turned back deliberately, for the express purpose of catching a man and having her way with him.

Or she may not be a she at all, just as the housebreaker isn't a man. The 1920s French production *Le Souris Noir* (*The Black Mouse*) finds a *female* burglar being startled by the man of the house when she enters the marital bedroom. Intriguingly, the wife has already had her sexual attentions rebuffed this evening, so when her husband attempts to punish the masked Mouse by forcing her to fellate him, the wife promptly joins in. Next, the husband insists the Mouse go down on his wife, only for his wife to switch positions within moments. Further interchange follows before the three settle down with a cigarette each, now the best of friends.

Not all housebreakers could expect so happy an ending. In a Danish stag from the 1960s, *Even Thieves Do It*, two young women appear happy to indulge the handsome housebreaker who disturbed them in the night — indeed, they totally exhaust the poor chap. Which, of course, is when they call the police and have him hauled away (before the police return and pick up where the burglar left off!)

Prostitutes, too, were a popular theme, with the borderline surreal *Crazy Cat House* standing among the most memorable American stags of the interwar years. Ostensibly offering up a glimpse into the average man's vision of a brothel, it opens with two bored prostitutes enjoying a little mutual cunnilingus, when a knock on the door announces a customer. They let him in and appear to be preparing to undress him. Then an odd thing happens: he disappears from view, and the girls are pleasuring one another once more.

It turns out he was simply watching, for he reappears with a broad smile and a bold erection, and the action follows on from there, all taking place beneath the bulging eyes of the Crazy Cat itself, a demented-looking Felix look-alike whose nodding head appears to be egging on the behavior of the humans.

Health professionals, doctors or nurses, dentists and chiropodists were also frequently portrayed. They were, after all, already in the position to give an intimate examination; now it could become even more so, with the added advantage of sex curing the most chronic ailment.

The woman who calls for medical assistance in *Call for Doctor Handsome*, for example, is so doubled over by stomach pain that she can scarcely make it onto the bed. But just a few minutes of ministration from the physician will cure all her ills, even if she does just lie there like a lump while he's working. Likewise the poorly lass who receives a house call in *Oh Doctor*, especially once the physician has diagnosed her problem. She is suffering from a serious case of "lackanooky" (the sexual euphemism "nookie" dates from the 1920s), but luckily he has the cure with him. Sometimes, as in 1934's *Dr. Hard-On's Injections*, the woman does not even need to be ill. She just has the hots for the doctor.

In fact, few situations were not exploited. *Clean Floors* finds a typically house-proud housewife enjoying a friendly threesome while continuing to scrub the kitchen floor. From around 1924,

Hycock's Dancing School sees the most fashionable new dance crazes executed both naked and as lewdly as possible. A decade later, as America began its fascination with keeping fit, *Coffee, Tea or Cum* explored the erotic possibilities of Melvin J. Anderson's recently patented Aerobic Exercise Machine.

Newlyweds were an obvious source of inspiration. From the late 1940s, *Honeymoon Cottage* is one of the better-known intrusions into a married couple's first night together, while the early 1950s' *New York Honeymoon* practically doubles as a tourism short, as its cast first wander the streets of the city, taking in such delights as Radio City Music Hall, the newly constructed United Nations Building and the observation deck on the Empire State Building. Indeed, it takes an age for the couple to actually arrive at their honeymoon suite — but once ensconced, they romp with becoming giggles and good humor, beneath the lens of a cameraman who clearly knows his trade.

These particular stags work from the premise that both husband and wife are sexually experienced. A post–World War II Italian stag, however, admits us to the chambers of a retiring virgin (who bears a striking resemblance to the older Diego Maradona), as both her husband and an obliging maid attempt to rid her of her absolute aversion to sex and, of course, succeed in elevating her to near-nymphomania. (A similar transformation is arrived at in the American *Super-Salesman*, where the virgin Dottie becomes "a whiz at the old profession" after just six weeks of tutelage from "the cue-ball salesman.")

Not one of these scenarios is, were one to be honest, especially imaginative. Working within the severe strictures of the stag medium, however, the modern viewer might almost consider himself fortunate that the makers even attempted to place the movie within some form of context, no matter how fatuous.

In *Bath Room Frolics*, from the late 1940s, a woman breaks off from some heavy petting with her boyfriend, so she can use the bathroom. There she discovers a naked man standing behind the shower curtain, so she picks up where she left off with him and, when the boyfriend comes in to find out what's keeping her, he's no more surprised to meet the intruder than she was.

As storylines go, again it's weak. But at least there was a plot, and a refusal to fall into the trap that awaited so many moviemakers of later years, who simply opened and closed their opus with the sex already in full swing, denying the viewer even the basic knowledge of the characters.

One can argue that "character" itself has no place in a stag film, and that might be true for some viewers. Yet, in the stags as much as the real world, it is the relationship between two people that flavors the sex that follows. Two long-time lovers, working their way through a dog-eared copy of the *Kama Sutra*, are apt to behave in a very different manner than two strangers thrown together by circumstance alone.

Likewise, the viewer will have a wholly different perspective of a beautiful spy paying her contact for some secret plans with her body (the Cold War–era *The Pay-Off*), as he would on two naked strangers already deep into a bout of rough anal.

In the earlier movies, the lovers are people with motives and desires (however crudely they might be rushed through in the opening minutes of the film). In later offerings, they are simply the objects on the end of their genitalia.

Another aspect of the earliest films that was subsequently lost was humor. Sometimes it was a running theme through out a film, as in *A Les Culs d'Or* and *The Goat*. On other occasions, it was employed as a punch line, such as the conclusion to *Keyhole Portraits* (a.k.a. *Keyhole Silhouettes*), in which a ragged little janitor discovers every room he peeps into is being occupied by lovers in various stages of sexual exploration, until he arrives at the last one, to find an equally ragged tenant crouched on the other side of the door. (The sights that the janitor witnesses, incidentally, were clipped from a variety of other movies, few (if any) of which are in circulation today; while the entire enterprise was proclaimed, amusingly, "A Warmer Bruz Stinkeroo.")

Sometimes the jokes were verbal (or, at least, inserted on captions representing speech). The young woman who applies for work in the early-1920s movie *Strictly Union* introduces herself with the words "Mike Hunt sent me" (say it quickly). Shot in what looks very much like a genuine dental surgery, the *Slow Fire Dentist* awakens a gassed patient by massaging her vagina, while a caption announces "a new way to revive them." And *The Hot Hotel* employs the Charlie Chan–like Detective One Hung Low to make sure that any men and women sharing a room are legally married; otherwise they can be busted for "fucking without a license."

But humor was also employed to disguise otherwise unfortunate incidents in the filming itself.

Playing on an advertising slogan of the 1930s and 1940s, *The Pipe Cleaners* first reminds us that "Kay Woodie says, 'a clean pipe is easy on the draw.'" (Kay Woodie was a very popular brand of tobacco pipe.) Unfortunately, the actress charged with making certain that the pipe before her meets those same standards is clearly unhappy about the tools she's been given to work with, a grandfatherly gentleman who simply cannot raise an erection, no matter how hard he — or she — might try.

And she does try. "Stripping the outer leaves to expose the bark," reads one especially graphic caption, while the glares she is now aiming toward the camera make it clear she is growing increasingly impatient with the charade. Matters are worsened when her partner chimes in — although it is a silent movie, he is clearly either making excuses or denying such things have ever befallen him in the past. But all to no avail, as the closing caption makes painfully clear: "Moral — have your pipes cleaned at least once a week."

Physical responses such as this are difficult to overlook. But facial expressions can also give the *viewer* an unexpected surprise, and in this department, a 1930s stag, *A Jazz Jag*, rises far above the competition.

A seriously inebriated businessman, Sir Crème de Cock, arrives at his hotel and, having lamented the fact that his wife did not accompany him on the trip, he phones a local escort agency to request the presence of his favorite girl, "the cute French maid Ala de Tit." Ala is indeed cute. She is also extraordinarily playful. "Help me undress," pleads her host. "I'm tight and I hope you are." They both strip, and Ala commences to fellate him, in a manner unlike any seen on screen before.

With comical exaggeration, she picks a hair (or something) from his glans. She pokes her tongue out at the bobbing serpent and thumbs her nose at it. Occasionally she raises it and, sighting down the shaft, aims it, rifle-fashion, toward the camera. Sometimes she pretends it's a microphone, sometimes it's a corn cob. The film is silent, but she is clearly maintaining a constant stream of chatter, putting on a truly virtuoso performance and enjoying every moment of it — a masterpiece of physical humor in every meaning of the phrase.

Such mad exaggeration is (perhaps understandably) rare in live-action stags. As early as 1928, however, the possibilities of animation were broached by *Buried Treasure*, a crudely produced but entertaining film that was starkly drawn in the then- fashionable style of Otto Mesmer, creator of that most remarkable of 1920s icons, Felix the Cat. (Some authorities even credit Bray Studios, makers of the original Felix cartoons, as the source for this and other erotic cartoons.)

Buried Treasure concerns itself with the misadventures of a man named Everready, whose impressively sized penis also possesses the power of free thought and perambulation. So when Everready takes it into his head to shoot an annoying fly that has just landed on his glans, his penis breaks free and takes shelter behind a nearby rock. It escapes again a little later, after being nipped by a large crab that had taken up residence in a passing woman's vagina (remember, this *is* a cartoon!), but it nobly returns when Everready really needs its assistance — to fight a duel with an equally well-endowed Mexican gentleman who refuses to share the donkey he is sodomizing. Everready wins the fight and the two friends — one man and his penis — head off for a new round of adventures.

Buried Treasure proved so popular it was even translated into French, as *Les Mésaventures de Monsieur Gross-Bitt* (or perhaps it is the American version that is the translation). It was also among the first, and remains the most frequently seen, of a number of cartoon stags. Many adhered to the same standards as *Buried Treasure*; others were so crudely animated (a train-board encounter between a masturbating man and a greedy-eyed flapper, for example) that they beggar belief. The best-known of all such efforts, however, are those whose very existence might well be apocryphal. Certainly they have never been seen by anything remotely approaching a reliable source.

Popeye fandom, for example, has long murmured of the existence of a stag-style sailor-man reel, which was allegedly created by employees of the real Popeye's own creators, the Fleischer Studio in New York. Why they did it can only be surmised, as can the reason why they then chose to screen the movie for their bosses, Dave and Max Fleischer.

A well-worn legend insists that all concerned were first fired and then prosecuted for the unauthorized use of company materials and equipment. The veracity of this tale is tested, however, by its similarities to the almost identical tale of Walt Disney's most unexpected birthday gift, a no-holds-barred encounter between Mickey and Minnie Mouse. Disney, it is said, laughed through the film and then asked who was responsible for it. Two of his animators stepped forward and were peremptorily dismissed.

For obvious reasons, neither tale has lost its ability to entertain (and, perhaps, haunt the dreams of) fans and collectors of Fleischer and Disney. If either is based on reality, however, it seems most likely that it is merely a garbled, and subsequently embroidered, account of a medium in which Popeye and Mickey Mouse — not to mention a host of other beloved characters, real and fictional — did indeed cavort with unabashed sexual abandon, in full view of the watching world.

The 1930s were the heyday of the so-called Tijuana Bibles, crude, hand-drawn and roughly printed cartoon booklets that circulated from under the counter of countless grubby bookstores, and whose sole preoccupation was sex.

Though they are most frequently described as a by-product of the Depression, a consequence of the cheap paper and even cheaper printing that characterized the genre, it is nonsensical to describe them as a symptom of the era. They were not, for example, cheap — a new Bible could cost anything from fifty cents to $5, depending on length (they ran from eight to thirty-two pages), availability and, as is so often the case with such materials, the personal appearance of the purchaser. If he looked like he could afford the higher price, that's what he was charged.

Neither could they be described as a rough and ready substitute for any other commodity that had been forced out of business by the prevalent economic climate. Rudely drawn but lasciviously detailed, both the best and the worst Tijuana Bibles can most easily be compared to a particularly well-decorated wall in a rundown public bathroom, all spurting penises and dripping vaginas, obscene comments and scurrilous rumors, all executed with absolutely no respect for anyone — least of all the celebrities and public figures who most frequently peopled their pages.

The term "Tijuana Bible" itself was a misnomer. Few, if any, were actually manufactured in Tijuana. Some, however, claimed to be, as a slim defense against any criminal investigations the U.S. authorities might care to launch. Others were purportedly printed in sundry European and Latin American cities; many offered no place of manufacture whatsoever.

Neither were they Bibles, although there was an audience that swore on them as a mirror of the excesses that the rich and famous were capable of enacting. And why not? How else would the inquiring mind discover that W.C. Fields' penis so resembled a banana that a Parisian showgirl once took a bite out of it? That both Laurel and Hardy and the Marx Brothers were inseparable, even in bed? That Greta Garbo's vagina tasted of vanilla?

Equally entertainingly, several of these sagas were based upon already circulating gossip. A Bible that depicted Joan Crawford being sexually serviced by Jimmy Durante's famously oversized schnozzle fed directly into a legend that was already well-circulated in New York, regarding Crawford's earliest years in the entertainment industry. Except it wasn't Durante whose nose the real-life Crawford enjoyed so much, it was MGM executive Harry Rapf, possessor of a proboscis, Crawford herself later laughed, that was "so big it kept his private parts dry in the shower."[8] And it was Rapf who first discovered Crawford, allegedly after witnessing a stag movie in which she was the star.

In later years, makers of stags would echo several themes broached by the Bible writers, and it is not unusual today to find animated stags described as Bible-like in their own right. The aforementioned apocrypha notwithstanding, however, few stepped further beyond the realm of make-believe than to hijack another of the Bibles' favorite themes, readily recognizable parodies of other Sunday Funnies–style cartoon characters. Among these, the greatest is surely *Sex-Capade Thru Comic Land*, a 1950s short that (re-) introduced viewers to Lil' Abnormal, Rick Dacy, Darn Ol' Duck and a Dogwood who delights, of course, in doing it doggy style.

In this particular universe, a philandering Popeye and a masturbating Minnie Mouse would not have raised an eyebrow.

The Sweet Smell of Vinegar

Sultan Slaves

The United States' most notorious single market for stags during the 1920s and 1930s was Kansas City. The self-styled Paris of the Plains boasted a flourishing Prohibition-era vice scene, where the aptly named West Bottom district was regarded as the best tenderloin west of Chicago. Edward R. Murrow once mused, "If you want to see some sin, forget about Paris and go to Kansas City. With the possible exception of such renowned centers as Singapore and Port Said, Kansas City probably has the greatest sin industry in the world."[1]

Located on the industrial riverfront, but spreading into the heart of downtown, West Bottom was a maze of speakeasies, honky-tonks and bordellos, with even the most exclusive-looking establishment a mere facade. One block from the federal courthouse, the Chesterfield was, to all outward appearances, a high-class supper club. But the waitresses wore only shoes, money belts and see-through cellophane aprons, and shaved their "pubic hair to represent a heart, diamond, club [or] spade."[2] Striptease and nude dancing were staples of the menu, and a warren of backrooms were reserved for both real and cinematic sex sessions.

For all Kansas City's countrywide renown, however, the films on show here would have been local productions, unseen beyond the immediate environs. With the exception of material emanating from such much-traveled hubs as L.A. and New York, a movie made in one locale rarely traveled far, unless an operator relocated to another part of the country, transported his collection with him and set up business in his new hometown. Small moviemaking operations existed in every city in America, and even smaller ones thrived in every community. Donald H. Gilmore recalls Wisconsin as a hotbed of production in the early 1950s, crediting a Racine filmmaker for shooting *"The Kotex King*, a popular satire,"* and a Spring Green operation for *Nights at George Sank*.[3]

Seattle was another city with a small but thriving operation, its early-1930s output dominated by a man remembered only as Sidney, and its biggest star a twenty-year old actress named Joan. Her experiences, as recalled across a series of informal interviews more than six decades later, offer a truly intimate insight into the world of prewar stag production.

With her thinning white hair, rosacea-tinted cheeks and a frame that struggled to squeeze itself into either of the armchairs that sat around her tiny apartment's television centerpiece, Joan looked like an advertisement for Mom's Apple Pie. Certainly it was difficult to equate this model of modern American grandmotherhood with any lifestyle beyond the Norman Rockwellian images that clustered in photo frames on every available surface — and almost impossible to believe that, sixty years before, she was something of a movie star.

"Nothing you would have heard of, though," she blurted out when pressed for detail, and the abruptness with which she changed the subject initially suggested that it was a topic she had no desire whatsoever to revisit, which was strange because almost every conversation she had revolved around her memories — for what else was there for an eighty-something-year-old woman to talk about, once the daily pleasantries had been exhausted?

She'd been a widow for a decade or more, but she wasn't lonely. Her family were regular and loving visitors and she had both grandchildren and great-grandchildren to dote on. And that, it transpired, was why she didn't want to talk about her moviemaking. Not one of her family knew about it, and she had no intention of ever letting them in on the secret. "I was young and it was fun" were defenses that simply wouldn't wash with her kith and kin; and, besides, she didn't have copies of any of her films, didn't even know what most of them were called or even how many she actually made. Only that the money was good — no, strike that; the money was sensational, and that made an awful lot of difference in those dark years immediately following the crash of 1929.

Joan was working at the local Woolworths when she first encountered Sid. "A friend of mine knew somebody who'd come into a movie camera and was looking for people — I suppose you'd call it 'auditioning' — who would make little pictures that he'd rent out to fraternity parties, clubs, the Elks, all those organizations. The Masons, firehouses, policemen's balls."[4]

Sidney specialized in filming dancing girls, "and that was all we had to do. Dance. It was a little suggestive sometimes — he liked us to run our hands over our breasts and below — but there was no actual touching, and we were clothed. Not the sort of clothes you'd want to wear on the street, but you couldn't see anything.

"He had a gramophone player, one of those Edison cabinets, although he wasn't recording the sound, that was just to give us something to dance to. Then he'd set up his equipment, and we'd dance on this little stage he'd built at one end of the studio. One record, one girl, so you'd be up there for a couple of minutes, and that was it, he'd hand you $10 and you were free to go."

The turnover rate among girls willing to dance for him was high. "You have to remember this was Sidney's business," Joan explained. "People paid to rent his films, and they wanted to get their money's worth. Which meant you couldn't just get up there and wriggle a little, you had to look like you were . . . well, getting excited. You had to dance to the camera. A lot of girls didn't understand that, they thought you could just hop around, run your hands across your stomach a couple of times — easy money. They were the girls who didn't get called back."

Joan, however, was not one of those. She'd had ballet lessons as a child, "so I knew how to move. And I went out dancing a lot. I enjoyed it, and I learned very early on that the more you moved, the more boys would look at you. So when Sidney started filming, I put it into my head that the camera was a crowd of boys — which, in a way, it was — and I had to get their attention. There were ten or eleven of us at my first audition, and I think Sidney only asked three of us to come back."

It was several months after her debut that Sidney's interests began to shift toward more erotic escapades. "I was nineteen when I first met Sidney and started dancing for him," she recalled, "and that went on for some months. In fact, I remember my twentieth birthday, because he did the studio up like a birthday party, and had me start out by jumping through a screen that had 'Sweet 16' painted on it [then, as now, youth was considered one of the greatest feminine virtues], and then go into my dance routine. So it was after that. Maybe six months."

He approached the subject in a circuitous, almost apologetic manner, Joan said. "Sidney was — not shy, but very reserved around us. He made it very apparent that we had a professional arrangement, which I think was important because some of the girls did develop something of a crush on him, which could lead to all kinds of problems. But I was at the studio one day, just dancing, and when I was finished he asked if I'd stick around to talk. Well, that was strange, because he'd never done that before. But I stayed while the last few girls danced; then, while he was packing up his equipment, he asked if I wanted to make some extra money.

"I thought he just had more dances for me, but then he explained that someone had seen one of my other films, and had asked . . . I wish I could remember the exact words, but it was along the lines of, 'Would you be interested in showing the camera what else you can do?' Something very innocuous. Well, I thought he simply wanted me to dance in the nude, so I told Sidney to let me think about it, which is when he told me that it wasn't exactly dancing, and I wouldn't be on my own."

Her initial response was one of horror. At the same time, however, $100 was an enormous amount of money, "more than I earned in I don't know how long at work. Plus, I also got the impression from Sidney that the request was not one that he was happy about turning down. So I said I'd think about it and I'd let him know later in the week, but I was waiting for the trolley home and I thought, 'To hell with it. Why not?'"

The actual physical mechanics of the situation "never crossed my mind." Joan said. Her initial assumption was that he would rope in one of the male dancers with whom he worked, shooting films to rent out for hen nights and similar, girls-only events. "Or maybe even it would be with him, because he wasn't a bad-looking fellow. So I ran back to the studio and caught him as he was locking up, and I said I'd do it, which I think shocked him more than if I'd said no, because he asked if we could go for a drink, and we went to a bar on First Avenue. I remember this so well, he was just asking again and again if I knew what I was agreeing to, and if I was sure, and what would my boyfriend think. . . . I told him I didn't have a boyfriend, so then he was worrying that maybe I was a virgin, or I wouldn't know what to do, or maybe I'd freeze on camera."

Joan, however, was "a very determined girl, and if I made up my mind to do something, I'd see it through. Like the dancing. The first time I did it, there was a moment of *What am I doing?* and then I put it out of my mind. If I decided I didn't like it, I'd not do it again. In fact, I was more worried about Sidney, because as much as it would be my first time, it was his as well, and I don't think it would have even crossed his mind if he hadn't been asked in the way he was."

She never did find out who Sidney's partners in this new venture were. "It wasn't the Mafia, nothing that organized, but they had the same ideas and methods, and I think that was who got to Sidney. And Seattle also had a very heavy Klan presence, they had their own lodge in town [the Klansmens' Roost, on Western Avenue], and they were always renting Sidney's dance films, so I wondered about them as well. Whoever it was, they knew someone was making money from that sort of picture, and they wanted to get a piece of it for themselves. And it wasn't as if they didn't pay Sidney well. I don't know if they had anyone else making pictures for them, but once

Sidney was on board, he was earning a fortune from them, all tax-free, no questions asked."

Sidney shared his largesse. "I was still living at home with my parents in Georgetown," Joan continued, "so I had to be careful about the money, I didn't want them to know I was earning so much. I was bringing home more in a day than my father was earning in a week sometimes. So I banked most of it, believe it or not, and didn't let on. Every so often, I'd come home with a 'bargain' that I picked up at the market, and I remember 'finding' $20 on the street one day, right around the time Dad needed some work done on his automobile, but they never did find out."

Joan shot her first stag in early 1931, on a Saturday evening after work. "It was bitterly cold, January or February, and I remember hoping the heating would be on in Sidney's building. I arrived, and we talked for a bit while he was setting up. Again, I think he was more nervous than I was. My partner was already there, and he wasn't my type at all — I mean, he was good-looking enough, and he was clean . . . that was something I told Sidney very firmly, they have to be clean. All over. But there was no chemistry at all between us.

"Sidney had what you could call a plot in mind, and I still think it was a clever one. He said there were a lot of films like this, where a burglar broke into a house, found a girl in the bedroom, and they'd start carrying on together. Sidney's idea was to reverse that. The man would be lying on his bed reading, he'd hear a sound and turn, and I'd be standing there with a mask on, breaking into his house.

"He'd stand and try to fight me off, but I'd overpower him. [A similar plot was used in the aforementioned French stag *Le Souris Noir*.] I had a shortish skirt on and no underwear, so Sidney wanted me to force him back and then sit over his face. The only trouble was, he couldn't get the camera in close enough to actually show what was going on! I was crouching there, with the camera lens pressing against my stomach, and I was wondering how anybody could watch this back and find it exciting?

"We tried this for what felt like hours, before Sidney finally admitted defeat, and asked if we had any ideas. The guy was saying, 'Well, we could [fuck] and you could film that,' but Sidney was still worrying about angles. . . . The next film we made, he had a whole load of new equipment, so I guess he said something to his new 'partners' and they set him up with the proper gear."

The original footage was not wasted, however Joan recalled. "It turned out that Sidney had caught enough action on film that he was able to turn in a ten minute picture, and they loved it. He told me he spliced in a few head shots from some of my dances, so people could see me enjoying myself, I suppose, and that was it."

A star was born.

"As I said, that first picture was a success despite all of our misgivings, and it could only have been about a week later — maybe a little longer, because I don't remember how long it took to get the prints made, although I know it was fast — anyway, he came by Woolworths one morning and asked me if I was free that evening. I said I was, and he told me there and then that 'they' — he always called his partners that — had loved the first film and wanted to know if there was anything else I could do. Again he phrased it in a way that made me wonder whether he was entirely comfortable working in this new way, but I said I'd see him as soon as I got out of work, because it was only a couple of blocks from the store to the studio, and there we were."

Joan had no idea precisely how many movies she made. "There must have been dozens that I actually shot, and then there were the ones where Sidney would take bits of one and bits of another, and splice them together. And others where he'd insert my head and shoulders into scenes I wasn't even part of. What was so wonderful was, he paid me for all of them, at least so far as I know. He'd just say, 'Oh this is for such-and-such,' even though I'd been nowhere near the studio all week, and he always paid me on the day when I was there. So I asked him and he said he got paid for every film he delivered, so it was only fair that I was paid for every one I was in."

She rarely saw her work once it was complete. "Believe it or not," Joan said, "I never actually sat and watched more than two or three of my pictures — it wasn't like they turned up at the local picture house, after all. Occasionally I'd ask Sidney to show me a scene, so I could see how something looked. It was the same as the dancing, you have to remember that the camera is your audience's eyes, but they're not only watching you, they're watching everything that you're doing. So you want to make sure they can see what you want them to. This might sound very conceited, but you also want to see what you look like from different angles, or doing different things.

"I remember one time, Sidney asked if I would do something, and we — Sidney, the guy and I — set up all these cues and warnings so I'd know what was going to happen, Sidney would be ready for it, everything was set up. And the guy forgot them all, so I had no warning at all. Well, I thought I got through it okay, but I asked Sidney just to show me back that part and it was horrible. I looked awful — cross-eyed, screwed-up face, just horrible. And I said, 'Sidney, if you don't cut those frames out and shoot it again, I will *never* make another film for you again.' It's the only time that ever happened, the only time I ever asked him to change anything, and he did it, bless him."

Birth control and infections were very real risks, and several of the girls working for Sidney fell prey to both. "We douched," Joan explained. "I still remember that, every time I smell vinegar. Religiously, after every shoot, I'd be in the bathroom with the vinegar. And I was lucky, I never fell. A couple of other girls did." Both, however, were back at work within a few weeks. "There were doctors," Joan explained simply. "Friends of Sidney's partners — well, probably not friends, but associates — they could treat most things, no questions asked, and it was all on the house, as well. At least, it was for me."

Joan knew only a handful of her fellow thespians. "There were a few you'd see regularly, but a lot who'd pass through just once or twice, and then they'd be gone. I know I was responsible for a few people only having the one shot, but the way I looked at it, we were professionals, we needed to behave professionally. Anybody who stepped outside of that had no business being involved."

Given the illicit nature of the filming, and the knowledge that it would take just a whisper in the wrong ear to bring the full weight of the Seattle Police Department crashing down on his operation, Sidney treated his cast carefully, especially when it came to saying goodbye. "He was very diplomatic," Joan remembered. "He always congratulated people on their performance, even if they'd been absolutely hopeless, he always paid them in cash on the day and, I do believe, if anybody ever tried anything on — making threats or whatever — Sidney's partners would soon have changed their minds. Plus, you have to remember what they were complaining *about*. It was hardly something they'd want advertised!"

For those who did make the grade, Sidney could be a demanding taskmaster. "There were no sick days. If there was a shoot scheduled, it didn't matter if you were feeling lousy. So long as it didn't actually show, and you weren't going to infect anybody else, you just got on with it."

As for what happened on-screen, Sidney frequently made suggestions ("He called them 'special orders'"), but would never push the cast, male or female, to do something they were not willing to at least try. "I said earlier that I'd had a certain amount of experience before I started with Sidney, but there were a lot of things I hadn't done, or hadn't even thought of doing, so Sidney would suggest something and either I'd laugh at the idea of it or he'd laugh at my expression. He called it my 'Little Miss Prissy' face."

One example that stuck in Joan's mind was her first lesbian scene: "The first time I went with another girl, it wasn't the actual physical thing that was bothering me so much as the fear that I was going to be shown up as a fraud. Anybody can give a man a good time, but girls can be harder, particularly if they're new to the industry, or they're not very good actresses. But you know where things are, and you know what makes them feel good, so you just empty your mind and get on with it. And it ended up being a lot of fun."

Neither was she averse to improvisation. "If Sidney asked me to have three orgasms, I'd have three orgasms. But if I threw in the occasional unscripted one, which did happen on occasion, then so much the better.

"Something I remember very well — it was my fifth or sixth picture, and in all that time, I'd only ever done things that Sidney specifically asked me to do, most of which involved putting myself in different positions. But there was one thing he'd never asked me to do, so I thought — well, let's see what happens. Because I'd never actually done it before. I did kiss a boyfriend there once, but it was just a kiss, a peck. I knew about it, though, because you do, girls just do.

"We were in the middle of a shoot, and the boy just couldn't stay hard, so Sidney told him to roll on top of me and pretend that we were doing it. I said, 'Let's just try something,' I pushed him over and put his thing in my mouth — he was soft, so it was scarcely difficult. And I'll never forget this, Sidney just went, 'Whooo!' at the top of his voice, and I saw that camera come right in, the closest of close-ups, and that was more or less the entire film.

"The funny thing was, he never did get hard. Sidney probably spliced on an ending from another film. But once I'd done it that once, Sidney asked me if I'd do it again, with someone who was more ready for it, and how far would I be willing to take it, so I told him to set it up and I'd show him."

From a technical point of view, Joan remembered these sequences as the most demanding of all. "You have to remember, even with all the money, the cameras and lights were still fairly basic, we were still doing a lot of things on the cheap, with natural lighting rather than proper studio lighting, so a lot of what happened was just lost when the film was developed. And it was really difficult to get that right; the camera would have to be positioned just so, my head would have to be just so, my hands, everything.

"Then I'd have to keep my mind on where my shoulder was, whether my hair was falling over my face, all those different things. So I'd watch those scenes back with Sidney, and we were at the stage of actually making diagrams of how I should be lying, how the guy should be angled, even what time of day brought the sunlight in best."

One stag movie, dating from some twenty years later, illustrates the difficulties that Joan and Sidney (and every other filmmaker) wrestled with. *The Cameraman* takes the viewer behind the scenes of a stag shoot, to capture all of the interruptions and intrusions that take place, together with the couple's own interaction as they first smirk, but then grow increasingly restive as the cameraman halts them again and again, to reposition a body part, demonstrate movements and positions, or any of the hundred other minor nuisances that can get in the way of a good view of the proceedings.

The sheer clumsiness of the sex act is revealed with astonishing candor. Even in the most amateurish-looking stag, one rarely gets to see the struggle to remove recalcitrant underclothing, the ungainly movements that precede the adoption of a new position, the need to get oneself comfortable before embarking on a new act — those are the moments, after all, where the camera is usually switched off. *The Cameraman*, however, captures them all and, were it not for the fact that another camera is obviously recording all the action (and the titular cameraman's own eventual decision to lay down his machine and join the action himself), one could believe one really was watching the creation of a genuine stag movie. And a genuinely well-made one, as well.

"It might sound peculiar," Joan said, "but we took pride in making these pictures, because no matter how secretive we had to be about what we doing — because it *was* against the law at that time, and no matter that people called them 'dirty movies,' we still knew that our films served a purpose, and were capable of touching people in a way that no other film was. Seriously. A romance might make you weep, a thriller might excite you. But our films reached deep inside people, and affected them emotionally and physically, which is an enormous responsibility. We could have just made boring films with bored people having bored sex in the shadows, but what would have been the fun in that?

"We wanted people to see what we were doing, as though they were doing it themselves, and if that meant spending an hour trying to work out how best to show five minutes, we did it. People appreciated it, as well. Sidney's people. Our pay went up — I could have given up Woolworths altogether, if it wouldn't have made people ask where my money was coming from, and this was during the Depression, when nobody was earning enough money. But Sidney and I were, and it was because we cared about the pictures we were making.

"It makes me laugh when I see people on the television saying that these sorts of films are degrading to women. I was living the life of Riley! If anyone was being degraded or exploited, it was the men who paid money to see the films. I don't know how much rentals were, but I know they weren't cheap — plus there'd be the cost of the hall, or wherever it was being shown, and everything else. And what did they get for their money? They got to watch me thinking about my radio serials, or what I was going to say to someone at work tomorrow. . . ."

Joan made her final movie sometime in 1934. "I stopped when I met my husband. I told Sidney straight, 'I've met this guy who I think I want to marry, and though I might tell him one day what I do, I'd rather not be doing it when I tell him.'"

In fact, she never did tell him. "I showed him a few of the things I'd learned, but it was [very different]. Sex as work or sex as love. We had love, so there was no reason to bring up work."

Neither did she regret giving up her career. "I missed the financial side of things, but my husband had a fairly good job, so we never went short. Plus I had my savings. We did okay, and when the economy picked up, we were fine. The only time I thought about going back to work was during the war, when he was away, but I'd lost contact with Sidney by then, and I simply didn't know how to get back into the business. So I never did."

Swedish Massage

Eureka! Mastophallation!

Home-movie-making equipment continued taking tremendous strides throughout the 1920s. But 1932 brought the most significant development yet. In that year, Kodak introduced the Cine-Kodak 8 camera, an ingenious device that ran a single strip of 16mm film through the camera twice, to be exposed one half (8mm) at a time. The film would then be split down the middle during processing and spliced together.

Three years later, Bell & Howell took the process one stage further with the introduction of the Filmo Straight 8, the first camera to employ true 8mm film stock. True, its advantages remained financially out of reach to many people, as unemployment and inflation continued to take their toll, but for those whose livelihood was not affected (and which might even have been improved) by the Depression, the Filmo rapidly established itself as the most economic home-movie camera yet developed.

Other innovations followed. Eumig introduced a built-in light meter in 1935, quickly followed by the first electric drive, to replace the unreliable clockwork mechanism of old. Cassette-loading cameras began to appear. The first amateur color film was in the stores; sound recording was a reality; and, although the latter developments made very little impression on the stag-makers, still there is an unmistakable ambience to the best stags of the 1930s, an almost surreal sense of glamour that was as tangible as that which pervades Hollywood's best-loved efforts of the same period.

In both a sexual sense and a broader cultural one, 1930s stags purposefully sought out situations their viewers aspired toward, and then let the action develop from there. The fact that many of these situations revolved around nothing more exciting than going for a job interview, living in a comfortable apartment and employing a maid is a reminder of precisely how desperate things were in the real world. Hollywood portrayed life as a series of increasingly flamboyant fantasies. Stags reversed the equation, transforming fantasy into what was once (and, hopefully, would again become) real life.

It is impossible to say with any certainty whether this was a conscious decision on the part of the filmmakers. After all, the same period also threw up many films that simply adhere to the basic rampage of the "beast with two backs." Even the title of the mid-1930s' *A Day in the Country* is misleading, in as much as the country, if not intended as a phonetic pun, is barely even visible (the odd patch of grass in the background should not count), for all the heaving flesh on display.

The erotic film genre's finest approximation of 1930s Americana would not be shot for another forty years, in the form of a lush parody of the equally redolent *The Sting*. The mid-1970s stag *The Bite* draws upon every popular visual stereotype the decade has bequeathed on modern culture, with a style and lack of self-consciousness that, in many ways, actually surpasses *The Sting* itself for period "feel."

Films of the period tended toward more mundane scenarios. Let Hollywood lionize the gangsters and confidence tricksters; stag films were more concerned with what their viewers really got up to.

"I was in my office one evening, when a young lady came in to get a job as my secretary."

How many fantasies open with such a sentence? How many hot detective novels? And how many films? Who knows, but one of the first movie versions, *The Interview*, dates from the early 1930s and even then the consequences were inevitable.

"I sent her into the back room for a more thoro [sic] interview. I wanted to make sure she could do more than just write letters. So . . ."

So he wrestles her out of her fur coat and, when she objects, defends himself with the claim "having studied osteopathy, I just can't keep my hands from roaming" — an explanation that, oddly, seems to satisfy her. Well, it's either that or the cunnilingus.

Later, we encounter another of those unscripted moments that give stag movies so much realism, as he unexpectedly ejaculates inside the applicant's mouth. The viewer sees nothing, but the woman is suddenly reeling around and rather hastily spitting something out, leaving him to simply hold his own apologetically. She clearly doesn't mind too much, though, because the next time it happens, she's ready and waiting, and devours it so greedily that the final caption tells us what we'd already guessed: "She's got the job!" If only employment was so easy to obtain elsewhere in the prevailing economic climate!

Scenarios built around gambling were popular. Bouts of strip poker were a regular launching pad for all manner of unclothed shenanigans.

The day-to-day business of living, too, featured heavily. One especially true-to-life drama, aptly titled *Making Up*, based itself around a married couple's steamy reconciliation, following a screaming row that sent both to bed in separate rooms. Neither of the actors is what one would describe as an oil painting, but the scenario would have struck a chord with most middle-aged onlookers; she settles down to sleep in the bedroom, he makes do with a sofa, and the icy silence might have gone on for days, had she not relented after a few sleepless hours and padded out to the living room to make amends.

Another movie, *Sunday Sunrise*, opens with a woman dressing for church, while she waits for her boyfriend, John, to arrive. When he does, she seems genuinely surprised that he has something other than worship on his mind (although the mask he's wearing should have tipped her off), but she peels off her Sunday best as enthusiastically as she donned it and, because it was too good a visual pun to ignore, she winds up on her knees regardless.

One emergent lifestyle that does not appear to have appealed to the stags of the 1930s was nudism, an omission that might initially seem surprising. After all, the starting point for almost every stag was the removal of the clothing; where better, then, to stage an event than in an establishment where everybody has already stripped bare?

But perhaps that was *why* nudism did not appeal. Since emerging fully formed on the domestic scene at the end of the 1920s (the first two organized movements, American Social Nudism and the American League for Physical Culture, launched in 1929), nudism had adopted a puritanical approach toward sexuality, a stance confirmed in December 1931, when the New York Court of General Sessions dismissed charges of public indecency against the ALPC (filed after police raided one of the organization's meetings), ruling that the meet was neither public nor indecent.

Nudity without indecency? It scarcely bore thinking about. But it was true, as the disappointed hordes that queued to watch the movement's first movies, the 1932 documentary *This Nude World* and 1934's *Elysia*, would testify. Both certainly offered acres of bare flesh to ogle (*Elysia* was even filmed at what was then California's largest naturist camp, Elysian Fields). But it was curiously antiseptic flesh, swathed in an asexuality that might, in the words of sundry disapproving censors, have *appealed* to prurient interests, but certainly did not satisfy them, which in turn was (and remains) an argument that committed naturists have been making all along.

With this absolute absence of eroticism in mind, it is no shock to learn that just one noteworthy period stag addresses the subject of nudism. *The Modern Pirates* (a.k.a. *Nautical Nudes*) features a quintet of girls who determine to open their own nudist colony on a deserted island, just outside the three-mile limit. They steal a yacht and are soon happily naked, playing beach ball and undertaking sundry innocent calisthenics, when the yacht's enraged owner (who followed them in a dinghy) arrives.

Seeing what is going on, he steals the girls' clothes and rows back to the yacht, leaving the girls marooned. He will rescue them, he says, only if they promise to do everything he asks of them. Of course they agree, but even as one of their number is submitting to his attentions, the others are plotting mutiny. And when he comes above deck to collect his next victim, they pounce, tossing him overboard and sailing away — proof that, no matter how inviting they might look, you shouldn't mess with nudists. Consequently, very few stags do.

Viewers of modern erotic movies are well aware that the industry is built around certain visual principles, without which the film might as well be scrapped before it is even processed. But there were few such conventions in the past.

Without entering into a debate regarding the makeup (both physical and emotional) of the modern "porn star" and his or her vintage counterpart, still there is a studied, even stony indifference to the twenty-first-century cast that was not present before: the sense that the actors truly are *acting*, and that every facial expression has been painstakingly rehearsed so as to illustrate precisely the correct level of desire, lust and hunger.

Particularly during the years when even "professional" stag-makers were essentially amateurs — that is, any time before the industry began considering itself an industry, during the late 1960s — there were few such demands made of the actors. It was simply a matter of getting on with it.

Likewise, though we know that certain moves may have been choreographed beforehand, there is no rigid adherence to any set sequence of events and actions. Even that most beloved (and literal) climax to the modern film, the so-called "money shot" of male ejaculation, was by no means guaranteed in the earliest films, while other so-called specialist interests rarely arose in the stags because, it was assumed, they rarely arose in the stag-viewer's own life — or, if they did, they tended to be something he kept quiet about.

Even between man and wife, anal sex was not a hot topic of conversation on the Detroit production line. Group sex occasionally occurred in films, but it only became a standard feature once the mainstream media discovered the cult of wife-swapping during the late 1950s. Male homosexuality was kept almost completely out of sight, except on those occasions where the positioning of a three-some left one of the men at a loss for what else to do; while lesbianism was generally treated as a mere appetizer for the arrival of the male. (Although some sensational exceptions do exist — from the 1930s, *The Three Graces, or the Torture of the Tickling Tongues* is often ranked among the greatest all-girls erotic films ever made. It certainly boasts some of the most word-heavy captions.)

In their own way, stag films were already pushing the envelope so far that any further expansion might well have proved fatal, for the audience if not for the genre.

For fully the first sixty years of the last century, sex education was, at best, a lesson either passed along from father to son or, more commonly, constructed from whispered sniggers in the locker room, and theoretical discussions around the nude models depicted in such magazines as *Screen Art Studies* or *Art Group Quarterly*, and the unclothed tribespeople who occasionally adorned *National Geographic*. And, even there, pubic hair remained fiercely censored until 1958, when it was finally permitted to blossom in the nudist press.

Other folk gained their knowledge by secretly leafing through their parents' copy of *Ideal Marriage: Its Physiology and Technique*. First published in the U.S. in 1930, Dutch gynecologist Theodore Van de Velde's guide to "increasing the forces of mutual attraction in marriage" was a worldwide best seller; by 1941, it had been translated into no less than twenty-five languages, including Yiddish, Hindustani and Chinese. It also journeyed into territory that no mainstream publication had ever before visited, offering frank (for the time) discussions on such hitherto unmentionable topics as female ejaculation, "karezza" ("insertion without ejaculation") and the vital importance of foreplay.

Forty years before *Joy of Sex* author Alex Comfort laid out those same preoccupations in the form of his gently bearded and pert-breasted pencil sketches, Van de Velde was gleefully holding forth on those occasions when "the man's reactions are less rapid, [and] the woman may with advantage take the more active part . . . and herself, most successfully give — instead of receiving — the genital kiss."[1]

Sex was a voyage of discovery, then, for even the most promiscuous-minded youngster. Nineteen-fifties pinup queen Candy Barr once claimed she'd been married two years before she ever heard of fellatio — "I wasn't even aware that people engaged in oral sex" — and she only found out then because she was filming a stag at the time.[2]

Most people, however, did not have that advantage. They gleaned knowledge from wherever they could and, short of experiencing the real thing, the stag movie — for those who encountered them — not only became an integral part of this voyage, it was also, quite possibly, the first practical demonstration of the sex act its audience would ever have witnessed. From the early 1930s, *Blends* even offered viewers an idiot's guide to the most basic sexual positions, with the reminder that, just as "blending improves such things as tobacco, whiskey and spirits," it can also "mix up screwing."

It would have been futile, then, for a filmmaker to have thrown his audience into the final chapters of the Marquis de Sade, when many of them were still coming to terms with the first lines of Dick and Jane. Several films from the late 1930s even close with what purports to be a message from "the management": "To the men. After seeing this picture, rush over to some nice girl and get taken care of." The instruction may seem brusque today, but for many audience members, any guidance was welcome. (Another stag from this time, *Swedish Massage*, demonstrates how to give a girl a feet-first tongue bath: "How this thrills them! Try it, boys!")

The lessons were not always well taught. A 1920s stag, *An Egyptian Adventure*, affects to offer viewers a crash course in the multitudinous sexual positions available to the more experimentally minded athletic types. But though the film is beautifully shot and sensually delivered, one cannot help but flinch as the man comes close, again and again, to dropping his partner on her head.

The concept of contraception plays very little part in the stag films. The occasional mention or unheralded glimpse of a "fish skin" (common parlance for condoms during the 1930s and 1940s) and one sighting of a diaphragm (in the 1940s' *Hillbillies Frolic*) notwithstanding, just two stags stand out as indicative of the genre's opinion of birth control.

A novelty condom, with a gently spiked tip, causes some merriment in the late-1930s film *Wet Dream*, while *Goodyear*, around twenty years later, introduced the unlikely spectacle of a door-to-door condom saleslady who cannot wait to demonstrate her wares. Unfortunately, no sooner has she applied the item to her prospective customer than he tears it off and they get on with the job without it.

Similarly, any attempt at lovemaking finesse, by either the actors or the camera, was generally frowned upon. As scholar Joseph Slade explained, "Stag productions generally aimed at an ineptitude that reinforced the genre's illicit reputation and served as an index of its 'authenticity.' Cameras intruded into frames, stagehands visibly adjusted lights, and performers clearly asked for direction or smirked directly into the lens; the glitches were left in the footage, as a way of underscoring that real sex was taking place between real people."[3] Which, in turn, guaranteed that the often hard-faced determination with which all but the most natural of modern actors and actresses deliver their goods is oftentimes replaced in older films by a veritable plethora of quite contrary emotions — nervousness, surprise, embarrassment.

Absolutely any inexperience or uncertainties that the cast may be suffering would be vividly revealed by the camera. The male lead's sudden inability to perform is the most pronounced side effect of shooting movies under the primitive conditions to which most stags were beholden, but it was by no means the only one. Even the most painstakingly planned shoot was conducted with one eye firmly focused upon the sheer impossibility of actually scripting every eventuality and preparing the cast beforehand for what might happen.

One of the most graphic such sequences appears in the 1960s British threesome *The Nightspot*, as one of the male participants fails to warn his fellatrix of his imminent ejaculation. A portrait of grace and harmonic beauty beforehand, she suddenly pauses for a split second, frozen in mid-movement. Her eyes bulge comically in surprise, and then she reels around as sperm cascades out of her mouth. Words are exchanged; she is clearly requesting some warning for next time. But she obviously doesn't get it for, as the movie approaches its climax, an almost identical scene is played out with the other male lead.

An actress would fall prey to a fit of uncontrollable giggling, an actor to a serious case of stage fright, but the camera kept rolling and the movie went on. A frequent criticism of the modern sex film is that it is too choreographed — you know what's going to happen before the opening credits have even finished. The corresponding condemnation of its vintage counterpart would be that it was too random. Even when the action is at its steamiest, anything might still happen.

It is this, many viewers concur, that ensure the stag movie's value as a sexual document, as much as an entertainment.

Dating from the late 1940s, the French *La Representante* (*The Representative*) features a door-to-door saleswoman who is rather brashly selling ladies' underwear to young men. Naturally, she has to model it for them, with a technique that invites them to admire both the look and the texture of the fabric. Things develop from there, but perhaps the most touching element of the film is the absolute bashfulness of the actress.

Without once looking as though she's regretting her decision to make the movie, it is clear that she possesses no more than the most mechanical notion of what she's supposed to be doing, and it's this, as opposed to anything else that's going on, that gives the film its most erotic quality. Once again, we are reminded that the figures on the screen are not actors acting. They are real people undergoing what, for them, is a real experience, no matter how surreal the setup may have been.

Such an observation is far removed from the most common criticism of stag films — that they are absurdly formulaic and sexually sterile. In truth, they are anything but. Although there are but a handful of basic scenarios from which almost every stag takes flight, that is true in most every other cinematic endeavor. Once the "action" starts, however, the actors are limited only by their own imaginations, the demands of whoever may be "directing" the film and the limitations of the camera itself.

The hand-cranked clockwork cameras with which the vast majority of amateur productions were shot were capable of filming around thirty seconds of continuous action before the built-in governor stopped the camera, as it began to slow down. It would then need to be rewound before filming could recommence. (One can identify these breaks in a movie's production by the appearance of a sudden lighter, flash-like, frame.)

Limiting though this factor was, it was also liberating, in that it allowed the moviemaker to reposition his or her cast without the need for the sometimes graceless — even clumsy — sight of the participants switching positions in full view of the audience. It also permitted him to vary the camera angle or move it closer to (or further from) the action. The zoom lens was little more than wishful thinking until 1932, while the concept of dismounting the camera from its tripod and moving it around while filming wasn't merely technically awkward, it was also (as *Inserts* reminded viewers) considered dangerously unconventional.

Very early on, then, the stag-makers learned that the straightforward missionary position was stultifyingly non-visual, and the quest quickly became to discover positions that would allow the camera the most lascivious view possible. For example, the so-called reverse-cowgirl position beloved by modern filmmakers for the unimpeded vistas it presents was already in regular use by the late 1920s, together with most attendant variations.

The simultaneous ejaculation by several men onto one willing female, an act now known by the Japanese term *bukkake*, was a lot more commonplace than the modern fascination would willingly let on; in fact, the only modern staples that do not seem to have been stumbled upon prior to the late 1960s or so (at least in any surviving footage) are double (simultaneous anal and vaginal) penetration and what erotic superstar Jenna Jameson rather unglamorously describes as "the internal pop shot."[4]

Of all the resources that the curious researcher can bring to bear on a stag film, it is the landscape of sexual positions that is among the most useful allies. No less than firmly situating a stag film in its geographical context, it is next to impossible to place more than a handful in any kind of chronological sequence.

Occasionally, of course, the movie will flag its place in history. *The Bookie*, for example, opens with its heroine reading what is presumably that morning's newspaper, with its front page consumed by the tragic collision of two aircraft, a DC 8 and a Super Constellation, over the New York borough of Queens on December 16, 1960.

Remove such obvious clues, however, and the researcher is often left foundering. The traditional methodology of studying the hairstyles, makeup, furnishings and so on is flawed, if only because it assumes that the set (generally either a hotel room or an apartment) had only just been fitted out; that the leading lady liked to keep up with the latest styles in coiffeur; that the randy motorist had only just picked his car up from the showroom; that the hip youngsters we meet in *Just Folks* have only just purchased their copy of Roy Hamilton's *You'll Never Walk Alone* LP.

These elements simply inform us of the *earliest* date at which a film could have been made, in the same way that we know a modern movie in which the hero wears disposable contact lenses could not have been shot before 1987.

One can, however, trace a certain evolution in the sexual techniques involved in a film. Nothing in the frame of human sexuality is new — man did not awaken one day and declare, "Eureka! Mastophallation!" But certain shifts in attitude do register on the serial spectator.

The smoking vagina — that is, the gentle penetration with a cigarette, cigar or pipe — is one fascination that modern viewers might find mystifying, although its grounding within opposition to a certain societal taboo does lessen that puzzlement somewhat.

The popularity of the image lies within what, in the years prior to the Great War, was a general disapproval of women smoking cigarettes in even a conventional manner. As late as 1910, no less a personage than President Roosevelt's daughter Alice was asked to leave a Chicago hotel lobby after lighting a cigarette, *not* because anybody feared the effects of her second-hand smoke, but because the only women who smoked in hotel lobbies tended to be prostitutes. Therefore, in the eyes of her disapproving peers, a woman who disavowed this nicety was one who probably disavowed many others.

The vice was tolerated during the war. But, in 1920, Mrs. Ella A. Booth, president of the New York chapter of the Women's Christian Temperance Union, announced that while "the cigarette . . . may have its uses on the battlefield, the war is over now."

Once again, the cigarette became a symbol of loose feminine morals, a slur that was rapidly developed as a very unmistakable form of visual code in both stag and conventional movies. If a woman smoked, there was no telling what else she might be willing to do — or what she might already have done. The so-called "missing sex scene" in *Casablanca*, for example, is flagged simply by the cigarettes that are lit "afterwards," while an even more overt sequence takes place in the 1927 movie *Flesh and the Devil*, as Greta Garbo approaches a young officer (John Gilbert) in search of a light for her cigarette. She places the cigarette dead center in her mouth, then removes it and places it in his. Then, when he has finally struck a very fumbling light, she blows out the match. It's an electrifying sequence, and one only partially fulfilled when Gilbert finally kisses her (she throws away the cigarette when he does so). Clearly, the passing of a cigarette from one orifice to another was already a recognized invitation for those orifices to meet more intimately.

Needless to say, many of the women in stag movies are avid smokers, and the puffing pudendum can be espied across the pre–World War II landscape, included in such efforts as 1938's *A Trip to Treasure Island* and the Cuban *Hot Rod*. (The imagery was still making sporadic comebacks as late as the mid-1960s with *How to be Pals*.)

The insertion of other foreign objects into the female and, less frequently, male body is considerably less pronounced. In *The Screwdriver*, a girl masturbates with the handle of the titular tool; *The Radio Repair Man* utilizes a pair of valves from an old radio;

another handymen tries out a light bulb (and seems surprised when it doesn't illuminate!).

Those old fruit and vegetable standbys are the most common phallic substitutes, however. Sundry mini-members of the marrow family have been caught on camera, alongside the ubiquitous banana; the 1940s' *The Bill Collector* reminds us of the aphrodisiac qualities of taste and scent when a bullying creditor is fed the same banana that two girls have just been masturbating with. No sooner has he devoured it than advances that he had brusquely rebuffed are now welcomed with open zipper. "He sure changes his mind quick!" marvels the accompanying caption.

In 1967, *Playboy* film historians Arthur Knight and Hollis Alpert conducted a statistical analysis of 1,000-plus stags, logging the incidence of every single sexual act over the course of almost half a century's worth of stag moviemaking.

They noted that lesbianism was present in close to one-fifth of the movies analyzed, which may or may not be an accurate representation of the number of men who actively fantasize on the subject, but were not at all surprised to discover that exclusive male homosexuality was even less prevalent than bestiality.

Two girls together will always find a fascinated male audience. Two guys together, on the other hand, tended not to appeal to a roomful of red-blooded manual laborers, unless the incident served a greater purpose. From the early 1930s, for example, comes *A Stiff Game,* a daring movie that set out to shatter as many societal taboos as it could, including homosexuality (Bill Hangnuts abandons scouring the Situations Vacant column in the local newspaper, in favor of becoming a male hustler) and interracial sex (his first trick is a black man, the unfortunately named Sambo). But, like the lesbians who are swiftly distracted from one another's charms by the arrival of a penis or two, the men are interested in one another only until something better comes along, in the shapely shape of two girls.

The subject of race is one that few stag movies cared to touch upon. Knight and Alpert found that fewer than one percent of films shot during the 1920s mixed black men with white women (although a healthier 6.8 percent reversed the roles) and, while they noted a steady increase in these figures as time passed, still the 1960s total of 4.4 percent was little more than double the number of woman-dog couplings.

Examples nevertheless abound. Mirroring *A Stiff Game*'s all-male scene, an early 1930s production, *Miss Park Avenue*, includes a mixed-race lesbian scene ("No depression here!" chortles a caption. "The stock market's down and so is the maid."), while *Love and the Ballerina* finds a black maid stumbling upon her mistress (a ballerina, although that is scarcely relevant) fellating a boyfriend. Stripping naked, the maid joins in, first taking over her mistress's position while the ballerina moves elsewhere, and then straddling the boyfriend's face, while the white girl takes his lap.

But the most enjoyable of the prewar mixed couplings, from the cast's point of view at least, was *The Handyman*, a 1930s encounter between a white woman, her maid and the black workman who visits to undertake some light repairs around the house. The maid and the handyman, in particular, spend much of the movie giggling toward the camera, clearly having a whale of a time, and the whole film is suffused with such an air of carefree enjoyment that it's plain that neither gives a damn for the cultural taboos they were so merrily shattering.

The corollary of this lightheartedness is *KKK Night Riders*, a stag that ostensibly depicts the rape of a black woman by a corpulent, robed and hooded Ku Klux Klansman. Yet the movie not only manages to convey an electrifying sexual fission, it also attempts to defuse the prevailing societal taboos concerning interracial sex, by concentrating its gaze upon the increasing tenderness of the Klansman's behavior, while asking its audience to square that with his professed doctrine of racial hatred. The captioned insistence that "all night riders must have their fun" does not defuse the implied hypocrisy.

Racial attitudes aside, many other trends emerge, both from the *Playboy* survey and from the stags themselves, to illustrate further fascinating sidelights of American sexuality.

Intercourse notwithstanding, according to Knight and Alpert's study, the most lastingly, and increasingly popular, routines in the stag milieu were fellatio and irrumation (the two terms are not synonymous). Thirty-seven percent of stags dated to the 1920s (*A Free Ride* among them) included a sequence, a figure that rose toward 50 percent on either side of World War II, then continued climbing to 68 percent during the 1950s, 77.3 percent in the 60s — and close to 100 percent since that time.

The same source then complains that "cunnilingus occurs in only 11.1 percent of the [presumably heterosexual] films produced in the Twenties, and just 12.6 of those made in the Thirties. The figure rises to 16 percent in the films of the Forties."[5] In fact, an admittedly less scientific study undertaken for this book reveals no shortage whatsoever of the act, and it would appear that, across the entire span of American stags, maybe three-quarters of the movies that depict fellatio also include at least a few moments of oral-labial contact.

The 1927 stag *Wonders of the Unseen World* describes cunnilingus as "the latest importation from Paris," and many viewers might well have believed that was so. But there was certainly no shortage of demonstrations to be seen and, if fans of the act do still bridle at the camera's obvious preference for fellatio over cunnilingus, be assured that the apparent unpopularity of cunnilingus had absolutely nothing to do with the popular sexological theories of male distaste for appearing anything less than dominant.

Of all the most popular sexual positions, fellatio is by far the most visual, for the audience if not for the participants. Indeed, any time somebody complains they've never had sex like a porn star, remind them that they probably have, and a lot more often than they realize. It's just that their eyes are in the wrong place to notice.

Other positions can certainly be manipulated into providing a dramatic eyeful, but prior to the advent (and, more importantly, the ready availability) of both powerful close-up lens and lightweight, maneuverable cameras, few directors or cast members would willingly risk the cramps and contortions necessary to the shot. Fellatio, on the other hand, can be successfully filmed from almost any angle and distance; therefore it was.

Visual aesthetics aside, however, certain sociological implications can be drawn from the statistics regarding oral sex; namely, that both the makers and the cast of the stags were responding to society's own (slowly) changing acceptance of oral-genital contact, itself a consequence of the increasing popularity of the "marriage manuals" that preceded the guides to sexual technique that litter the modern bookshelf.

Hardly surprisingly, Van de Velde's *Ideal Marriage: Its Physiology and Technique* was the act's most vociferous proponent. Within little more than a decade of the book's American publication, a sex act whose slang names ("gamahuche" and "French" for fellatio, and nothing whatsoever for cunnilingus) had remained unchanged in generations, was now undergoing an unprecedented linguistic revolution. The terms "blow job," "muff dive" and "giving head" all date from the early 1940s and, as they became better known, so the practices they referred to became more widespread (or, at least, were acknowledged to be more widespread), off-screen and on.

Further evidence for Van de Velde's surely unexpected influence on the stag movie can be gleaned from the corresponding decline of practices that his book does *not* discuss or that he pointedly speaks out against.

Remaining on the theme of oral sex, there are very few pre-1960s movies that depict the willing acceptance — much less ingestion — of male ejaculate, a practice that *Ideal Marriage* explicitly warned against by counseling the loving wife against "approaching that treacherous frontier between supreme beauty and base ugliness." Indeed, in any comparison between modern erotic fare and its vintage forebear, the most pronounced remains attitudes toward ejaculation during oral sex — a debate that the 1980s and beyond essentially ended with the industry standard of "down the hatch."

In earlier times, however, the decision rested very much with the actress herself; consequently, it's such a rarity that, when it does occur, even the camera laps it up. The earliest surviving example, in terms of absolute visual certainty, takes place in *The Modern Gigolo*, shot in Buffalo, New York, in 1928 by the immortally named Fuckaduck Films; further samplings appear in *Miss Park Avenue Takes a Bath* and, briefly, *KKK Night Ride*. But the most unexpected tasting takes place in the final moments of *Two Hot Chicks*, a movie that initially startles for the ease with which it crosses the generation gap, a true spring-autumn affair.

The movie opens with an elderly male servant coming across some lewd playing cards in his female employer's bureau. He is also much taken by the texture and scent of her underwear and has just started masturbating when the lady of the house and one of her girl-friends walk in. One assumes he will be disciplined; instead, the two girls pounce upon the wrinkled retainer (and *his* wrinkled retainer — they seem most enamored with his scrotum) and much jollity ensues. But not once is the old gent permitted to orgasm, not until one of the girls produces a cup and bids him masturbate into it. They then force him to raise the cup to his lips and drink.

One wonders what Van de Velde would have made of *that*?

The Melty Man and Other Non-myths

Miss Park Avenue
Takes a Bath

If Theodore Van de Velde can be credited with popularizing some aspects of sexual behavior, he can likewise stand accused of dismissing certain others.

Many cultures regard human (and other creatures') urine as an aphrodisiac — in September 2001, the *Indian Express* newspaper reported on the use of cow urine for this very purpose at the Gau Seva Sangh naturopathy hospital in Durgapura. Well into the 1930s, many people in the United States shared a similar belief (or, at least, accepted the same urban myth), which a handful of stag films happily propagated.

Urophilia was already a familiar image in erotic photography when *Miss Park Avenue Takes Her Bath* introduced it to the world of moving pictures. Having been interrupted during her bath by the arrival of her classics teacher (there is no explanation why he, too, should be naked), the pretty debutante is busy fellating him; the proceedings are suddenly interrupted when the tutor is stricken by an urgent call of nature.

Rather than turn toward the toilet that was surely just a few steps away, however, he instead urinates over Miss Park Avenue's breasts, an action heralded by a caption announcing "The Golden Shower." (This now-common term might actually have been of the filmmaker's own creation; first popularized in gay circles, the expression is otherwise unrecorded prior to the post–World War II era.)

Likewise dating from the early 1930s, *The Farmer's Daughter* finds its heroine seducing a hired hand after urinating into a pail and handing it to him to drink, while similar consumption is featured toward the end of *A Stiff Game*.

Even more extreme was *The Passionate Farmhand*, a movie that culminates with the laborer Rufus placing girlfriend Lena in a bathtub and urinating over her, although only as the final act in a seriously weird sequence of events; he has, by this time, already inserted candles into both her vagina and anus, which he then proceeded to light — a procedure that a caption describes as "the old candle trick but in a modernized way called flaming youth." There is also a scene of her wiping his ass before inserting her tongue (accompanied by the caption, "You must have had spinach for dinner"). The fact that he saved the urine till last, however, indicates that audiences, as well as Rufus, clearly viewed it as a fitting climax to the earlier debauchery.

Within a few short years, however, urophilia was a dying delight, an assassination that can be placed firmly at Van de Velde's door. The much-thumbed pages of *Ideal Marriage: Its Physiology and Technique* speak out with a morbid obsession against the sharing of urine, citing it as one of the most infection-prone hindrances to successful sexual relations that any couple could ever indulge in.

It would be misleading to portray *Ideal Marriage* as an unofficial "how to" guide for the aspiring stagmaker. But one final example cannot be overlooked. Anal sex was utterly ignored by Van de Velde and, correspondingly, the act rarely appears in period American stags. Indeed, on the few occasions when it does, the angles are usually such that it is difficult to be certain exactly what is taking place.

Perhaps predictably, given the film's head-on assault upon all boundaries of sexual taste and convention, the act is implied during the latter part of *Miss Park Avenue Takes Her Bath*, both visually and via the captions that both herald the scene ("He asses her [a] question") and conclude it ("She's a three-way girl"). It is also shown in *Strictly Union*, an early-1920s stag in which one character suggests, "Let's detour and try the dirt road." But such sequences are atypical of both the period and the American side of the genre as a whole.

But if stag films served only as a mirror to American sexual mores through the first half or so of the twentieth century, how great an impact could they have had on the average red-blooded male? To be truly effective, they needed also to play on the unfulfilled fantasies of their audiences, and do so in a way that permitted the viewer to dream that he, too, might one day find himself in a similar situation (or, given the environment in which the films were viewed, boast that he regularly did).

A perhaps unintended aid to these particular fantasies lay in the sheer normalcy of many of the couples featured in the stags. The modern erotic film prides itself in the desirability of its cast, with cosmetic surgery happy to dispel any last, lingering blemishes that Mother Nature may have inadvertently thrown into the mix. The actors and actresses who make these films are a lot of things to a lot of people, but very few of them are actually attainable.

It would be unreasonable to say that stag films set their sights lower when selecting their stars. But it is also true to say that the words "homely," "cuddly," "kinda cute" and "not so bad" are more likely to spring to the viewer's lips than any outright declarations of Goddess-driven lust.

For example: *Under the Parasol* takes place precisely where it says, with a comfortingly-ordinary looking couple making good use of the same lawn furniture so many households had in their own yards. "This," the film is saying, "could be you," and that's a terrific psychological gift to the audience. Jenna Jameson might spend large tracts of her autobiography bemoaning her misbegotten quest for love, until every red-blooded reader yearns to hold her tight and pledge undying devotion, but really, how many of them are ever going to get within a $20 Polaroid shot of her? The mumsy-looking brunette who works out under the parasol, on the other hand, could easily be your neighbor, your workmate . . . your wife!

No matter what profession they might ordinarily ply, underemployed prostitutes or unemployed actresses, part-time dancer or full-time housewife, the females in the majority of stag films, particularly those dating from the 1950s and before, are the girl, the woman and, occasionally, the middle-aged spinster next door; the actors are the guy who works in the store down the road, the delivery boy who you've never really noticed, the butcher, the baker, the candlestick-maker. They are Everyman, and every man can identify with them, while at the same time reveling in the pure escapism of sexual fantasy.

Sandy Brody, described by *Man's World* magazine as head of PR for a Hollywood-based moviemaking operation called the JB [John Braker] Sales Company, recalled the erotic film trade of the late 1960s: "Hiring . . . wasn't hard. John advertised for them in local trade papers and he got all the girls he could use. Very few women who answered the ads turned down the money. And John was very fair. He gave any woman who showed up at least some work, even if she were aging and not particularly attractive. 'In this business,' he said, 'there's no limit to the number of different tastes. We have customers who prefer seeing the old bags to seeing beautiful young girls.'"[1]

Of course, realism can be taken too far.

Viewers of writer Steven Moffat's British television comedy *Coupling* (the BBC original, not the appalling remake misguidedly unveiled by NBC) will doubtless remember the episode that concerned itself with the uninvited ability of an erect penis to suddenly flop away to nothingness for no apparent reason. The episode was called, with perhaps unnecessary clarity, "The Melty Man Cometh," referring to a dread fiend who, at the very mention of his name, "will rise from his shadow dimensions to do his evil work inside your terrified pants." This, as the episode winds on, is precisely what happens, and the Melty Man's hapless victim is suitably mortified.

Certainly he does not even consider the possibility that things could have been worse. Far, far worse. After all, he needed perform only for the woman he loved. Imagine if there was a cameraman looking on as well, maybe a director, certainly a naked stranger and, inevitably, a nagging voice that bellowed, just as subsidence commenced, "Don't stop now! We're in the middle of a take!"

"How to Make It as a Male Porn Star," an anonymous Q&A sequence within Jenna Jameson's *How to Make Love Like a Porn Star,* features "one of porn's leading men" confessing, "It's tough when you're on set and there's a thirty-person crew sitting there waiting for you, and a girl filing her nails saying, 'Don't look at me like I'm your girlfriend.' It's a lot of pressure for a guy to get hard."[2] And sometimes he doesn't.

Captured for posterity in behind-the-scenes footage from British director John Lindsay's early-1970s stag *Wet Dream* (and included in his 1974 documentary *The Pornbrokers*), one of the actors is utterly unable to coax himself into an even passable imitation of an erection. He is banished from the set (paid off with a £5 cancellation fee), and Lindsay later admitted that similar disappointments happened with such regularity that he himself was now something of a stag veteran, despite having no desire to appear in any of his own films. "I was never into it myself," he insisted. But sometimes he'd be halfway through shooting, "and now needed a prick that was hard enough to stick up the girl. [So] I had to stand in myself . . . because I didn't want to waste the film."[3]

That was a pressing concern, particularly in those days before "fluffers" came along. Much is made, in other writings, of the sheer *cheapness* of the majority of stags, how a short could be shot for just a few hundred bucks, which included paying the cast and printing the film. But often (although not necessarily in Lindsay's case), those few hundred bucks were as much as the makers could actually afford, until the film was completed and delivered onto the circuit. Until then, what they spent was all they'd got, and film — which was already the most expensive component of the entire exercise — could *not* be wasted under any circumstances.

Neither was an erection the sole demand male performers were expected to live up to. Ejaculation, too, needed to be planned — or, at least, heralded in such a way that the camera could get into position. Veteran actor John Holmes explained, "With a lot of guys, the director will say, 'Okay, please don't come. If you feel like you're gonna come and you can't hold it, tell us and we'll shoot it somehow. And so the guy'll say, 'Okay, I can't hold it, I'm gonna come,' and the director yells, 'Hold that motherfucker out,' and the guys with the camera are trying to focus. Some come shots you've seen are always out of focus and fucked up — that's because the guy said, 'I can't hold it.'"[4]

In the days when there was no cutting-room floor upon which to consign such unscripted moments, the filmmakers just got on with their job as best they could, camouflaging the incident wherever possible, but seldom capable of wholly disguising what had happened.

Taking its lead from the massive success of the 1933 Garbo/Barrymore vehicle *Grand Hotel*, the stag *The Girls from Apartment 13* introduces "two girls, who are fugitives from the Grand Hotel," inviting a couple of men to their apartment for a party.

Arriving, we are told, "in peppy form," Mike and Ike "below the belt look just alike," and it seems they love alike, too. At least, they would if Mike (or Ike) hadn't just been paid a visit by the Melty Man, a misfortune that leaves his female partner with little to do but flop the flaccid organ in the air, presumably until the director calls for them to *pretend* it's working. A few moments later, we flash on the fact that Ike (or Mike), too, is undergoing an equipment malfunction, and the film is almost over before any penetration is achieved. What can be celebrated is the good humor with which the incident is accepted, and the obvious rapport among the cast. Even at the most desperately floppy stage, the smiles and conversation are genuine.

Somewhat less indulgent is *Tom Boy*, a late-sixties English film that establishes its title character early on, as she plays a rough-and-tumble variation on rock/paper/scissors with a male friend and, just to make it interesting, agrees to take off her top. Naturally, he loses all interest in the game at this point, and soon the pair of them are naked.

Unfortunately, nakedness is all he has and, far from having their voyeuristic fantasies fulfilled, the audience is instead subjected to a study in inhuman humiliation, acted out through the expression of absolute disdain, shot through with lingering upward glances of long-suffering boredom, with which the Melted Man's ministrations are met.

He nuzzles her nipples. She rolls her eyes heavenward. He kneels between her legs and licks her. She tips her head back and stifles a yawn. Now, bearing in mind that he is completely oblivious to all this (his face being occupied elsewhere), he should be in a considerable state of arousal by now. But no, he remains as soft as an otter's overcoat, which means our Ice Princess can really kick into disparaging overdrive.

Occasionally, something that happens (or is said) off-camera brings a broad smile to her face. Then it fades again, and she's looking up at the ceiling, or round at the walls, anywhere but in her co-star's direction, not even when the roles are reversed and she's trying to blow some life into him. But time's a-passing, people, and film's a-wasting. If he can't get it up (and he seems to be getting softer all the time), she'll just have to fake it. And so, with some judicious use of shadow and a lot of long-range shots, they might *just* have got away with the subterfuge, if someone hadn't decided to put the girl on top, because you can still see her expression, still see the absolute boredom in her eyes, the sheer ennui with which she regards the entire affair. When the film finally runs out, it's not merely the end of a movie. It's a mercy killing.

Thankfully, some actors were able to make a virtue . . . even a plot device . . . out of their nervousness, as "Rich," a frequent stag-watcher during the 1950s, recalls: "One of the very old films I remember well was a guy laying on his back in a hospital, naked, with a soft cock. The nurse came in and he very animatedly showed her his prick, almost crying and complaining that it was limp. She picked it up in her hand and let it drop, and it was very soft. She removed her uniform and started rubbing it on her tits and then sucked on it a little and rubbed it in her hands. Then it began to swell a little and he sat up all excited and pointing at it, and she continued until it was up to full hardness. I laughed, it was so funny."[5]

The Radio Man, from 1931, likewise raises a smile as a visiting repairman is relieved of his wilting manhood by a dose of Dr. Pep's Erection Tablets, "guaranteed to stiffen a limp prick and replace lost vitality." More than sixty years before the arrival of Viagra, just two of these (sadly fictional!) pills would ensure a one-hour hard-on, while four could keep it up for a full day and night. The radio man devours a handful and is, indeed, good to go, at least until the end of the film.

The strongest (and the cruelest) commentary on the subject, however, was delivered by an early-1930s stag, *Ecstasy in Platinum*, in which a wife's infidelity drives her impotent husband to murder . . . or, at least, attempted murder. Spying on her latest liaison, he grabs a double-barrel shotgun and opens fire at close range, only to discover, "My God, the gun's empty!" No surprise there, one can imagine the wife replying.

One can both condone and condemn the stags' open acknowledgment, whether intended or otherwise, of the problems of "real life"; it is, after all, a debate that has raged for several decades in discussions of the escapist nature of modern erotic cinema.

Leaving aside the inescapable truth that, if one is truly seeking reality in an erotic movie, it would be shot in pitch darkness and over in three minutes, the critics point out the extraordinarily high standards to which the average viewer is convinced he must aspire, and ask why the industry rarely focuses on the flaws to which all male flesh is heir.

The answer to that is the same as one would get for asking why there's never any out-of-tune singing in a Hollywood musical or why you never hear the bum notes on a major-label CD. Because that is not what such vehicles are in the business of preserving.

Forty, fifty and more years ago, however, they had no alternative and, in truth, may not have needed one. An audience would swiftly grow restless if every stag on the evening's bill revolved around the unscheduled arrival of the Melty Man. But once or twice in a full evening's fare not only did little harm, it also offered a supremely lighthearted break in the action, a chance for the guys to laugh at the onstage stud's discomfort and, just as likely, take solace from the knowledge that it really does happen to every man.

It was, after all, one thing to read Van de Velde's caution that "temporary and occasional apathy is, so to speak, quite normal . . . a natural self-defense of the organism against exactions and excesses." It is quite another to see a healthy-looking hombre in the same predicament, no matter how hard his partner is striving to raise the dead.

Where the stags are at their most successful, then, is in conveying some sense of the sex act's natural realities, psychological, spiritual and emotional — areas habitually lacking from modern efforts. Few of the men and women seen onscreen were what would today be regarded as "professionals"; fewer still were sufficiently accomplished as actors to mask their natural feelings from the camera. The emotions they experienced on the set are those that are captured on the film, a reality that completely restates the traditional thespian roles of viewer and performer, to become voyeur and exhibitionist.

A FREE RIDE

APPLE KNOCKERS COKE

A STIFF GAME

ATTACHMENT

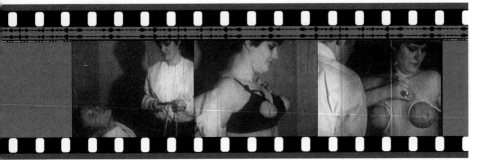

BABYSITTER

CRAZY CAT HOUSE

BLACK MARKET POTATO HOSEN

CASTING COUCH

DR. HARDON'S INJECTION

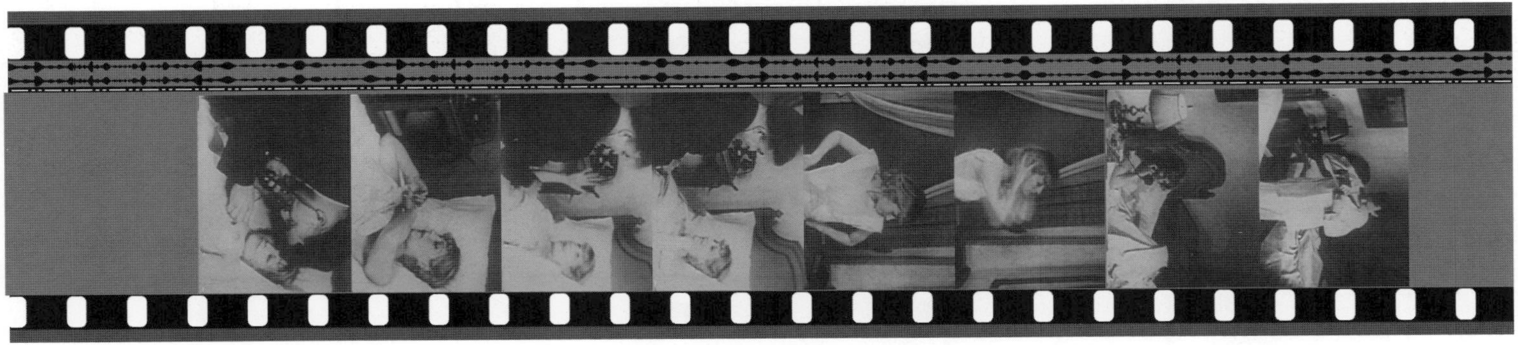

DETECTIVE ONE HUNG LOW

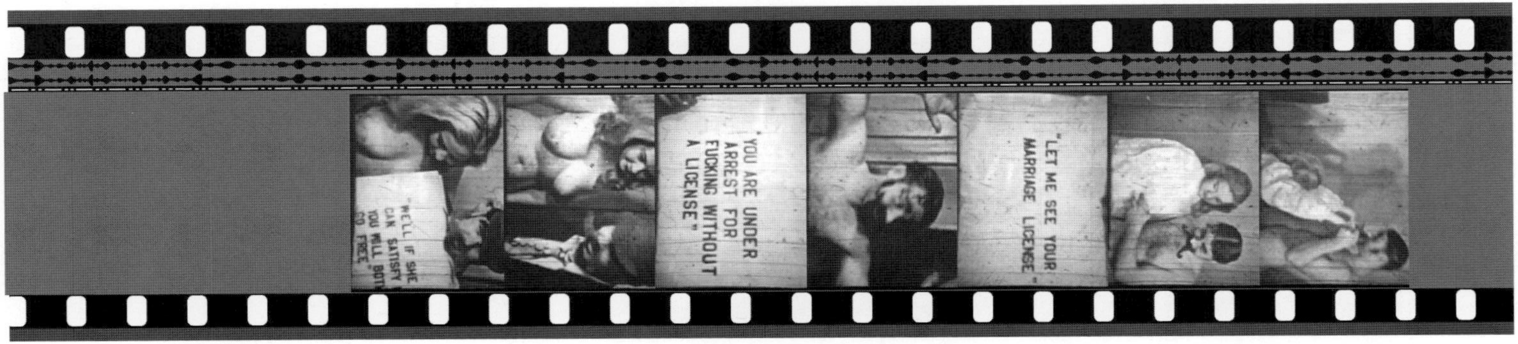

JUNKIES AND THE NIGHTMARE

KEYHOLE PORTRAITS

MISS BOHRLOCH

NEW YORK HONEYMOON

MISS PARK AVE TAKES A BATH

MODERN PIRATES

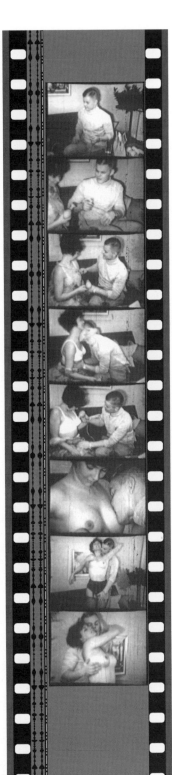

NIGHTSPOT

SATAN'S CHILDREN

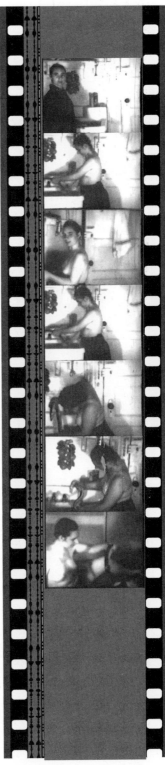

SULTAN SLAVES

SWEDISH MASSAGE

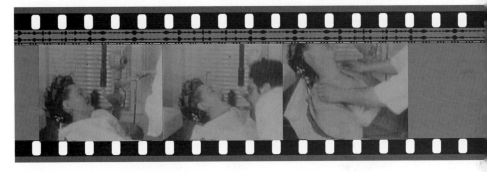

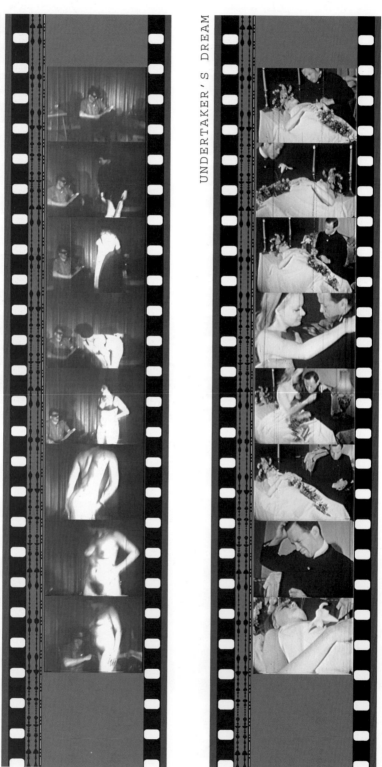

Don't You Know There's a War On?

*Black Market
Potato Hosen*

The United States entered World War II in December 1941, following the Japanese attack on Pearl Harbor. And, as the attentions of the country as a whole shifted, so did the focus of American erotica.

This shift is best documented by the wartime stag *Torchy, the Red Hot Red Head*. The movie is touchingly conventional and extraordinarily tender, which are vital commodities during wartime, when many of the film's audience — soldiers serving overseas — could get all the kinky sex they wanted from hookers and the like, and now wanted nothing more than to be reminded of the sweet girls they'd left behind Stateside.

The change is even more pronounced on the printed page of the era, in the form of the so-called male magazines that dominated the pulpier end of the newsstands. A far cry, visually and stylistically, from the jizz mags of today, such publications rarely traveled beyond the realms of innuendo and cheesecake. But even these pleasures were to be revised once the nation went to war. Nudity faded from even the most daring girlie magazines of the period. Strippers became showgirls, hot blondes became homely brunettes. Many publications even abandoned photography altogether, transforming themselves into military-themed cartoon digests. And all so wholeheartedly abandoned even the merest hint of shocking licentiousness that, as author Dian Hanson observed, "when strippers did appear . . . [they were] stripping off their nylons, to be recycled into parachutes."[1]

For anybody who did continue filming through the war years, there were manifold difficulties to be overcome, most notably the scarcity of raw film stock. Many enterprising producers attempted to circumvent this by recycling their existing collection of movies into compilation-style films, a practice popular since the 1920s (*Keyhole Portraits* and the French *Le Trou* — a 1928 hotel stag that should most certainly not be confused with Jacques Becker's 1960 prison drama!), but which now took off in a big way.

Some spliced together scenes from a variety of different stags to create a new one, with only the vaguest suggestion of an interlinking device to explain how the blonde woman in one position suddenly became a brunette in another; others took to creating what we might call "specialist" compendiums, similar to the *40 Squirting MILFs Volume 73*–type compilations of today, with all the action focusing upon one particular sexual act.

Others still, assuming their audience would accept sexual rationing with the same stoicism as they accepted gas and food shortages, adapted other kinds of movies altogether. Old burlesque routines were a favorite, spiced up with the addition of a few moments of spliced-in sex, as though the dance or pose beforehand was simply the foreplay to the main attraction.

Manpower also became a problem, as the military whisked away many of the men who had hitherto been cranking away on one side of the cameras or the other.

While a market for stag films continued to flourish on the home front, there was even greater demand for them at bases overseas. Several published accounts of wartime military service reflect upon the popularity of stag films at late-night screenings in sundry postings and, while military rules frowned upon such gatherings, they do appear to have been tolerated by the authorities.

One British Royal Air Force veteran, Campbell Muirhead, even recalls sexually explicit material (stills, on this occasion) being employed during official lectures aimed at refreshing the men's aircraft-identification skills: "As minds wandered, the instructor would drop in the occasional nude. . . . He promised more 'once we've done *ship* recognition.' A few destroyers and pocket battleships later . . . 'on came a shot of an orgy in full flight.'"[2]

Of all the films made in and around the war years, the most interesting are those that reflect the mood of the moment. *G.I. Joe Returns Home* is littered with military references, a clear gauge as to its intended audience. The film opens with "Miss Bombshell" masturbating alone, using "a radar tube to find the depth of her box." Her "G.I. Joe" appears, to offer the newly rechristened "Miss Atom Bomb . . . a mouthful of bologna"; another board cautions "one way not to ride a jeep — poney [sic] style."

The film includes some fascinating diversions. In one shot, G.I. Joe is clearly wearing a condom; in the next, it has vanished. We also sight Miss Bombshell penetrating herself with a cigarette, an extraordinarily late-in-the-day reminder of that once-popular fetish. But the most unexpected moment comes when a caption announces, "The cameraman finds it tough to keep his mind on the work" and another lens swings in to catch him masturbating as well.

One also gains a taste of the times from *Black Market Potato-Hosen*, a movie that might also lay claim to the most mystifying title in the entire stag canon. What does it mean? What *could* it mean? Although this is certainly an American production, "*hosen*" is German for "trousers." Potato trousers? Watch carefully!

A 1940s housewife, carefully perched beneath the cornflakes, answers the door to a deliveryman who, having brought her regular groceries, also has a bonus extra. Yes, black-market potatoes! But the housewife, having already paid for her original order, is now flat out of cash. Perhaps he would take payment in kind? Of course he will — stag deliverymen always do.

In terms of the acting, it's clearly the first time out. Both actors are in constant need of direction; the viewer can almost hear the director calling across, "put your hand there . . . no, not there —

there." You catch their eyes uncertainly seeking out instructions, or else they nudge one another . . . "Hey, I think he's talking to you." Even those things that should come naturally — like taking off his vest — seem to require a lot more effort than it ought to, while the deliveryman is in such a hurry to get to one scene that he quite forgets there's another one beforehand, until a poke from his co-star sends him scurrying back into position. But it's a delightful movie, all the same.

The war was also responsible for two of the most intriguing of all the mid-century stag films. *Adventures Abroad* and *Swastika in the Hole* were both what we might term propaganda films, part of the vast corpus of anti-Nazi material pumped out by the Allied studios during World War II, although Frank Capra's *Why We Fight* never looked like these.

Dating from sometime before the United States entered what had appeared a predominantly Eurasian conflict, *Adventures Abroad* opens innocently enough, with two girls sitting around their apartment, when the telephone rings. A caption announces the return home of Lulu, "just back from her trip abroad," and Lulu herself then arrives to show her friends where she's been and, more importantly, what she learned there. A similar travelogue approach had already been utilized in the early-1930s film *The Gay Count* (titled in the days when "gay" merely meant "lighthearted").

With the aid of a conveniently placed globe, Lulu reminisces about her visit to the Soviet Union, while one of her now-naked friends mounts the other and rides her "Cossack" fashion. Lulu points to France and cues a bout of enthusiastic cunnilingus — "Paree," as the caption puts it. And finally there was Germany, and "the Dictator's Special": mutual masturbation followed by much Heil Hitler-ing, while now moist fingers are placed beneath the nose, in imitation of the Führer's moustache.

Adventures Abroad mocks; *Swastika in the Hole* assaults. A raunchy all-American brunette seduces Hitler himself, albeit in the form of a short man wearing a saggy rubber mask. They have sex, and the Nazi leader is obviously impressed by his partner's pubic hair, shaven into the shape of a swastika. His performance, however, is clearly less than she expected from a member of the self-appointed master race, a criticism she spells out in such livid terms that the shamed and demoralized Hitler picks up a nearby revolver and (with remarkable historical precognition) shoots himself in the head.

In the same way that one views Mexico's post-revolution output as political artifacts, one could argue that films such as these went some way toward legitimizing stag films amid the culture of the times, "doing their bit" to negate the Nazi menace, proving that even perverts (for who else, demanded polite society, ever watched such films?) could be patriots.

Unfortunately, the scarcity of these two films both on the modern collectors market and within the wealth of duplication-heavy VHS and DVD anthologies that now circulate suggests that even among the traditional stag audience, neither was particularly popular. Besides, as the Allied war machine began pushing its way across Europe (the troops made landfall in Italy in 1943 and in France the following year), an entire new world of entertainment was opening up, as brothels and private houses alike fell into the liberators' hands, and with them, some very unexpected treasures.

The work of those giants of the prewar French stag industry, Nathan and Dominique, was still in circulation in 1940s France, together with the vast corpus of work produced by so many other filmmakers. As the Germans commenced their long retreat and, *ville* by *ville*, life returned to a degree of normalcy, so the liberating Allies were introduced to a breed of stag that their homeland had scarcely aspired to.

It would not be Francophiliac to describe French stags as "classy" — and even if it were, that would not alter the truth of that statement. The spellbound Allies who were now introduced to this rich repository of undreamed of delights not only discovered, as Al Di Lauro and Gerald Rabkin put it, "that French filmmakers were working for a more sophisticated audience than the Americans,"[3] but their output was also "much more exotic in theme and setting," more concerned with plot and a lot less prone to coarse humor than their transatlantic brethren.

One would like to think that, among the thousands of GIs who must have seen, or at least had described to them, these fresh horizons, there would be a handful who would return home and apply these new values to the American stag. And one would be correct in doing so. Although the term "revolution" might be too strong a word for it, the 1950s at least witnessed a minor sea change in the nature of homegrown erotic movies, one that would gather speed as the decade unfolded, before opening out into the seemingly limitless pastures of the late 1960s.

The majority of these would-be auteurs remain as anonymous today as they sought to become at the time. We have no way, for example, of knowing who shot the early-1950s gem *The Mirror*, in which a couple's lovemaking is viewed, indeed, via its reflection in a looking glass. It is not altogether a successful film; the actors clearly didn't consider their positioning and angles before the filming commenced, and too much of *The Mirror* shows writhing bodies alone. But it was an interesting experiment and one hopes that its director went on to greater things.

French stag production, having ceased altogether following the German invasion in 1940, was likewise not slow in resuming operations in the months that followed Liberation. One of the earliest postwar efforts was *The Reporter*, in which a journalist is dispatched to investigate the lewd goings-on at a nearby hotel — an excuse for much squinting through secret peepholes, through which the action (namely, excerpts from a handful of prewar stags) can be viewed.

It was a primitive start when compared to the majestic gems that France had hitherto been renowned for, but the straitened nature of postwar France was not the only obstacle the moviemakers were faced with as the country returned to normalcy. A new foe had arisen in the form of a crusading government determined to wipe away all traces of the country's prewar decadence.

Anxious to secure a scapegoat for the calamitous collapse of their nation in the first year of the conflict, the authorities cast around France's prewar society and settled upon decadence and moral decay as the primary causes of Hitler's triumph. Especially wounding to national pride was the knowledge that, following the fall of Paris, many high-ranking Nazis were regular visitors to the brothels; that

Herman Goering had lusted where once Cary Grant had played, while German soldiers stood guard outside Le Chabanais. Clearly, *les maisons closes* not only symbolized the corruption that had consumed the once-ferocious French soul. They were also largely responsible for it.

A new phrase entered the vocabulary. *Collaboration horizontale*, or horizontal collaboration, applied to any woman (or man — many male brothels likewise remained in business throughout the occupation) who, under any circumstances bar rape, accepted a German invader into her bed.

Paris councilwoman Marthe Ricard led the charge, and was already garnering considerable support for her mission when Madame de Gaulle, the wife of the newly elected French president, revealed her own personal dislike of France's brothel culture. That was the end for the embattled bordellos. On April 13, 1946, the proclamation of a law named for Ricard officially closed down France's most beloved tourist attraction.

Prostitution did not end. Even Ricard conceded that the closures were little more than "a step toward abolition." As occurred in America thirty years earlier, the brothels simply shifted underground and, as much as possible, carried on as before. The stag movies that emerged from these now-straitened circumstances, however, reflected the new, hard-line attitudes toward love and life, just as the venues where they were now available were some steps further down the social scale from the palatial surroundings in which they were once viewed.

"The axis of Marseilles–Lyon–Paris is the base of these circuits in France," Ado Kyrou revealed in 1957. "Public exhibitions generally take place in the back rooms or the cellars of certain coffee bars and in rudimentarily furnished hotel rooms." Like the secret cinemas of the pre–World War I era, "these venues change very regularly, for fear of the police force. In Paris, the prices reach as high as 10,000 Francs (around $3,000 U.S., at the then current exchange rate!) for a single half-hour meeting."[4] Private screenings, incidentally, were legal, provided the host did not issue printed invitations to his guests.

Some filmmakers continued exercising their prewar fixations. In

Femmes Infideles, the heroine is aroused by a work by the turn-of-the-century German humorist Freiherr von Schlicht, *Treulose Frauen* (*Perfidious Women*). The camera closes in on a handful of the book's lightly amorous illustrations, before following the reader to bed, where she undresses, climbs between the covers and falls asleep. But what dreams she has, of dancing naked around the room, of ecstatic masturbation and, produced from who knows where, a penis that is hers to do with as she pleases. And all this overlaid on shots of her still sleeping form.

Equally ambitious, but somewhat more representative in subtext, is *Un Realization de Mézig* (French for "ejaculation"), *La Femme au Portrait* (*The Woman in the Portrait*). Dating from around 1952, this jewel offers up a variation on a theme that has been utilized in any number of other, non-sexual, and even non-cinematic, media, as a character from a painting (in this case, a statuesque Spanish-looking beauty) comes to life to assist a frail and put-upon housewife get her own back on her thoughtless husband.

This they achieve by forcing him into sex with each of them, before discarding him as useless and continuing their session alone. Then, as he awakens the following morning, the pair vanish into the painting together. As the film ends, and the bewildered man slumps to the floor in front of the painting, the señora reaches out to plant a massive bull's head on his shoulders.

From around the same time, *Petit Conte de Noel* (a double entendre that can translate as either "a little Christmas story" or "a little Christmas cunt") initially looks like a straightforward tale of a wicked Santa. Clambering down the chimney, he is astonished to find a naked woman masturbating on the couch, alongside his milk and cookies.

At first, he is as shocked as one would hope him to be. Clearly as nice as she is naughty, however, the woman quickly wins him over with her sad tale of an unfulfilled lesbian encounter earlier in the evening. But Santa's first thought, of allowing her to take out her frustrations on his own sizable erection, is dismissed by the sudden appearance of a mortified Christmas angel. So he fashions the girl a dildo machine instead, utilizing the rest of the household's presents (including a bicycle, whose pedals power the device), at which point the angel returns and, delighted by Santa's self-control, treats him to some very heavy petting while they watch the machine in action.

Neither film offers an exactly conventional view of sex — in one, it is revenge that fires the main action; in the other, it is unfulfillable lust. These, however, were the themes that postwar France appeared to have selected as indicative of the national libido; and, hand in hand with the whip and chain, it was these that would dominate the local stag industry for the next decade and a half.

Bondage and domination had featured in stags in the past — the country that birthed the Marquis de Sade could hardly have chosen to ignore either. But now they became an obsession. *Esprit de Famille* (*Family Spirit*), a film dating from the late 1940s, is fascinating in that it is one of the few to utilize genuine street scenes, complete with members of the public curiously watching as the actress and camera cross the street. What, you can imagine them asking, is being filmed here? And will we see ourselves on the silver screen?

Well, ladies, yes you might. But only if you take yourself off to the sort of establishment that cares about the consequences of a young lady paying a visit to her sister and, through no fault of her own, finding herself obscured behind a curtain just as her hostess arrives home with a man and clambers straight into bed with him.

The unwitting interloper remains hidden behind the curtain and watches, shocked at first but with quickening interest, as the pair make love. Inevitably she starts masturbating; equally inevitably, she is quickly discovered. Of course she must be punished, a routine that includes a mild whipping and rear-entry sex, before the sister, in turn, is trussed and beaten, then forced to watch while her visitor has all the fun.

An historical slant on the flagellation theme is provided by *Roman Jail*, a film that manages to titillate its audience at the same time as pushing all those religious buttons that so much French art enjoys depressing. In this instance, an escaped slave saves a woman from crucifixion, but not before having sex with her while she still hangs suspended from the cross.

Numerous other French flagellation flicks dating from this period — *Dressage au Fouet* (*Rising with the Whip*), *Sous les Caresses du Martinet* (*Under the Carresses of the Martinet*), *Flagellation en Bord de Marne* — tend to feature women only, while those that do allow men in the room usually grant the female dominatrix the leading role when it comes to disciplining another woman.

This allows for some unusual twists. *A la Français* includes a scene in which the "victim," while firmly trussed, is placed between the man's legs and ordered to fellate him while the *other* woman holds the penis in one hand and continues the beating with the other. At that point, the bound girl is cast to one side, and — presumably sufficiently aroused — her tormentors then have sex on their own. *A la Français*, incidentally, might well rank among the most oft-seen of all stags, thanks to the inclusion of a short sequence within British director Nicholas Roeg's 1967 (released 1970) movie *Performance*.

Another favorite vehicle among French directors inverted the old male trick of "slipping something into her drink" by having the female slip something into *his* and reducing him to the status of hapless victim.

Serves Après Vent finds a respectable-looking woman drugging the store owner who, having sold her a dildo (!), then followed her back to her home. She is just getting to grips with her new toy when he gets there, but we do wonder precisely what he was intending to do, for nothing actually happens until she hands him a drugged drink. He passes out, at which point she steals his wallet, then proceeds to debauch him with the dildo.

He awakens to find her fellating him, but that is nowhere near as great a shock as the discovery that he's been robbed — at which point, any attempt to maintain the plot seems to fly straight out the window, as stage fright takes over where an erection once quivered, and the woman is reduced to posing in some quite undignified positions, while one arm gestures furiously and her silent lips part in some kind of instruction: "Get your fat ass over here, or you'll never work in this town again," perhaps.

The most intriguing of this particular sub-genre, however, is

Attachement, a movie shot with an exquisite eye for close-ups and sufficient assurance on the part of the actress that it is obvious she's done this kind of thing before. And so she has. This strikingly attractive brunette also appears in the same period's lesbian shaving demonstration, *Un Rasage en Douceur* (*A Shave and a Douche*).

Again, she spikes her male visitor's drink, as a prelude to tying him to a chair and beating him. Semiconscious, he makes several attempts to escape his bonds, although his tormentor really doesn't seem as intent on whipping him as she is in simply immobilizing him in readiness for a remarkable blow job. Binding her own breasts with rope and then securing his penis in her cleavage, she sucks him to orgasm just as the film ends.

Love on the Home Front

The Shiek

The end of World War II in 1945 not only
flooded the cities of America with several
hundred thousand young men versed in the
ways and wiles of European sexology, it also
unleashed a tsunami of military surplus
equipment — everything from clothing
and water bottles to typewriters and tanks.
And filmmaking equipment. Lots and lots
of filmmaking equipment.

The military first acknowledged the usefulness of film with the
establishment of a special department within the Signal Corps in
1894 and, by the outbreak of World War II, the service boasted three
separate facilities for film and still-photo processing, the photographic laboratory at the Army War College in Washington, D.C.,
and two motion-picture production facilities, in Fort Monmouth,
N.J., and Wright Field in Ohio. Photographic training took place at
the Signal Corps training center at Fort Monmouth.

The army's first four Signal Photographic Companies were
organized in 1942. The 161st, 162nd, 163rd and 164th companies
were each divided into teams of one lieutenant and six enlisted men,

comprising still and motion photographers, drivers and one clerk. Two further companies, the 165th and 196th, were formed during 1943; more were created as the war continued. Between them, these companies shot an estimated 200,000 feet of combat film per week, until, by the end of World War II, the men of the Signal Corps had produced no less than 1,338 films, a literal baptism of fire that, upon demobilization, turned out its own small army of trained and experienced moviemakers.

Many of these automatically gravitated into professions that reflected their training. Some went to Hollywood; others returned there (directors Darryl Zanuck and Frank Capra were both commissioned for wartime service as Signal Corps officers). Some became professional photographers; some found themselves shooting industrial films for private companies. Some opened camera or photography stores and studios. And a handful decided to combine their knowledge of filmmaking with some of their other European experiences.

As the military commenced disgorging its overstock of cameras and projectors to the army surplus stores that made it available at seriously knockdown prices, the stage was set for an absolute boom in home-movie production. By far more stags films dated to the late 1940s and 1950s exist today than for the entire thirty years beforehand, and while this can in part be put down to the simple laws of survival (the older something is, the more chance it has of expiring), it also indicates the comparative ease with which anybody so-minded could obtain the means to make a movie.

Developing it, however, remained problematic. It was illegal for any lab to process film stock that depicted nudity, sexual activity or anything else that could be construed "obscene material"; anybody dropping such film off would be promptly contacted and asked to give permission for the prints and negatives to be destroyed (it was also illegal for a lab to destroy a customer's property without their express permission).

For many would-be filmmakers, this presented an intractable problem. When aspiring young director Russ Meyer (himself a veteran of the 166th Signal Photographic Company) shot his first movie of a topless Tempest Storm in 1952, for example, there was only one place he could take the 200-foot roll of 16mm Kodachrome, and that was to an official Kodak processing laboratory. But that was out of the question. "Bells would ring," Meyer later recalled, "lights flash, a big sign probably went on and off on the wall winking 'tits tits tits.'"[1]

But there was a way around it, and one that Meyer was probably not alone in considering: "The film was delivered very personally by a sexy young French girl named Susie, who gave the Kodak lab man a little something extra for sneaking the film through."

Indeed, the very fact that so many stag films were produced in the United States in the postwar period indicates that the letter of the law was seldom upheld by any but the most conscientious processors. Private photo labs were popping up all across the country, one- or two-man operations whose margins were so thin that they would not turn down any work, provided they could be guaranteed anonymity. As late as 1972, the classified ads in the back of certain magazines were lousy with such entrepreneurs, all offering to develop "anything under the sun, no questions asked" for as little as $15 for an 8mm film.

These characters were running considerable risk. The perils of being caught in possession of undeveloped material (positive film) were no different from owning finished stag films (negative film) — were, in fact, even greater, as an operative caught with the latter could claim he was merely a traveling exhibitor with no knowledge of, where, when and by whom the movies in question were made. Possession of the former, on the other hand, tended to indicate the suspect was a distributor or even a manufacturer.

Roy Blick, a D.C. metropolitan police inspector, detailed one such bust in November 1954. Having received a tip that a carload of pornographic materials was entering his jurisdiction, he pulled over the suspect driver. "On the back seat of the automobile was fourteen rolls of film, eight reels of positive, six reels of negative, about 10,000 feet of film altogether. And he was on his way to some place — would not divulge where he was going — to have 80,000 feet of film made from the positive film."[2] The driver was charged with "possession of pornographic films," and Blick was unequivocal when asked to define what he meant by "pornographic": "Male and female sexual relations, abnormal or cohabiting in the nude. It was filth."

The sheer quantity of stag films that would be cranked out of American backroom studios over the next twenty years would not have any bearing on their quality. Indeed, if the genre can ever be said to have become either hidebound or fossilized, it was now, as the earlier comparative handful of filmmakers was joined by a battalion of joyous first-timers, all attempting to penetrate a market that simply couldn't get enough films.

It was a word-of-mouth trade, generally entered either through knowing, or finding, somebody who was already involved in some fashion. According to Arthur Knight and Hollis Alpert, one unknown studio on the east coast turned out upwards of thirty stag movies during the immediate postwar period, with such titles as *Night School, Merry Go Round, The Dentist* and *Midnight Till Dawn* conjoined by the appearance of the same "portly male" star in almost all of them.

The same authorities also credit a Nashville operation for a series of films highlighted by *Dice Game, The Butcher Boy* and *I'll Cry Tomorrow,* while one unnamed Chicago area wholesaler was alleged to be routinely pulling in more than $35 million a year from stag rentals alone, a staggering amount that one surely needs take with a large pinch of salt.

These are impressive statistics, but they are misleading, in as much as they reinforce the impression of some vast, nefarious organization pumping out movies on a more or less professional basis. In fact, the reality was often very different and considerably smaller scale.

The manner in which the majority of stag films have come down to the modern viewer, via the video and DVD compilations of the 1980s and 1990s, is deceptive, lending the impression of some vast clearing house for films, from whose vaults these anthologies are collated. In fact, any collections that do exist tended to be constructed piecemeal during the 1970s and 1980s by enthusiasts who realized that a major part of America's sexual history was being allowed to rot, unnoticed, in attics and cellars across the country. The origin of each film, at that time, was not even of academic interest. It was enough, simply, that it would now be preserved.

Many of these plucky survivors were gathered from the discarded stock of merchants who had, in the past, either sold or warehoused their holdings. But, like archaeological remains that are carelessly hauled out of their environment and disseminated, undocumented, around the museums and collections of the world, their point of origin has long been forgotten. In these instances, the seller was unlikely ever to recall whether the movies came from this warehouse in Kentucky or that one in Delaware. And with the loss of that piece of basic information, so is lost any hope of tracing even the basics of a given production's origins.

Other films that circulate on the modern collectors' circuit were not even intended as stag films per se to begin with. Many first came to modern attention within private hoards of home movies. Dad has just taken delivery of his first home-movie camera and, having already filled a dozen reels with birthday parties and baby's first steps, he finally asks Mom if she'd like to make a little film of their own.

Perhaps she is uncertain, in which case he could first show her *Home Movies*, an early-1950s study of a couple watching stags in their own home. We do not see the films they are viewing, but their effect on the couple is obvious. Three reels and four ideas later, one or other is suggesting, "Let's try that position we saw in the film."

The mid-1960s film *Candid Camera* documents what might happen next. They get drunk, they get frisky, they prop the whirring camera somewhere where it'll record all the action. Wifey poses, squeezing and fondling her breasts until her stubbornly sunglasses-clad husband can't stand the teasing any longer. The camera is forgotten, they go at it like gangbusters and, before you know it, there's a lockbox at the back of the wardrobe, and neither of them ever mention the subject again. Then the years pass and things get thrown out or donated to the thrift store, and that little reel of film resurfaces in someone else's hands. Now it's no longer a midnight secret between husband and wife, it's a hot one-on-one genuine vintage stag.

Not all home movies that are labeled "erotic" necessarily reveal the sexual techniques of Mom and Pop. The makers' own thoughts on the subject are, nevertheless, likely to be the same. Writing in *The Moving Image* in 2005, archivist Dwight Swanson documented one such discovery, found within a donation to the Northeast Historic Film society's collection of regional home movies.

"There were sixteen reels of home movies . . . of [which] two reels were labeled 'Private Showing Only,'" wrote Swanson. "These turned out to be a reel that showed the grandparents on the beach with a topless (but not very revealing) shot of the grandmother and a second reel of a sailing trip that the grandfather had taken with some friends of his — again with some mild nudity."[3]

Of course, for every comparatively innocent moviemaker, there would be another who knew precisely what he was getting into.

"George," demobbed (although not from the photographic corps) in 1947, was working in a north New Jersey bottling factory when one of his workmates asked if he knew how to operate a movie camera. "I didn't, but I told him I did," he recalls, "and the following night I met him and his girl at his apartment, where they wanted me to film them fucking. We started and it was so boring, because he was just lying on top of her pumping away. I suggested they do something else. I didn't know about the close-up lens or anything, or how to stop the camera filming while they changed positions, and we probably ended up with about thirty seconds of actual footage where you see what was happening. I don't think he even bothered getting it developed.

"The next week, I went to the library and got out a book on cameras, then told the guy we should do it again, and I'd pay for the film and everything. I also made some notes of what I wanted them to do, and timed it out . . . two minutes this, three minutes that and so on, and when it was done — it was funny, I don't think either of them actually got off while I was filming, because they were too busy listening to me telling them what to do, but the guy, he knew someone who could get the film printed, and he brought it home and showed it to me and it was so fucking hot, it didn't matter whether they enjoyed making it. Everyone we showed it to loved it, and that's how we got started."[4]

Over the next four years, until he was busted (on an unrelated matter) in 1954, George reckons he produced in excess of fifty "real fuckin' and suckin'" movies, a run that ended only when "I got greedy and tried to move into other [unspecified] things." Most of his movies were shot using the same clockwork Bell & Howell camera with which he made the ill-fated first film; most were printed by the same contact. The cast, however, shifted as George introduced various friends and acquaintances to what quickly proved a lucrative line of work.

"There were four or five shops within an hour's drive that I could take films to, who I knew would pay a fair amount, cash up front, and I used to play them off against one another — 'Well, the guy over in Englewood said he'd give me a hundred for it,' that kind of thing. And, as I got better and I knew what I was doing," George explains, "I used to do things like cut sequences from one film and edit them into another; that was one of the reasons I liked to work with the same people, because the faces . . . well, not just the faces . . . remained the same, but the action kept changing, so you never knew if you'd seen the same film or just recognized the couple."

George never kept copies of his films: "If I wanted to get hold of one to mess with, I'd buy it, same as any other guy. I figured this way, if I ever did get busted, the most the cops would find would be my camera, and whoever got busted for owning a camera? Of course, every time I bought a film, the quality would be several shades of shit worse than the time before, because they were just duplicating and reduplicating those suckers, and you'd get these really harsh extremes, where I cut, say, a blow job from an old movie into one of the later ones or added some new footage to it. But it wasn't like today, there was none of this digital remastering crap. If the picture got fuzzy, someone in the audience would shout at the projectionist to fix the focus, that's all."

How the film reached that audience, George again claims not to know. "So far as I was concerned," he says, "the chain ended when the guy in the store handed me the money. What happened after that was none of my concern." He adds that he never used his real name in these transactions. "If the store was busted, the only thing the cops would get would be a description of a guy who came in every couple of months with a few films, in a gabardine suit and glasses." He would collect his money and then leave.

In fact, the film could then travel in any one of several different directions, on its way to its place within what one U.S. Congressman stated, around 1956, was "a $300 million dollar a year industry"[5] — a figure he can only have pulled out of thin air.

Having run off what they considered to be a suitable quantity of copies, some storeowners would simply add them to their own repository of under-the-counter materials for sale to certain trusted customers — road-show operators in the main, but also a few private enthusiasts. Others would place copies within a wider pool of films shared between several organizations; others still would sell them to a regional distributor — or even an international one. For many American men, after all, their first glimpse of a stag took place not in some rented hall or a friend's front room in Anytown, U.S.A., but in Cuba.

Throughout the 1950s, at least until Batista's government was felled by Fidel Castro, Havana was as popular a destination for U.S. business conventions as Las Vegas is today — and for many of the same reasons. Certainly no trip to the city was complete without a visit to either the Shanghai or the Monte Carlo Theater, eighty-cents-a-head nightspots that offered both a stag-movie show and, later in the evening, a live floor show, both of which could be interrupted at any moment by one of the prostitutes who haunted the floor deciding to take matters into her own hands.

Cuba's own stag industry dated back at least to the 1920s. One of the earliest known island exports, dating from around 1925, was a lavishly costumed effort titled *The Shiek*, in which a clearly powerful Arab chieftain and a favored concubine set out to sample as many sexual positions as they can in the allotted time. The actual setting of the film is as spartan as any desert tent, but the costumes (for however long they are worn) and the bearing of the actors confer a dramatic stateliness to the proceedings, albeit one that few subsequent Cuban productions would be able to emulate.

Some years before American stag-makers opted to dispense with storylines and plunge straight into the sexual action, the vast majority of Cuban efforts offered little more than a festival of rutting (and not particularly imaginative rutting at that), with their most remarkable moments deriving from the script more often than the action.

Unforgettable, for example, is the sequence in which a woman completes her morning toilet (with much rubbing of bare breasts and crotch), then wanders back into the bedroom to discover her sleeping husband's erection bursting through his pajama bottoms. "Cojones!" exclaims the Spanish-language caption. "It's a dead tapeworm!" A tapeworm that she can deal with only by sucking hard on its head.

Another noteworthy intrusion into the run-of-the-mill demeanor is offered up by the late-1940s film *La Señora y la Criada* (*The Lady and the Maid*), in which the stereotypical notion of the male as the dominant sexual partner is struck down with resolute force. Two women are making love when they are disturbed by the arrival of a swarthy young stud who insists that he alone can supply what they patently lack — "Aquí lo que hace falta es una buena morronga": a good hard piece of meat.

The lady is unimpressed, casting doubt on whether Renato could even get it up ("La señora duda que a Renato se le pare") and then cutting him down altogether. "A mamar carbon . . . que te llegó la hora" ("Suck my cunt, that's all you're good for").

Kensey Report

Damned Dirty Stuff!

The 1950s explosion in home-movie technology saw many dealers begin to retail reels direct to the public. Many homes possessed a movie projector now and many had amassed sizable film collections, just as modern consumers own DVDs and VHS tapes. For the first time, it was possible to view a movie without waiting for the road show to come into town, and slowly a way of life began to die.

The 1970 Commission on Obscenity and Pornography reported, "The operators of the 'road shows' found their services required less and less, so they became the first distributors, wholesalers and retailers for this market. As . . . more outlets for the films came into existence, the so-called 'traveling road shows' began to die out and, as of 1970, are relatively infrequent in most parts of the country."[1]

In terms of both the number of movies available and the amount of money generated by their sale, the erotic end of the rental market was tiny in comparison to the family-oriented side of things. It was also a difficult business. Most operators preferred to handle all transactions in person — "a wholesaler who is usually otherwise employed in a business that calls for a great deal of travel (such as a salesman or truck driver) ordinarily purchases 100-200 reels of film from a distributor and sells to retailers along his regular business route. Clandestine retailers are . . . found in bars, gas stations, barber shops, factories, etc."[2]

Sometimes, however, a distributor would aim for a larger market. Movie rental services had been around since the early 1920s — the first, Kodascope Libraries, was established in 1923, following the introduction of 16mm film stock. The retail-based Kodak Cinegraph followed in 1929, after which a wealth of private distribution companies set up to capitalize on the booming home market.

For the most part, these enterprises concentrated on harmless family fare — cartoons, comedies, dramas, series and newsreels. A handful, however, maintained a more adult stock for the use of certain discerning viewers — the series of naked dancing girl "featurettes" produced by the San Francisco–based Cine-Art Productions, for example: artistic modeling movies, nudism features and so on. And a few traveled even further. The name and logo of one of the country's most successful rental companies, Castle Films, appears at the end of several 1950s-era stags, although at least one correspondent insists that this insertion was simply another cunning ruse, designed to confound any would-be investigators.

No matter who was retailing or renting the movies, advertisements for such material, as published in the pulp magazines of the period, were by necessity circumspect. Many did not even state precisely what was being sold — rather, they would publish a list of titles that could have been books, postcards, or even ceramic salt and pepper shakers, for all the unsuspecting reader knew. Regular customers would understand, however, and would scour the ad in search of likely titles. (Tijuana Bibles were advertised in much the same fashion.)

Placing such a movie into the mails was likewise a fraught exercise, a stark contravention of the U.S. Post Office's restrictions on the passage of obscene materials. Imported films were similarly challenged by the 1930 Tariff Act, with its express prohibition on the importation of obscene materials, and Arthur Knight and Hollis

Alpert report on a subterfuge that American Customs once came across: "A cardboard tube of the kind used for protecting a rolled-up photo or poster. In this case, it was the print of an illustration from a Hans Christian Andersen fairy tale, and could be seen by opening the end of the tube. But upon removal of the brown wrapping paper, the examiner found that still another wrapping had been tightly wound around the outside of the tube and sealed with plastic tape. Beneath it he found a 200-foot length of stag movie film wound in a spiral around the tube."[3]

No less a personage than sexologist Alfred C. Kinsey, working through the late 1940s–early 1950s to build his eponymous institute's collection of sexual materials, regularly ran afoul of these regulations. Every week, the mail would bring him fresh erotic photographs, films, slides, prints, etchings, paintings and drawings, and every week, another federal employee would crack open a package and recoil from the obscenities that glistened within.

"Damned dirty stuff," one customs official told the *Indianapolis Star*. "Nothing scientific about it." One can only imagine the outrage these worthies would have suffered had they known that Kinsey was not only importing his filth, he was also producing it, beavering away in his Indiana attic to create what he described as a visual record of his researches.

Kinsey's movies were never intended for public viewing; they were for his and his research staff's eyes only, as they sought to answer the questions, solve the mysteries and quash the myths that surrounded both male and female sexuality. Thus, a film depicting several hundred men (Kinsey had hoped to recruit 2,000, but ultimately fell short of that target) masturbating together in the same large room was intended to prove that the majority of male ejaculations dribble rather than squirt — and so it did, with fewer than 30 percent achieving blastoff.

Yet, although Kinsey's intentions were undoubtedly scientific, his subjects — primarily institute staff members and their families — felt themselves to be under just as much pressure as the wantons and victims that urban legend insists were forced to make the stags. Although a few certainly shared their employer's exhibitionist streak, and some went even further (Kinsey himself often insisted on taking a part in the experiments, to the exception of his chosen partner's own spouse), others agreed to be filmed having sex only because they believed they had no alternative. The wife of one unnamed Kinsey employee complained to an interviewer of "the sickening pressure" she was under to have sex on film with her spouse and other staff members: "I felt like my husband's career at the institute depended on it."[4]

Altogether, Kinsey is estimated to have produced over fifty films during the early 1950s, of which around half focused on masturbation, twenty highlighted homosexuality (usually with some sadomasochism thrown in — not at all coincidentally reflecting Kinsey's own sexual preferences) and the remainder featured heterosexual couples. (Later in the decade, William Masters and Virginia Johnson likewise shot a number of movies while researching their landmark textbook *Human Sexual Response*.)

Naturally, these films were kept firmly under wraps, their very existence acknowledged only on a strictly enforced need-to-know basis. Some rumor of their creation does, however, appear to have circulated. One midwestern gentleman clearly recalls, sometime around 1960 ("I remember that because it was just after I left the Navy"[5]), being shown "several" films that were purportedly shot by Kinsey and his cameraman Bill Dellenback, in the attic at the institute: "To be honest, they were a lot duller than I'd expected."

The likelihood of these films having been the real McCoy is slight. More likely, he witnessed the early-1950s stag that shamelessly mistitled itself *The Kensey Report* after the institute's best-known work, and which gained its own notoriety after it was publicly named during testimony delivered to the U.S. Senate Judiciary Committee later in the decade. (Later, the same film would have its opening sequences shaved away and be fobbed off as a Marilyn Monroe stag!). Still held by the Kinsey Institute, even today Kinsey's movies are primarily available only to accredited researchers.

Not every institution that kept such materials under firm lock and key could be relied upon to remain 100 percent secure, however. "Rich" grew up in Oakland, California, and recalls seeing his first stag around the middle of the 1950s, courtesy of an obliging member of the local police department.

"A friend of mine would get a few guys together for a showing at his house," Rich recalls, "and we watched films that had been confiscated from backroom porn stores by the Oakland police department. He had a friend who was a policeman. We each kicked in a dollar to cover the cost of paying the guy who got them out of the impound office. We normally watched two or three movies."[6]

In a scene replayed with vivid clarity (if absolutely irreproachable good taste) in director Delbert Mann's 1957 film *The Bachelor Party*, the movies were shown at a private house, and half a century later, Rich was still able to recall the salient details, not only of the movies on display, but also of the floor show that was staged beforehand: "The guy I knew who had the connections set up a showing for a few of us guys, and he had a couple show up to provide a bit of live entertainment. The female, young, blonde, slender, well-built, was offered to us for pussy-licking only. Most of the guys gave her a good licking and tongue-fucking (not me), and then the guy who came with her had us watch him fuck her. He lasted for about five minutes and pulled out and shot his load on her belly. When the film started, it was the same couple in the flick. They had filmed the same kind of thing we had just done with another group of guys!"

Despite the complicity of the police department (unofficial, of course; had the officer in question been discovered, he would have been dismissed at the least, and probably hit with a barrage of charges as well), "the guy who showed these films was always very nervous and very careful not to get caught. The law was very strict then about full frontal nudity, much less fucking and sucking. However, they didn't seem to be as strict about child porno as long as the actors weren't too young. For instance, some films depicted Girl Scouts selling cookies as a start for sex, and I would guess their age to be maybe fifteen or sixteen at the most. Nowadays, a film like that would be a disaster!"

"George" agrees: "I never involved anyone in my movies who hadn't been around the block a few times, mainly because I couldn't afford to waste film on inexperience and nervousness. But there were definitely a few movies around where you had to wonder how old the girls — and sometimes the boys — were. I never saw anything involving really young kids, but there were definitely a few borderline cases."[7]

Few, if any, of these questionable films are known to exist today, at least among American examples of the genre, and those that have been suggested as likely candidates — the mid-1950s' *The Babysitter*, for example, or any of the putative schoolgirl romps produced in the U.K. a decade later *(Schoolgirl Lust, Pussy Galore, Free for All)* — give up any pretense the moment the girl undresses. The British stag *Do It Yourself*, for example, revolves around a father's efforts to interest his surly and fully uniformed schoolgirl daughter in hanging wallpaper. The more she messes up, the angrier he becomes, until he rips down her panties and spanks her behind, before being overcome by remorse and kissing the afflicted buttocks better. Finally the couple disrobe, and anybody seeking evidence that it is the uniform and not the age of its wearer that propels this particular fetish, will find it in the garish tattoos that adorn the arms of the "schoolgirl."

It is debatable whether any genuine examples of such films have truly been lost, or whether collectors who possess them are simply mindful enough of current legislation to keep their existence a well-guarded secret. But it was also true that American stag-makers seldom strayed too far from the sexual straight and narrow, and that few of the specialty themes so enjoyed by modern audiences receive more than a token airing in stags.

In part, this was because the market for such themes was exceedingly difficult to penetrate. Many filmmakers had a difficult enough time making a living from straightforward heterosexual movies. Without an already proven entrance to the field, why would he even waste the film stock on a movie whose target audience he did not even know — especially when there was a distinct possibility his regular crowds might well be horrified to discover what can go on in the bedroom, beyond the "usual" activities?

Di Lauro and Rabkin speculate that the paucity of juvenile sex films might well stem from "the middle-aged smoker crowd's aversion to watching girls the age of their daughters cavort sexually,"[8] an observation backed up by the anonymous midwestern distributor quoted by Knight and Alpert. Discussing *The Private Lives of the Sexy Sexteens*, a foursome comprised of three teens and an older man, the distributor shuddered, "You get to know your audience. If I showed up with that reel for a smoker at the local Kiwanis or someplace like that, they'd skin me alive."[9]

This is quite possible, although the generalization itself certainly flies in the face of findings delivered by the Senate Subcommittee to Investigate Juvenile Delinquency, in 1954. According to Senator Estes Kefauver, ranking minority member on the four-member panel, the testimony of so-called experts in the field not only confirmed that "pornography is a contributing factor, and a substantial one . . . in the increase of juvenile delinquency," there was also evidence that teenage girls were increasingly "being used in making pornographic films . . . [while] girls in their upper teens not only see these films, but actually engage in their manufacture and sale."[10]

Man's Exploits magazine concurred, in a 1957 exposé of the stag trade: "[The] latest gimmick worked out by the smut-peddlers involves teenage kids. The muck moguls line up good-looking youngsters ranging in age between 15 and 20. They supply a place where the kids can stage an orgy, furnish the liquor and marijuana — and set up lights and cameras. 'It's like a documentary, a newsreel, see?' leered one trash tycoon not long ago. 'The kids go wild — and so do the audiences later!'"[11]

Behind the sensationalist language, there was some cause for concern. A police officer named Barnes described for the Senate Subcommittee an elaborate "three-dimensional and four-color" film in which "acts of sexual perversion between men and women and women and women" involved "a girl 16 and . . . a girl 17."[12]

Even more alarming was the case of Ivan Jerome. On June 12, 1955, local emergency services responded to a report of a fire at the fifty-nine-year-old multimillionaire's estate in Massapequa, Long Island. A Russian immigrant, Jerome was credited with being present at the birth of the helicopter and with inventing the automatic record changer for phonographs. He was also one of the area's most respected figures.

The building was already engulfed in flame when the fire brigade arrived; Jerome himself drove up soon after, and of all the possessions on the premises, the ones he seemed most concerned about were some canisters of film he claimed were related to some work he'd done for the government. He offered an on-the-spot reward of $500 to any fireman who could rescue the precious canisters. He said not a word on the subject to the police.

The first film canister removed from the gutted wreckage the following morning was handed not to Jerome, but to the police. Suspicious of the man's concern for its contents, the officers fixed up a projector and screened the film onto a wall. What they saw was certainly sensitive, but it could have had little relationship to any government project. The film showed a series of explicit sexual encounters involving Jerome and an estimated twenty different girls, all aged between eleven and seventeen.

Jerome was indicted on no less than sixty counts of staging filmed sex parties with underage girls and producing "depraved sex films . . . so bad that local police refused to allow even reporters to take a peek at them."[13] However, when he was freed on a $100,000 bond, he promptly jumped bail and, despite being reportedly sighted as far afield as South America and the Soviet Union, he was never apprehended.

Cases such as this understandably created an upsurge in concern for the well-being of America's youth. Despite the vast amount of publicity they engendered, however, there was little evidence to prove that such incidents were either endemic or (perhaps more importantly) produced for anything approaching public consumption.

In 1970, *The Report of the Commission on Obscenity and Pornography* cited some seventy case histories, dating between 1957 and 1969, in which juveniles either committed or were the victims of sex crimes, and in which sexually explicit materials were found in the perpetrator's possession. No more than five cases implicitly involved motion pictures (including one where the molester was a projectionist at a movie theater); far more implicated copies of *Playboy*, the nudist magazine *Sun* and topless playing cards.

Pedophilia was not the only line in the sexual sand that was rarely if ever crossed in American stag films. Violence, too, was seldom portrayed, a taboo that might seem surprising to those who would condemn the stag as a misogynistic fantasy, but which loses that impact when one considers the true nature of the fantasies the films tapped into.

The whole point of stags was to portray life as their audience believed it *should* be, with their womenfolk as lustful and libidinous as the men themselves — or, to put it crudely, why resort to physical threats when what you want is already being offered on a plate?

A handful of American stags do venture into threatening territory. From the late 1950s, *Double Date* focuses on a house-proud woman who has just finished making the bed when she is disturbed by a man wearing sunglasses and, improbably, a fez. Heedless of her admittedly diminishing protests, he half-strips the bed and then completely strips the woman. Only as time passes, and her enthusiasm increases, does one realize this is not the crude assault it initially appeared to be, a discovery that is confirmed when a second man enters the room and is invited (by the woman) to join in the fun — at which point, somewhat old-fashionedly, her original partner departs.

Similar scenarios appear ready to play out in a handful of other stags, built around the surprise intrusion of a burglar, but again the woman's initial disinterest and fear is quickly overcome, and lust not only triumphs, it often leaves the intruder wondering quite what he let himself in for.

It is for similar reasons that few American stags ever investigated the more esoteric sexualities posited by certain foreign productions. Audiences completely failed, for instance, to climb aboard the French preoccupation with bondage — one reason, perhaps, why so few of that country's productions made it into circulation in postwar United States. (The only pre–World War II American production of any note is 1930's *Beat Me Daddy.*)

It might also be said, however, that New York publisher Irving Klaw had already tied up this particular market, via the range of films and photographs he produced with burlesque legend Bettie Page. These films were originally intended to help promote Irving and sister Paula Klaw's thriving mail-order fetish-wear business. Between 1951, when Page first began posing (for stills) for the Klaws, and 1957, when she announced her retirement from both modeling and the public eye, the model is estimated to have made over fifty films for the siblings, while garnering such attention that she became *Playboy's* first Playmate of the Month for 1955.

Page's films, although undeniably sexy, did not involve sex. The leather, whips and chains were for decoration alone, as Page danced and posed across the screen. Their appeal, then, was in their promise and, for many actresses and models, the line that Page refused to cross was indeed regarded as the final Rubicon.

Burlesque queens Virginia "Ding Dong" Bell, the aptly named Busty Brown, Tempest Storm, Lili St. Cyr, Wilma Wescott, Blaza Glory and Rita Grable all joined Page on the screen (one Klaw production, *Buxom Beautease*, even brings many of them together). But while Klaw would eventually be busted on a charge of distributing obscene material and many of his films and photographs destroyed by the authorities, that line remained unviolated.

Likewise, any existing market for bestiality was more than sated by the stream of such films that came into the country from south of the border. Live dog and donkey shows had long been staged for the delectation of both locals and tourists in search of fresh depravities, and several films emanating from this particular mind-set gained some notoriety in the U.S. during the 1950s and 1960s: *Rin Tin Tin Mexicano*, *A Hunter and His Dog*, *Rascal Rex* and *El Perro Masajista*.

France and the United Kingdom, too, produced a handful of animal movies. According to film historian H.C. Shelby, writing in 1969, "There are at least two [English] stags of some vintage that employ ponies and women,"[14] while a decade earlier saw a French film, *Nuits* (*Nights*), introduce a live snake into the proceedings. According to Donald H. Gilmore, *Nuits* was filmed "in the back of the Krazy Horse Saloon in Paris in 1959, and starred the younger sister of a very famous French actress."[15]

The closest that period American moviemakers came to the same subject, however, was *The Slippery Eel*, a late-1940s stag that was shot as a dare. An anonymous correspondent, claiming familiarity with the movie's creator, writes, "It was the girl's idea to bring the eel onto the set, and she was going to do all manner of things with it. She got cold feet at the last minute, though, but they were already filming, so one of the guys on the set had to come on and do her, and then he used the eel on her right at the end, when she was good and ready for it."[16] The unfolding action and, even more pertinently, the girl's facial expressions and body language certainly back up this explanation for a highly unusual movie that is, likewise, very much an acquired taste.

Other American bestiality-style movies were considerably more lighthearted. *Ping Pong* is a *circa* late-1950s movie in which a gorilla of that name escapes from a zoo and makes his way to a suburban home, where he espies a young woman undressing. Nobody, however, could doubt that the ape is anything but a man in an ill-fitting monkey suit, and the first glimpse of his penis confirms this. (From around the same time, *The Wolfman* is constructed around a similar concept and suffers from identical drawbacks.)

The conclusion that has to be drawn from this is that, once one has accepted the basic premise of the American stag film (that is, two or more people having abandoned sex on camera), the genre itself is remarkably pure. Let the Latins and the Europeans throw themselves into the later pages of the *Kama Sutra* and its ilk. The American stag remained as straightforward and, for the most part, conventional as any respectable married couple, with their well-thumbed copy of *Ideal Marriage* by the bedside, might expect their own sex life to be.

Wake up, light a cigarette, scratch your balls, take a leak — and then hop into bed with the missus. Yes, it's time for *Daily Duty: The Only Work We Never Fuss About,* and so what if hubby's a big, fat, hairy chap? He's just as attentive as the younger studs, and one of the few who chooses to reverse the normal fantasy flow and awaken *her* with some oral.

Another typical film from the era is 1952's *This Is the Life*, a stag that might have been one long, luxurious advertisement for the sixty-nine position, were the couple's evident enjoyment of oral not interrupted by the director's demands that they do something else for a while. They comply, but only briefly, and then it's back to what they do best. The final scene, meanwhile, delivers the punch line that the film's title didn't actually need. Relaxing with a cigarette each, they both pick up a magazine to read. It is the latest issue of *Life*.

With this loving gentleness in mind, it is scarcely surprising to discover that the one subject that appeared to intrigue the American male was the woman being susceptible to the same lustful stimuli as he was. The manifold etiquettes of the day had so successfully subsumed this actuality beneath her higher role of homemaker that it might as well have been the most unrealistic male fantasy of them all.

The Dreamer is a bedroom drama in which a boyish-looking vamp awakens and tries to arouse her sleeping husband. She is still working at it when a second man enters the room and treats her to all the pleasures she was hoping for — even more, in fact, as her husband suddenly bounds into action alongside him. But then the scene shifts and she is alone again, emerging from a fabulous dream to discover her husband is still asleep and still uselessly flaccid. Disgusted, she lies back down and returns to sleep.

The Cuban *Las Dos Amantes* (*The Two Lovers*) finds its two heroines growing hot and bothered over a series of erotic drawings, while the latest in a long line of American films called *Peeping Tom* zeroes in on its titular hero spying on a woman masturbating to a copy of Martin Dibner's 1958 novel *Showcase* (steamy goings-on behind the scenes at a major department store!).

And, finally, *Solitude* is just one of dozens of stags that cozy up with a single woman, alone in her bed (or her bath or her favorite chair . . . wherever!) with just a dildo for company. Barely is she warming up, however, than there appears by her pillow a naked man, his semi-erect penis so unerringly pointing toward her mouth that she barely needs raise her head to accommodate it. Fully erect, her visitor scurries around to fuck her, only for a second man to take his place at the head of the bed. Had the film not run out shortly after, one can only imagine the line that must have been forming at her door.

CHAPTER
FOURTEEN

*The Apple,
the Knockers
and the Coke*

Show business always fascinated the makers of stag movies. Whether they were bona fide Hollywood stars or the denizens of some rung lower down the entertainment ladder, the life of the public performer was, if the stags are to be believed, one long and livid bacchanalia. And so it may have been, at least if we heed the adventures of Blondie Blondell.

Among around forty stags that have been ascribed to an anonymous Chicago producer who operated during the 1930s, several starred this extraordinarily photogenic blonde actress, describing her as having arrived "direct from the London Gaiety Theatre." This billing is either an outright fabrication or a typographical error; the Gaiety was demolished around 1903, to be replaced by the *New* Gaiety. Nevertheless, it is quite possible that Blondie was one of the latter venue's dancing girls; she certainly has the body and charm for the role, and she emerges from such stags as *The Modern Magician* and *Matinee Idol* in the company of the era's most memorable performers.

The Modern Magician zeroes in on the conjuror the Great Hokum and his attempts to impress Blondie with a succession of, admittedly, eye-opening stunts. He compliments her on the color of her underwear and, when she asks how he knew, he produces the items from his pocket, then causes the rest of her clothing to vanish. He retrieves a rabbit from between her legs, followed by a rapidly inflating balloon, and performs what he styles the Detachable Prick Trick. But his favorite trick — and Blondie's too — is when it's time to "make the magic wand disappear."

Matinee Idol stars Blondie as a showgirl graciously succumbing to the seductive technique of Lord Fuckem, in the company of her ele-phantine maid, the facetiously named Wee Wampus. A jolly three-some ensues, while we catch a very smart cultural reference as Wee Wampus turns her most formidable charms upon the hapless lord. Sci-fi serials were all the rage in early-1930s America and, although we have no evidence of any stag movie actually blasting its cast off into deep space for the duration (the amorous adventures of *Flesh Gordon* would not materialize until 1974), Wee Wampus's Tit Rays would have raised a cheer regardless.

Magicians and conjurors appealed to stag-makers because of what they could do (the disappearing-clothes trick was still in use forty years later, in *The Magician*). Hypnotists and mesmerists, on the other hand, were fascinating because of what they could cause their audience to do. Boasting a female lead who bears a striking resemblance to the black maid in *Miss Park Avenue*, *The Hypnotist* features the mysterious Madame Cyprion working her skills on a young couple. Both are hypnotized into removing their clothing; then, while they remain entranced, they are seduced, first individu-ally and then together.

Hypnotism also takes center stage in *One Enchanted Evening*, as a canoodling couple are interrupted by a passing trickster. The boyfriend is rendered motionless, while his partner is transformed into a willing (or, at least, wordlessly compliant) partner for the hyp-notist.

The stage was not the only arena within which a performer could strut his stuff, and *The Aviator* recalls the showmanlike glamour that attached itself, during the 1920s and especially the post-Lindbergh 1930s, to the aviation trade. Utilizing genuine footage of an auto-gyro, the direct ancestor of the modern helicopter, *The Aviator* opens with a contemplation of the sights a pilot might enjoy from his lofty perch (although most of them seem to demand that young women live in homes with glass roofs). Eventually, one particular woman catches his eye. He lands his machine and plunges into adventure with an extraordinarily pretty brunette whose virtuoso performance would surely have endeared the film to every audience that saw it — and the cameraman knows it. The movie is awash with captivating facial close-ups, even when the "serious" action is taking place at the other end of her body. Indeed, the late Jim Holliday's *Adult Video Almanac and Trivia Treasury* ranks *The Aviator* among the "hottest" of all 1930s stags, an attribute he credits wholly to "the inspired lead female."

The most pernicious of all the stags' show-biz fantasies, of course, was the legend of the casting couch, the fabled daybed that was a standard piece of furniture in every talent scout and casting director's office. In fact, the earliest stag ever to take its lead from the legend also lifted its title from that same, much-used and abused piece of furniture.

The Casting Couch opens with an archetypically sleazy-looking director berating a young would-be actress (rumored in some circles to be a young Joan Crawford) for not including any bathing suit shots in her portfolio. "If you have one here, I will try it on and show you how I look," she suggests, but when she goes to the room where he told her she'd find one — surprise! She has stripped down to her underwear before she even thinks to look for the costume, and she seems genuinely surprised to discover that it's not there. The agent, however, is kneeling at the keyhole watching her and, natu-rally, enters the room to help her look.

But when he oversteps the mark, as he inevitably does, her response stops him cold: "Stop! I came here for a part, not to do that."

"Alright," he responds, as he walks out of the room. "But see how far you get by being that way."

Disgusted, she picks up a pamphlet lying nearby, titled *How to Become a Movie Star*. Moments later, "Oh, Mr. Casting Director?"

As usual in such films, the rooms in which the action takes place are sparse. But clues strewn throughout *The Casting Couch* demonstrate just how difficult it can be to correctly date a stag and the lengths to which a careful filmmaker might go to throw prospective bloodhounds off the scent.

Perhaps the most intriguing of these is the opening glimpse of an advertisement placed by Kalem Studios, calling for girls "to interview for a big part in motion pictures." One of the major movie producers of the early silent era, Kalem was responsible for close to a thousand conventional films between 1907 and 1917, starring such names as Mary Pickford, Alice Joyce and Helen Holmes. The studio was then bought out by Vitagraph in 1918.

Beyond the obviously (and atypically) very high quality of the movie, there is no suggestion that *The Casting Couch* was in any way connected to Kalem. So how is it that its name features so prominently in the opening moments of the movie? Either somebody purposefully set out to locate an ad referring to a long-dead studio — at the sight of which, any enterprising detective would hopefully lose interest — or it was clipped from a current issue of a movie magazine and thrown in to add veracity to the situation. Or the movie really was shot at the Kalem Studios. In either of these latter instances, *The Casting Couch* would unquestionably merit the title of "America's oldest extant stag" that sits so uneasily on the head of *A Free Ride*.

Unfortunately, the latter two scenarios are both unlikely, as an examination of the terminology used in the film's captions makes clear. According to *The Historical Dictionary of American Slang*, the term "casting couch" was unrecorded prior to 1931, while "fish skin," the would-be actress's term for a condom, dates from 1936 (in contrast to "eel skin," which was in common parlance as far back as the Civil War). But the costuming and furnishings then turn the clock back to the 1920s, and when the New York Museum of Sex dates the movie to 1924, it is a compromise based around all of these factors.

The couch's reputation never paled. A decade after *The Casting*

Couch, the uncompromisingly titled *Cuntinuity* is set on the (fictional) P.I. Studio lot, where Minnie and Mary are "always willing to take the hard parts in movies." *Revels of 1940* features a showgirl "auditioning" beneath a poster for the Don Terry movie *Dangerous Adventure*; and, deep into the 1960s, much the same scenarios were still playing out with stubborn regularity, perhaps because they allowed the conscientious stag-maker to hit back at his own sordid reputation for exploiting the innocents who strayed into his grasp.

The TV Casting Director is as duplicitously slimy as any fictional smut-peddler — the viewer knows that the moment he appears onscreen. But the babes all love him . . . of course they do, for how else are they going to get the parts they crave? So, when he calls up the next young lovely and invites her down for an interview, naturally it will require her to show a little more leg, flash a little more cleavage . . . oh, and let's see you in your underwear, just to make sure you're right for the part.

Only when he asks her to remove *that* does she balk, so he waves his hands disgustedly — "Then you might as well leave right now." She changes her mind when she hears those words, demurely removing her bra, at which point the panties have to go as well, and his job is done. Unprotestingly, she sits on his lap, proffers him a breast to suck, unbuttons his shirt, flicks off his beret (she leaves his shades) and, before you can say, "Oops, my mistake, I've just remembered the part's been filled," she's on her knees before him, giving the performance of her life.

The greatest of all stag mythologies, however, is the involvement of known and named celebrities, usually at the dawn of their careers, when any chance to get before the cameras was one worth taking. Part of the appeal is the storyline's adherence to the principles of the American dream, clawing one's way out of the cultural gutter on the way to the stars. But there is another, darker side to the fantasy.

For as long as man has elevated a select few of his peers to celebrity status, a parallel need has existed to catch those celebrities, both figuratively and literally, with their pants down. The Roman historian Suetonius delighted in echoing back the most salacious gossip about the emperors whose lives he was chronicling and, whether that gossip was true or not, the sexual and violent excesses he documented have become a part of the historical record.

Excess itself plays a significant role in this need. Ordinary people do ordinary things. Glamorous people do glamorous things. As late as the 1960s, it was not day-to-day junkies shooting up on street corners who were accused of turning kids onto drugs. It was the pop stars who gave the lifestyle its contagious allure and whose own trials, tribulations and, very often, deaths became headlines not because the events themselves were at all out of the ordinary, but because their victims were.

Hollywood has never wanted for sensationalism, on either side of the lens; indeed, the nature of the beast demands it, for it is sensationalism that sells the product to the public in the first place, and the need for regular refills that keeps them coming back.

It did the 1932 Jean Harlow and Clark Gable movie *Red Dust* no harm whatsoever when the rumor circulated that the pair had shot a series of hardcore stag-style inserts for inclusion in prints destined for certain specialist movie theaters in Latin America. Four years later, Greta Garbo's *Camille* became the subject of similar whispers, which reached a deafening crescendo when it was reported by one source that MGM head Louis B. Mayer had fired "a number of assistants, as well as a hapless double of Garbo" for their part in an after-hours stag-style enterprise.

The lesson, then, was clear to all. If the stars won't deliver, the public imagination will, and the bigger the star, the riper the imaginings.

The most pernicious of the ensuing rumors surrounds Marilyn Monroe's alleged involvement in at least three extant stag films, and several others which, conveniently for the storytellers, have since been lost — assuming they ever existed.

Of them all, the best known and the most seen is a softcore short known to collectors as *The Apple, the Knockers and the Coke*. And the Monroe claims continue to lure in the unsuspecting punters even today, decades after the movie's blonde star was revealed to be Arline Hunter, one of several statuesque strawberry-blondes who spent the 1950s being touted as either the "new," the "next" or even the "surrogate Marilyn Monroe."

Hunter is best remembered for her appearance as only the ninth *Playboy* centerfold, in August 1954 (in which she appears in a remarkable facsimile of Monroe's famous nude calendar pose — itself the star of *Playboy*'s debut issue). She also enjoyed roles in Klaytan Kirby's low-budget thriller *A Virgin in Hollywood*, the Bob Hope and Joan Fontaine comedy *Casanova's Big Night*, Dale Robertson and Lili St. Cyr's *Son of Sinbad* and episodes of the television series *Perry Mason* and *My Three Sons*.

But she never shook off the mid-1950s tag of "the poor man's Marilyn Monroe" that she acquired after her *Playboy* appearance, and sometimes even that term was shortened by certain unscrupulous souls.

Sometime before the *Playboy* session, Hunter's life on the very fringes of Hollywood saw her shoot a handful of short, mildly provocative and occasionally topless movies for one of the many local companies then specializing in glamour films. The purpose of these movies was twofold. Included in a portfolio, a private screen test of sorts, they offered potential employers a more intimate introduction to the actress than mere photographs ever could. But they could also be sold to the public as a means of further publicizing a young talent, and countless aspiring thespians took this route toward possible fame. Few required their star to do more than wriggle a little (the more adventurous souls might throw in some dance steps as well); bare breasts aside, none were anything less than wholesome. But they were popular with fans and oglers alike and, deep into the 1970s, advertisement proclaiming "See the stars before they were famous" were still appearing in magazine classifieds.

No record exists of precisely how many of these shorts Hunter made; undoubtedly, however, each was as innocent as another. In *Casbah Slave*, for example, she is first seen chained to a lattice wall. Breaking free, she embarks upon an extravagantly teasing dance, baring all down to the flimsiest of coverings. But that covering is never removed.

Hunter also appeared in *Uncover Girl*, an epic of wriggling and writhing that allows her to play up her Monroe resemblance to the hilt. But her best-known short — indeed, her best-known piece of cinema, full stop — was an innocuous eight minutes of fun in which the topless Hunter is primarily engaged in rolling an apple through her cleavage and down her torso, and drinking from a bottle of Coke. It is mild titillation at its most harmless. One would like to know what kind of off-camera instruction causes her to splutter with laughter at one point and dribble a mouthful of soda down her front, but the film is no more or less revealing than any other she appeared in.

Somewhere down the historical line, however, a print emerged that had been shaved of its opening credits — those frames that would have introduced Hunter by name and given the movie a title. In their stead, there appeared a new title, *The Apple, the Knockers and the Coke*, and a new identity for the now-anonymous star — a very young Marilyn Monroe.

It is unclear precisely when this switch took place. Rumors of a Monroe stag film circulated throughout her career, continuing unfettered even after her death in 1962, a holy grail among viewers and exhibitors alike. It would have required very little imagination to simply snip off the opening seconds of the reel and send the remainder onto the circuit with a whispered suggestion of who the star really was, and very little time for those whispers to become an accepted fact.

Certainly the film was in circulation by the late 1960s. One correspondent recalls, "My frat used to stage stag shows from time to time, and there was one with Marilyn Monroe in it that was always popular. Nothing actually happened in it, compared to some of the other movies we watched. She was drinking Coke and messing around with an apple. But nobody doubted that it was Marilyn, and I don't think it hurt her popularity at all."[1]

Indeed it did not. Even posthumously, Monroe's status as America's number one all-time sex goddess remained firmly in place, with even crude, second-generation reproductions of her own photo shoot passing gleefully from hand to hand. The existence of a piece of film that not only depicted Monroe in the flesh, but also revealed almost *all* of her the flesh, was tantamount to Camelot for those fans who were able to see it.

By the time the clip showed up in director Bill Osco's *Hollywood Blue* compilation in 1970, where it was tastelessly intercut with scenes from Monroe's funeral, neither distributors nor viewers doubted that it was indeed Marilyn. (A second copy of the film, absent Osco's additions, but still devoid of its original captions, moved onto the American college and cinema circuit, distributed by Grove Films within a collection of stags and early experimental shorts.)

Hollywood Blue was conceived as a celluloid equivalent to Kenneth Anger's *Hollywood Babylon* exposé of Hollywood's darkest secrets — at that time an almost mythical beast, published in France in 1959, but doomed to remain unavailable in English until 1975. Osco had spent much of the late 1960s shooting stags in Los Angeles, at one point averaging fifteen to twenty new productions a week, and several of his own movies show up in the course of the feature, a by-product of the unfortunate discovery that, while the Hollywood gutter was littered with legend, actual celluloid evidence of its straying stars was very hard to find.

Much of the film is consumed by either decidedly non-blue news footage of Jayne Mansfield, Evelyn West, Shirley Temple and Ronald Reagan, or once-controversial scenes from released films — Hedy Lamarr's naked swim in *Ecstasy* and Fay Wray's disrobing in the original *King Kong*.

The opening moments of *Hollywood Blue* do offer a glimpse of a gay stag that purportedly stars a sailor-suited Chuck Connors enjoying a raunchy romp with a soldier — the future TV cowboy is said to have supplemented his earlier career as an athlete (he played basketball for the Boston Celtics and baseball with the Dodgers and the Cubs) by taking starring roles in such films during the late 1940s.

But that — and *The Apple, the Knockers and the Coke* — notwithstanding, *Hollywood Blue*'s greatest notoriety (and box-office allure) rested upon the inclusion of a bestiality-flavored encounter between an unknown girl and her pet Saint Bernard, which was in any case deleted before the film even left Osco's own Eros Cinema.

The Apple, the Knockers and the Coke is not the only pseudo-

Monroe stag to have surfaced over the years, although the majority have been shot down very quickly — author James Haspiel, a close friend of Monroe's, correctly identified the Arline Hunter fraud very early on.

Shortly after Monroe's death in 1962, however, rumor of her involvement in one particular stag grew so loud that her second husband, Joe DiMaggio, offered $25,000 for the original negatives and all prints of the offending film. (A close friend following their 1955 divorce, DiMaggio continued protecting Monroe's interests long after her death.) The film was said to date from 1948, shortly after Monroe was released from her first movie contract, with Twentieth Century Fox. Her earliest steps into cinema, via minor roles in *Scudda Hoo! Scudda Hay!* and *Dangerous Years*, were already behind her and, consumed by insecurity, she fell back on the modeling career that had helped sustain her beforehand.

But Monroe may have also tried her luck as a call girl, and as an actress in a clutch of hardcore stags. The only substantive evidence for this would appear to be what her many biographers have referred to as her later (post-fame) fear that her past might one day resurface to destroy her reputation. But it was certainly a pervasive image — so pervasive that, soon, DiMaggio was not the only party interested in procuring a copy. The U.S. government, too, was anxious to view the movie, as part of the FBI's ongoing investigation into Monroe's purported relationship with John F. Kennedy, and the events that led up to her death. An increasingly stubborn rumor insisted that her partner in the film was either John or Robert Kennedy.

The Kennedy angle was debunked on February 10, 1965, when an FBI informant, supervised by agents in the bureau's Albany, N.Y., office viewed the movie in the presence of its owner. An FBI memorandum issued the following day references "a motion picture which depicted deceased actress Marilyn Monroe committing a perverted sex act on an unknown male," but confirms that neither Kennedy brother played the role of her partner.

A week later, the actress's involvement, too, was quashed when a second memorandum noted, "The laboratory has no information concerning Marilyn Monroe's participation in [this] film." Thus ended the FBI's interest in the affair, with DiMaggio withdrawing his own offer shortly afterward.

The movie the FBI witnessed (and which has since been included on several underground DVD anthologies of purported Monroe stags) was, in fact, nothing more than the 1951 (or later) *The Kensey Report*, shorn of an opening sequence in which "Marilyn" (and the woman does look a little like her) opens the door to a well-dressed young man, armed with a very arousing questionnaire. The most commonly circulating print, however, opens with the cast already in action, making out on a couch.

Having gone some way toward undressing one another and attempting sex in a seated position, they pause to pull out the sofa and fold it into a bed. The "perverted sex act" follows a few minutes later, as "Marilyn," seemingly less than impressed by the initial intercourse sequence, makes her way slowly down her partner's body and treats him to some very enthusiastic and conclusive fellatio, an act that one of Monroe's closest friends later described as both the actress's favorite sexual position, as well as a key element in the breakdown of her marriage to DiMaggio. He, apparently, considered it unnatural, and refused to indulge his wife's passion.

The session ends with "Marilyn" laying the now-flaccid organ back on his thigh and then very peremptorily dressing and seeing her visitor to the door.

With *The Kensey Report* frequently numbered by other commentators among the most popular American stags of the early 1950s, it seems incredible that the Monroe fallacy could have survived as long as it did, let alone draw the attentions of the FBI. Nevertheless, with both Monroe and Kennedy's involvement now firmly debunked, it was assumed that film and rumors alike would vanish from view. And so they did for a time. In 1980, however, they returned with a vengeance.

That March, readers of Sweden's *Fib Aktuellt* gossip magazine were introduced to a young Swedish photographer who had discovered a single copy of what was now being described as "the world's rarest stag film," a seven-minute reel in which a young and somewhat plump Monroe effectively fulfilled every male fantasy she was ever to induce.

Swedish experts instantly pronounced the film to be the real thing; they were even able to establish an approximate date for its production, that sad interregnum around 1948.

Despite many (and continuing) claims to the contrary, the so-called "Swedish movie" was *not* the one the FBI investigated. Clad in black teddy, chunkier than in her moviemaking prime and a lot more coarsely featured, the blonde actress first poses and then plays with a proffered electric vibrator — the kind that had to be plugged into the wall. She and her watching co-star then fall into a none-too-vigorous sixty-nine, and have intercourse in a variety of positions. The movie ends with the couple sharing a cigarette and a drink, and then embracing, smiling at the camera.

Perhaps the most remarkable feature of the movie, however, is just how non-explicit it is, as a combination of poor camera angles and atrocious lighting render any attempt to study detail all but impossible.

Was this girl Marilyn? There are certain sequences — in particular, those that were farmed out to the world's media in 1980 — where the resemblance is striking. But it is a resemblance to the older Monroe. The weary-looking woman who stares out from the celluloid bears no resemblance whatsoever to the fresh-faced, ringlet-festooned youth immortalized in other photographs of the same period. Two and a half decades and several tons of newsprint after the film's discovery, Monroe's involvement in this, or any other stag, remains dubious.

Of course, for those people who want it to be a Marilyn Monroe movie (and there are many), no evidence or testimony will ever shatter their beliefs, just as none will ever rid the rumor mill of its other celebrity participants, and a roll call almost as old as the movies themselves.

By 1924, Joan Crawford, then a twenty-year-old Texan named Lucille LeSueur, was already a popular dancer at New York smokers and stag parties. She had made her Broadway debut as a dancer in *Innocent Eyes*, but her dream of graduating to cinema seemed doomed. Three times she screen-tested for Marcus Loew, owner of the Loew theater chain, and three times she failed. So, it is said, she made it onto the screen from another direction, by taking the lead role in a series of stag movies.

Little is known about any of them. She has been credited with appearing in the aforementioned *The Casting Couch*, but one look at that movie's heroine should dispel that particular fantasy. Another movie allegedly involved her in a lesbian situation; another saw her initiate and exhaust a gang bang; and another, *The Plumber*, is said to have paired Crawford with vaudeville comedian Harry Green, a former lawyer who would go on to a small degree of cinematic success.

Green was apparently no stranger to stag movies. He is one of several stars (Harold Lloyd is another) credited with playing the bespectacled dupe Anthony Browning in *On the Beach* (a.k.a. *The Goat*), a lighthearted seaside romp in which Browning, a simple soul "who still believes in mermaids and fairies," persuades three sunbathing beauties to have sex with him.

Innocently, he assumes it is bashfulness that prompts them to insist he can only have them through a hole in a fence. In fact, the secrecy is down to the fact that they have just located a goat — and that is what the poor sap winds up having sex with.

On the Beach frequently turns up on anthologies. *The Plumber*, however, has vanished from view. Indeed, beyond the obvious connotations of its title, we know nothing more about it, allegedly because Crawford purchased every existing print in 1929, around the same time she married Douglas Fairbanks, Jr. Just one copy of *The Plumber* is said to have escaped the purge, and that was held in the private collection of the Quiet Birdmen of America, an exclusive aeronautics club that numbered Charles Lindbergh among its members.

Out of sight does not necessarily ensure something remains out of mind, however. Actor Ted Jordan, best remembered today as the man in black who is shot down by Marshall Matt Dillon during the opening credits to *Gunsmoke*, recalled discussing Crawford's past with Marilyn Monroe in the late 1940s, as the aspiring actress continued her struggle to make an impression on Hollywood.

Norma Jeane was undergoing one of her periodic bouts of self-pity and insecurity, chaffing at being the butt of much slanderous gossip, most of it targeted at her willingness to sleep her way into a contract. On this particular occasion, Crawford was the target of her rage.

"I don't hear whispers about her like I hear about me," she complained. "Hell, I didn't fuck six guys in a stag movie like she did."[2]

Neither, she doubted, would she receive the break that Crawford's efforts won her. Jordan explained, "When [Crawford] was trying to break into the studios, she got nowhere until several . . . executives were given a private screening of her stag film. They sat open-mouthed as they watched the woman with the slim figure wear out a group of men. The movie became the hottest item on the underground screening-room circuit around Hollywood and, in short order, Miss Crawford won a studio contract."[3]

A similar story appears in Monroe's own *My Story*, ghostwritten by Ben Hecht shortly after her marriage to Joe DiMaggio in 1954, but unpublished for twenty years thereafter. Crawford is not mentioned by name, while the content of the stag itself is diluted considerably from Jordan's description, to become an albeit "vulgar and suggestive" two-reel nude dance. The end result, however, was the same.

"Every movie producer or director who saw the stag film became haunted with the nude performer," Monroe recounted. "They vied for her services as if she were the only female on tap, and the only full set of secondary female characteristics in Hollywood. She became famous in a few months, and is still famous today."[4]

Crawford herself denied the tales, even after word of her supposed spending spree became common knowledge on the Hollywood grapevine. Neither would her denials halt the whispering. On October 11, 1935, on the night that Crawford celebrated her second marriage, she received an anonymous phone call from a man offering to sell her another of the films in which she had supposedly starred — rumor has it that this was *The Casting Couch*.

Crawford promptly referred the caller to the legal team at her studio, MGM, who viewed the film and loudly pronounced it Joan-free, a stance vindicated in later years, when film historian David Thomson declared it was studio executive Harry Rapf and/or his colleagues at MGM who started all the rumors swirling in the first place.

"Joan was an ideal working girl, someone with a past to hide, perhaps," writes Thomson. "And the studio publicity people painted that picture vivid. They spread stories that there were stag movies in existence — from hot Texas days — of a very young Joan doing unspeakable but very watchable things."[5]

Crawford's denials were no more convincing than Monroe's to the audience whose personal fantasies were made flesh by the supposed existence of these films. Neither were those issued later in the decade (and beyond) by supporters of those other celebrities who supposedly supplemented their pre-Hollywood earnings with a quick dash through the stag scene, all the more so since those protests invariably relied on one basic truism to prove the individual's innocence. As *Man's Exploits* magazine airily sniffed, "Once [a stag reel is] released, the members of the cast are cooked for straight parts. They can only work for the sex-film makers."[6]

Occasionally, however, a celebrity can shake off the rumors by actually stepping out and demonstrating precisely how he or she differs from the celluloid doppelgänger.

The late 1960s saw many viewers of *The Personal Touch* convince themselves (or allow themselves to be convinced) that the movie's female lead was a young Barbra Streisand. Aired in heavily censored form by Al Goldstein's New York public access TV show *Midnight Blue* in 1974, *The Personal Touch* is an unremarkable effort that might have been completely forgotten had the "Streisand connection" not been drawn. But even believers had to acknowledge that spotting the resemblance required a lot of imagination, as Streisand herself pointed out.

"When I first heard the rumor," she said, "I thought it was a put-on. But these people you never can seem to find were selling a film, and claiming it was me. I couldn't resist the temptation to see what the actress looked like, and also to check out her performance, so we got a copy.

"The film, naturally, is very blurred. The girl has long hair, like I did back in the sixties, although she was chubby, while I was very skinny. But the dead giveaway came when the camera zoomed in on her hands around the guy's you-know-what. There they were: short, stubby fingers! Definitely not mine. So all you would-be buyers, don't waste your money. Actually, the idea of me in a pornographic film is preposterous! Me, right? Who was an usher in a legitimate theater, and hid my head so nobody would remember, after I became famous, that I had showed them to their seats!"[7] (Interestingly, the same couple that shot *The Personal Touch* appear in another movie, *Auto-Sex*, which has never been ascribed to Streisand.)

Mistaken identity is an easy trap to fall into. Viewers of adult movie star John "Long Johnny Wadd" Holmes' earliest stag movies, in the late 1960s, were so taken by his resemblance to (appropriately) *Leave It to Beaver* star Ken Osmond that both Holmes and Universal Studios were prompted to issue denials. The real Osmond, the studio added, was now happily married and working for the LAPD.

Tab Hunter has been linked with the mid 1950s *Love Me Tender* (no relation to the Elvis Presley movie) and Kim Novak with the late-1940s pair *The Call Girl* and *The Barker*. The young Jayne Mansfield was purportedly captured going at it with a breathtakingly unglamorous paramour in the mid-1950s stag *Ding-a-Ling*. Here, however, the scandal-mongers are certainly grasping at straws. Although the woman's hairstyle certainly matches the future actress's earliest blonde mound, her other most renowned attributes are decidedly absent. (Mansfield makes a less contentious appearance in *Rendezvous*, an American stag that warms up its female lead with the summer 1956 issue of *Cabaret Quarterly* magazine, of which Mansfield was the cover star. Jayne is promptly discarded, however, once the girl's male lover arrives, and the pair prepare to hurtle through no fewer than fourteen different sexual positions in a little under nine minutes.)

The carnival of denials that normally surrounds these films is not endless, however. Pinup queen Candy Barr was still known as Juanita Dale Slusher when she was convinced — or, as she put it, coerced — into co-starring in *Smart Aleck!*. Born in 1935, she was a runaway at thirteen, married to a Dallas safecracker at fourteen, and just sixteen when, she later claimed, a man she met at a local club drugged her and forced her to perform, at gunpoint, in a stag film he was making in his hotel room.

It is a horrific scenario, but little of that is apparent in the movie. Barr appears neither stoned nor scared, and her interaction with her partner has a sparkling energy that suggests she was enjoying every minute of it. Neither does the movie's own setup appear as slapdash as Barr makes it sound, as a hitherto straightforward sex scene suddenly demands that both participants stop screwing and start acting instead.

The man demands a blowjob; Barr demurs.

What follows ranks among the most oft-discussed sequences in the annals of stag, although it is possible to read way too much into it. Generalizing furiously, reviewer Phil Hall insisted, "In all stag films, women gladly do what men demand of them. In *Smart Aleck!*, not only does Barr refuse, but she literally fights back. When the man tries to force her mouth between his legs, she punches him back! Who wears the pants in this skin flick?"[8]

In fact, there are a number of other films where the woman visibly refuses to accede to one or another of the director's commands (or purposefully makes such a poor job of it that she might as well not have bothered). Neither is there any suggestion that the scene was not carefully scripted beforehand — or, if there is, it is quickly defused when Barr steps to the telephone and calls up a friend, who arrives within moments to gladly perform the act.

Barr may not have been a willing accomplice in the film, but neither was she the ferocious scene-spoiling hellcat her apologists so blandly credit her as.

In fact, the sequence was simply an ingenious way of introducing a third character into the movie, and *Smart Aleck!* plays out as a riotous threesome. (Barr's co-stars continue their relationship in the less confrontational *The Sleepwalker*.)

Barr put the trauma of *Smart Aleck!* behind her. She told the French magazine *Oui*, "It happened and I've had a lot of flak about it. People say, 'what the hell, it's only a fuck movie.' Well, that was 1951; I do care what the hell. If I had done it by choice, then I would have had some mechanism to adjust it into my lifestyle. But I didn't do it by choice. . . . I wasn't lured. I was taken, done and that was it."[9]

Nevertheless, she continued reveling in her sexuality, as an actress, stripper, dancer and nude model. Elected one of *Playboy*'s 100 sexiest women of the twentieth century (Marilyn Monroe and Jayne Mansfield topped the poll), Barr made her final unclothed appearance in that same issue of *Oui* in 1976, at the age of forty-one.

That same year, Al Di Lauro and Gerald Rabkin proclaimed Barr "the first pornographic star," a subverter of official morality on a par with Lenny Bruce, and described *Smart Aleck!* as "the single most popular film of the genre."[10]

They do not, unfortunately, back this claim with any evidence, but amid the flurry of Internet postings that followed Barr's death in Victoria, Texas, on December 30, 2005, there was sufficient mention of *Smart Aleck!* — complimentary, excited and aroused — to justify at least some of the hyperbole. Besides, as the first actress ever to admit to a past in stag films, how could any other "pornographic star" be credited with preceding her?

Read It in Books

"Melody enjoyed working before the hot eye of the camera. As she applied the final touches to her makeup, she wondered how many stag films she had made? Fifty? Sixty? At least that many, she decided." — Sheila Faye, *Hold That Pose* (Midwood, 1964)

If whisper, rumor and innuendo were responsible for forging the greatest of the mythologies that surrounded the world of stag films, the printed page was equally liable for the wealth of misinformation, suspicion and disdain that formed around the nuts and bolts of the business.

The first mass-market author to broach the subject of stag movies was noir screenwriter and novelist Horace McCoy. Born in Tennessee, McCoy's earliest stories were pure pulp, published in the likes of *Black Mask*, *Detective-Dragnet*, *Action Stories*, *Battle Aces* and *Western Trails*. The Depression saw him relocate to L.A., where he briefly entertained dreams of an acting career; he wound up working as a bouncer on the Santa Monica pier and returned his attention to writing.

His experiences, however, were not wasted. His debut novel, *They Shoot Horses, Don't They?*, drew heavily upon autobiography, and the same mood carried over to *I Should Have Stayed at Home*, the 1938 Hollywood exposé that set the stage for every subsequent work from *The Day of the Locust* forward. And it is within those pages that the rapt reader first discovers how Hollywood's own glitterati employ stag movies — as a means of seducing the sweet young things that fall into their hands, in search of their first "lucky break."

Ralph, the novel's hero, has tumbled into the clutches of the rapacious Mrs. Smithers, a fading beauty who attracts young aspirants with bountiful pledges of stardom, but seldom advances their careers any further than her own boudoir. Solid, shy and stubbornly Southern, however, Ralph is proving a tougher nut to crack. Mrs. Smithers resorts to 16mm home movies.

"Who's in this picture?" he asks, as she sets up the projector and screen.

"Don't be curious." And, a moment later, "I don't want you to be frightened at this. Remember, it's just a motion picture."

She snapped off the pilot light on the projector and started the picture. Their Night Out, the title said.

Two men were sitting at a table playing cards. There was a knock at the door. One of them got up and opened it, admitting two girls. They didn't kiss or shake hands or anything else, they all started taking off their clothes. One of them literally tore his shirt off.

"They don't waste time, do they?" I said, just to have something to say, to try to cover my self-consciousness.

"That's to save footage," Mrs Smithers said. . . . "Look at what they're doing now."

I looked — and I was thankful the room was dark so she couldn't see my face.[1]

While McCoy explained where stag movies frequently wound up, crime writer William Francis Urell (he abandoned his surname when writing) explained where they came from in the first place when he followed McCoy into the world of clandestine movie-making with the publication of *Rough on Rats* in 1942.

"Tough, good-looking private eye" Anthony Martin is on the trail of some missing film reels, at the same time pursuing a relationship with a pretty young actress named Jerry, who appears in the films. Initially, he is ignorant of what the movies actually entail; it is only as he finds himself increasingly ensnared within a rat's nest of murderous intrigue and lies that he learns the steamy truth.

He is also shocked (as, indeed, was the reader) to discover precisely how much money was bound up in the trade.

"They're valuable?" he asks the films' owner, as they discuss the loss.

"Yes," comes the reply. "It would cost about $50,000 to produce them again. It was a year's work. Any studio would charge a great deal for the processing alone. The actual investment in material is small, of course, but getting people to act in them costs money, and everyone connected with them has to be well paid to keep quiet."

The mourning mogul goes on to explain that such movies could be made for a lot less money: "A great deal are made in hotel rooms. They are made on home-made outfits. Poorly lighted and really don't sell very well." But the material that Martin is pursuing was "high class . . . a script and a story . . . settings . . . costumes for the actors. Good-looking girls."[2]

Martin never actually watches the movies he spends the entire novel pursuing, and the reader is never offered more than a glimpse of what they contain. That glimpse, however, was sufficient, for who among the author's audience had not heard the whispered accounts of the kind of films that can involve such danger and induce such secrecy? And who would not pay their own small fortune to get their own hands on more of the same?

Despite Francis's reputation (he was still a teenager when he published his first short story, "Three Lives for $27,000," in the weekly detective magazine *Flynn's* in 1928, and went on to establish himself as a regular contributor to *Colliers* and *The Novel Magazine*), *Rough on Rats* was not a best-seller. Pulp paperbacks rarely were. It was also, perhaps, a little ahead of its time. American publishing, if not

America itself, was not yet ready to investigate the world that Francis revealed. A decade later, however, the industry was undergoing a major seismic shift. It was time to get *Rough on Rats* all over again.

In 1951, Signet Books reprinted *Rough on Rats* (coincidentally, alongside a new edition of McCoy's *I Should Have Stayed at Home*), this time under the title *I.O.U. Murder*, and now there was no doubting the story's subject matter. "Death Stalks Stag Party Girls," screamed the subtitle, while the lurid back-cover blurb only heightened the anticipation. "Jerry," it announced, is "a screen actress. But you've never seen her in the movies. She appears only in pictures shown at smoky stag parties."

The impetus behind this brave new boldness was the birth, in the late 1940s, of an entire new breed of men's magazines — the logical successors to the prewar pulps, but each one imbibed with a rugged twist of savage reality.

The troops were returning home, but they were very different men to those who had gone off to fight. Prewar men's magazines, although racy enough for their time, were no longer of interest to the average Joe. Back then, his life had revolved around the ideals of the American dream — a nice house, a pretty wife, a good-looking car and a brood of kids — and even the pulpiest reading matter (detective, crime and science-fiction ruled the roost) was little more than a diversion.

Now his horizons had changed. He knew how to kill, and he had seen death first hand. Before the war, patriotism meant saluting the flag on July 4. Now it meant something more, something brutal and real, something the folks back home could never comprehend, and which the new postwar world simply couldn't accommodate. How can you transition from slitting throats in Far Eastern jungles to riveting car parts in a mid-America factory; from the experienced whores in Europe to the girls next door in Wisconsin?

It was an impossible task. But this new wave of pulp magazines at least sought to make the transition easier, by returning the reader to that not-so-long-ago time when war was hell, but hell was for heroes; where the women were game for anything, and even the hardest decisions were laid out in black and white. By the time the Korean War ignited in June 1950, returning the fighting man to at least a semblance of "normality," several dozen titles had arisen (and fallen) in pursuit of the disenfranchised vet, and more were emerging every month.

The overall appearance of magazines like *Man to Man, Battle Cry for Men, OK for Men, Man's Adventure* and, most archetypal of them all, *Stag*, evinced little more than a graphic eye for blood-boiling, eye-popping, sinew-straining violence. When one delved within those cheap newsprint pages, one was as likely to discover whether "abnormal hang-ups are destroying your sex drive" as to learn how it feels to be "chewed to death by giant turtles," and for every "Massacre off Zanzibar — the day our decks ran blood," there was an exposé into "teenage lust orgies — America's latest scourge."

Neither did it matter that, after a few months, the stories all seemed to blend into one another ("Radioactive koala bears can sap your manhood"). The magazines sold well when they first appeared during the 1950s, and they were still selling healthily two decades later.

Stag movies slipped effortlessly into the manly milieu, not only because they represented the closest that many readers were now likely to come to the carnal extremes described elsewhere in the magazine but because, like the shared experience of war and combat, they offered like-minded men a bond that could rarely be discussed, let alone shared, with the average passerby, one that existed only within the closeted, smoky world of a fraternal lodge.

The pulps' fascination with criminal masterminds, underworld sleaze and depraved adventure, and the accompanying fission of lawlessness and danger, only added to that bond. Not every man could be Dick Tracy or Perry Mason. But maybe he could be a bit player in one of his adventures.

Lurid exposés were the nature of the game, a monthly parade of shocking stories ripping the lid off one illicit practice or another, and relying, in equal part, on delirious fantasy and brutal exaggeration for their sources. The shocking saga of wealthy pedophile Ivan Jerome, for example, was employed to illustrate the depraved depths to which *all* stag producers might sink, even though Jerome's collection was intended for private viewing only and had no correlation with the movies being made for commercial distribution.

Occasionally, however, the pulps got lucky, not only stumbling upon a genuine exclusive, but — by so doing — opening up what had once been a cult into something approaching a mainstream fascination.

In 1957, the New York-based magazine *Mr.* ran a feature centered on a few half-gleaned semi-facts, concerning some peculiar goings-on in and around certain military bases. They called it "Wife-Swapping," although "Wife-*Sharing*" would have been a more appropriate term.

According to rumor, the activities in question dated back to World War II, when the traditionally close and fatalistic fellowship that existed among active military personnel — particularly air force pilots — adopted a new perspective, in the form of an informal (but nevertheless solemnly sworn) pledge to continue caring for a colleague's wife, in the event of "anything" happening to him.

That these duties included taking care of her sexual needs was, initially, unspoken, but as time passed and the conflict grew more ferocious, so these original parameters shifted. Now personnel on the eve of shipping out to the war zone would supplement the usual going-away parties with more intimate farewells, with their friends as well as their spouses.

The popularity of such soirees faded once the war wound down — there was, after all, no longer a need for them. The outbreak of the Korean War, however, reignited the sense of weary fatalism that had once consumed America's military, as they returned to the front lines to fight and, presumably, to die. Those unspoken pledges, and all the other activities they entailed, returned with them.

The war ended in 1953, but this time the arrival of peace did not curtail the cult of wife-swapping. Rather, it simply encouraged it to develop further. Already the popularity of the parties had spread from the military bases where they were once most prevalent, into the neighboring suburbs where both military and civilian personnel were living. With that expansion, there came a new informality.

"Key clubs" became popular: at the end of an evening, the assembled husbands would place their house or car keys into a pile in the middle of the room, to be drawn at random by the wives. The owner of the selected key would become the woman's partner for that evening. (A typical key party is depicted in Stanley Long's 1965 movie *Primitive London*; another features in Rick Moody's novel and subsequent movie *The Ice Storm*. March 2007 saw one very entertainingly portrayed in the BBC series *Life on Mars*.)

Mr. magazine outlined all of this, but did so without a second thought for the subject — "wife-swapping" was just another feature in a magazine that constantly sought out new scandals and sensations with which to titillate its readership and which, having done so, would then move onto the next month's exposé.

This time, however, was different. No sooner had that issue hit the newsstand than the incoming mailbag was suddenly bulging with enthusiastic responses from *Mr.* readers. Some were already regular swappers; others wanted to know how to become one. And more were members of even more exclusive sex clubs, devoted to three-, four- and even more-somes, husband- and wife-only societies, and any other permutation that their circle of friends could devise.

It also turned out that a lot of these folks were handy with cameras, filming their group's cavortings and then trading them with other clubs on a circuit that consumed almost all fifty states.

A number of stag movies circulate today that purportedly show the activities of the wife-swapping and like-minded swinger scenes (office parties were another popular theme), many of which appear to be genuine documents of an evening's entertainment that somehow transitioned from private collections to the public domain.

Others, however, were certainly staged events, manufactured specifically for sale to the general public. One especially suspect film (shot during the mid-1960s, to judge from the LPs left casually scattered in one corner of the room) not only features faces familiar from several other period films, it also suggests that only the best-looking, best-built and best-endowed youngsters were members of this particular club. There is not an ounce of middle-aged spread in sight.

Truer to life are those movies where the assembled cast run the gamut of suburban society — the young marrieds, of course, but also the elderly swingers, the middle-aged businessman and his over-cosmeticized wife. The denizens, in fact, of Any Suburb, U.S.A. and, by the mid-1960s, the U.K. as well. July 1970 saw the release in that country of the full-length (eighty-six-minute) *The Wife Swappers*, a dramatized documentary exposing what, in the pages of the British tabloids, was one of the most sordid American imports yet to shake the bastions of traditional English life.

Producer Stanley Long explained, "I was reading the *News of the World*, and [the] story . . . just leapt off the page. I knew immediately that it could be a massive hit if I turned it into a movie."[3]

Directed by Derek Ford and narrated by David Gell, an original host of TV's *Ready Steady Go!* pop-program, *The Wife Swappers* was purportedly compiled from the "real life" stories of genuine swappers and is shaped by the stark warning that "it is a feature of most couples established in the so-called 'swinging set' that they will constantly seek to involve others, a feature they share with drug addicts and alcoholics."

There was even a so-called "eminent London psychiatrist" on hand to place the sexuality into the social and cultural context required of a documentary, although Long later admitted that he, like the swappers onscreen, was actually played by an actor. (Quietly unobtrusive amid the bustle of the soundstage, incidentally, the movie's stills photographer was a young Scotsman named John Lindsay, destined to become one of the U.K.'s most infamous makers of stag movies.)

The Wife Swappers' wife-swapping was staged, and the aforementioned flood of other fakes ensures that it is difficult today to determine a genuine swapping event from a faked one. But all have one thing in common — a perception of disrupted domesticity, the knowledge that any of these people could have been one's own neighbors, and that they very possibly were.

In 1966, a swapping circle in California accepted into its ranks a new recruit, delegating him their cameraman for an evening, assigned to film their activities for a short movie to be shared among the club members.

What they proposed was not illegal; the California Supreme Court had already ruled that the private production of sexually explicit photographs and home movies was legal, provided they were for personal use only. Step beyond that line, however, and the law was merciless, as this particular circle discovered when it transpired that their cameraman friend had not only consigned a copy of their film to the stag circuit, he had also been busted by the vice squad. And now the cops were after them as well.

The club members were arrested, and the charges mounted up. Not only were the swappers complicit in the creation of a commercial sex film, they were also guilty of adulterous behavior and of indulging in sexual perversions — oral sex was, at that time, illegal in California.

None received any harsher punishment than probation and suspended sentences, but the accompanying newspaper coverage ensured that they suffered far greater than that. As one of the wives explained, "We are now second-class citizens. My husband's claim for unemployment insurance [he was fired when the case became public] has been denied, and also his application for life insurance. His chances of finding a decent job are very remote. I have been on the verge of a nervous breakdown since our arrest. This mess has ruined our reputation, taken our life savings and caused grief and humiliation to our children and other members of our family."[4]

Whether explained or exposed, wife-swapping became an intrinsic component in the pulp DNA, both in magazine form and, increasingly as the late 1950s rolled on, in book form. No less than the monthly press, American publishing had a long and proud history of the pulp novel and, where the magazines first trod, the books were quick to follow. The headline-hogging advent of wife-swapping was a boon to the industry — cash-in titles rolled onto the bookshelves as fast as their authors could turn them around.

But it was not the only subject worth tackling. In among the plethora of what we might call standard sex tales — infidelity, adultery, promiscuity and so forth — any number of other sexual concerns and societal ills were ripe for the literary plucking, and the more shocking (to mainstream America), the better. Homosexuality, bondage and domination, transvestism . . . all became the themes of presumably best-selling pulp titles.

The pulps' favorite topic, however, was the sex trade — prostitution, escort agencies, seedy photographers and, of course, stag films.

"She stood on the movie set wearing only a sheer negligee. 'Now, young lady,' Hugo said. 'This is a silent film. We'll add any sound effects later.'"[5]

Thus is the reader is drawn into *Stag Starlet*, a 1961 novel by Paul V. Russo (one of several pseudonyms employed by author Gilbert Fox) that helped inaugurate a series of *Stag . . .* titles for the publishers Midwood. *Stag Model* (by James Harvey) and *Stag Stripper* (Mike Avallone) appeared the same year, investigating the equally seedy worlds of photography and nightclubs respectively.

The plots continued to revolve around the basic staples of crime, intrigue, death and sex. A halfway-valid criticism of 1960s pulp paperbacks was that, although the titles and the names of the characters changed, the stories themselves rarely did. As with the genuine stag movies, there were only so many variations an adventure could pursue, with the easiest by far being those that built upon the stags' existing reputation for lawlessness, by incorporating further crimes into the scenario and allowing the movie theme to slip more or less into the background: "She was more than just a passionate pawn in the hands of the smut film merchants — but her sizzling lusts led to blackmail . . . and murder!"[6]

Even *The Blue Movie Murders*, the last-ever Ellery Queen mystery from 1972, could have told much the same tale without the added frission of a secret stag factory deep within the bowels of the otherwise respectable Mann Photo Service. But for many readers, it was the subplot that mattered the most, the impression that the author had somehow tapped into the very heart of his subject and was now laying bare all of its secrets.

These roles were occasionally reversed, as the stags gazed in on the purported effects of the pulps on their readership. The late-1950s stag *Tonight at 8* is one of several in which the heroine warms up for her date by reading a spicy pulp, while *Let Me Love You* opens with a young lady, Mary-Ann, engrossed in what is clearly a torrid magazine short story and placing herself in the position of the tale's heroine. It is unlikely, of course, that any newsstand publication would have devoted an entire story to the delights of prolonged cunnilingus, but that is beside the point. Utilizing all the ambiguities of the English language, such acts were scarcely veiled in print; why should they be disguised on film?

Further food for thought is offered by *An Author's True Story*, in which hardbitten 1930s pulp author "Bob, from *Pussy Chasers* magazine," is writing a short story about his girlfriend's sexual prowess. When Bob drops by in search of fresh inspiration, he discovers her enthusiastically demonstrating it with another man. The notion that the hottest tales could be written only from real-life experience was one the pulps desperately attempted to uphold. *An Author's True Story* loaned itself seamlessly to that conceit.

For all this daring experimentation, still the marriage between stag and story remained in its infancy. But there were other currents moving through American publishing at that time, seismic shifts that would allow the printed page and the moving image to merge closer than they had since the heyday of the Tijuana Bibles.

That's Not Porn, It's Psychology

*Junkies and the
Nightmare*

In 1957, the Supreme Court handed down the landmark determination that, while obscene material was *not* protected by the First Amendment, art, literature and scientific research were. Therefore, if a work could claim to be of artistic (or literary or educational) value, it didn't matter what else went on within its pages. It was protected.

The ramifications of that decision were slow in filtering through. A full nine years later, in 1966, the State of Massachusetts was still attempting to prosecute the publishers of *Fanny Hill*, a 200-year-old novel whose reputation for bawdy licentiousness by now certainly outstripped its actual content.

Referring back to its 1957 decision, however, the Supreme Court lost little time in shooting down the authorities' case, and this time the legal eagles of the publishing world were just as swift to translate the ruling to plain English. If a publication could reasonably claim to have any redeeming quality whatsoever, no matter how insignificant that might be (a quote from a sociologist would suffice), then it was protected.

The floodgates opened, and once again the world of stag movies was at the forefront of the deluge. Except now, the books were no longer fiction. They were textbooks.

Author Anthony Crowell's *Stag Films '69* was the first off the block. Published (at a then-weighty $1.95) as "a Barclay House Psycho-Sex Study," its stated premise was to educate readers into the mores of the "modern" erotic movie. (Other titles in the series included *Dangerous Lovers, The Auto-Erotic Female* and *Adultery 70*.)

"Stag films and motion pictures of definite pornographic character have been made for a long time," announced the introduction. "But never as they are made today." The industry ("and it *is* an industry," Crowell declared) "has come of age and today's films use only the most beautiful girls, the most handsome studs, and there are always more applicants for such work than the market can handle." Why this should be, however, "is something for the psychiatrists to figure out."[1]

Crowell was not a psychiatrist. He shared, however, that profession's appointed curiosity regarding the lives and morals of the men and women who acted, made and distributed stags. His cast of characters was drawn with casebook precision: Karen T., the beautiful blonde from Detroit who chose to make stag films because "she is a dedicated hedonist and decidedly over-sexed"; Larry G., the handsome young bisexual who stumbled into stag movies after his wife took a lover; Warren B., a forty-two-year-old college graduate whose dreams of a legitimate Hollywood career were put on hold when he discovered he could make a comfortable living from stags; Marsha and Vinny, Doug and Tisha, the moviemaking wife-swappers . . . and so on.

And all told tales of such graphic detail that it was sometimes easy to forget this was *not* a collection of short erotic fiction, albeit one with a scientific eye for perverse detail: "that damned horse had a cock as big around as a beer can."

In fact, the veracity of the stories mattered little. The situations Crowell outlined, both onscreen and off, were based on some degree of fact. It *was* cheaper for some California filmmakers to work in Mexico than in the United States; some people *did* simply fall into the trade by accident; some would-be directors *did* expend considerable time and effort offering potential cast members a crash course in the basics of moviemaking.

As a reference work, *Stag Films '69* paled anemically alongside Arthur Knight and Hollis Alpert's then two-year-old *Playboy* article. As a standard-bearer for a wave of future stag exposés, high on incident if not information, however, it was peerless. But it was also one of many books that hit the stands over the next couple of years.

The educational worth of Larry Harris's *The Stag Film Report* might best be summed up by the chapter documenting the state of censorship in various countries around the world: Italy, Mexico, Great Britain, Australia, Africa — yes, the whole of Africa, neatly defined as a single country, "so highly diversified and complex," whose censorship policies were at the "whims and fancies" of whichever "political party [is] in control at the time." If a book cannot differentiate between a country and a continent, what other misunderstandings might await the unsuspecting reader?

Again, the tell-all interview was the heart of the book, in this case the reminiscences of one Harvey Franks, as he recalled the January 1970 creation of a 1920s-style stag set in the baronial mansion of Lord and Lady Kraze-Cock.

The film itself, unfortunately, appears to have vanished from view (if it even existed in the first place). But the procedures and processes Franks explains are so universal that any film could have been under discussion, so long as there was plenty of sex to describe in loving detail, as lush accompaniment to the eighty-two color and black and white exquisitely explicit (and occasionally miscaptioned) movie stills that doubtless complemented *The Stag Film Report*'s educational mission.

Of all the books published around what was now being described as the stag-movie phenomenon, just one appears to have treated its subject not only with the respect it deserved, but also as something other than the vehicle for an endless stream of erotic fantasy. H.C. Shelby's *Stag Movie Review* grandly endeavored to offer the stag viewer the same service Leonard Maltin had recently gifted mainstream viewers (the first edition of Maltin's *TV Movies*, the forerunner of his *Movie and Video Guide*, appeared in 1969).

Promising both "the basic plots and the dialogue of those 'sexy movies' you see advertised,"[2] *Stag Movie Review* is extraordinarily selective in the movies précised. Just forty 8mm/200-foot films were discussed and reviewed, as compared to the 500-plus full-length features described in the similarly sized first edition of *Video Times Magazine's Your Movie Guide to Adult Video Tapes and Discs* a decade and a half later.

What it lacked in quantity, however, it more than compensated for in detail, as Shelby painstakingly logs every last nuance — visual, verbal and even technical — of the movies he chose. Critiques followed each movie entry, commentary on the quality of the acting, the camera work and so forth: "the forest setting is impressive, but the sun creates havoc with the exposure at one point." But the heart of the book lay in the summaries.

Indeed, so deeply did Shelby luxuriate in his subject matter that several of his descriptions are at least as arousing as the movies themselves, which was perhaps the most important consideration of all. After all, few of the movies he covers were available *à la carte*; one could not simply call up the local retailer and expect him to have a copy of *Skin Lollipop*. But if you read Shelby's description of it, you probably wouldn't need to.

"Cheap wallpaper and a drab décor envelop the couple on the bed," Shelby recounts. "The brunette lies on her side with her right leg sprawled forward. The mattress sways as a slim man penetrates her from behind."

Stag Movie Review was an invaluable guide to the movies that were already out there. Where, however, could one turn for information on those that were still to come? In a modern industry dominated by such titles as the monthly telephone-directory-sized *Adult Video News*, it is difficult to envisage a time when one could not simply peruse the "new release" sheets to discover what delights were coming next month; when one was forced instead to wade through the small-print ads at the back of men's magazines.

Such ads were not always screamingly visible, squeezed as they were amongst a veritable firestorm of correspondence courses, dating agencies, teeth whiteners, wholesale gadgetry, stamp approval services and so on. But for many readers, they were the only ones that mattered.

The authorities must have loved it. So much smut, so little time. Between 1957 and 1969, U.S. Post Office inspectors conducted some 100,000 investigations related to obscenity passing through the mails, resulting in almost 5,000 convictions. But there were ways around even the tightest law (the discreet "plain wrapper" not least of all), while the authorities' attempts to break the back of the business through the magazines that carried the advertisements were likewise doomed to frustration.

Rather than accept direct advertising, most publications instead sold blocks of pages to freelance adjobbers, who then filled the spaces through their own efforts. They also assumed the corresponding risks, and rapidly found ways of avoiding them. "Warren B," distributing stag movies in L.A. in the late 1960s, explained that police raids "only get what we want them to get. They don't steal any of the good stuff. It's like everything else, you know they are going to come in, you have to leave them something to grab, so you get all your bad reels, old stuff that you've rented out, or the dealers have . . . you rent them out a few times and then they come back spliced, the good scenes snipped out by some smart bastard; it's junk. After a while, these cans pile up and the boys in blue take them off your hands for you. No problem."[3]

Neither could the authorities be guaranteed a glistening haul on the occasions that they did conduct a successful surprise raid.

Many — the vast majority, in fact — of the movies being sold through the back pages of the pulps were little more than discarded screen tests, or the same portfolio-style shorts that Arline Hunter made back in the early 1950s. Some might unearth a scantily clad burlesque routine, a Bettie Page bondage commercial or a vaudeville striptease, all of which were shocking enough to an audience unaccustomed to such things. But they were scarcely the hardcore filth the local district attorney (and, presumably, the mail-ordering public) was dreaming of. What a typical ad called "Frisky, alluring routines" remain, after all, in the eye of the beholder.

From Toronto, Ontario, Supreme Films offered "French stag movies, direct from France 8mm/50ft for $6." From a P.O. Box in L.A., Studio 722 offered "ten great stag shows" for $2 and threw in an 8mm movie viewer for just another $5. The Movie Club Guild of Burbank offered "the startling and dynamic party films formerly seen only by Hollywood's inner circle of sophisticated producers!" The Hollywood Color Club pledged, "We'll do anything to please YOU, our valued customer," and Titan Stag Films promised the world's "greatest adult movie bargain — ten stag movie subjects for only 20¢ each."

The Trade Descriptions Act might have been bent somewhat by the wording of the ads . . . and if one assumes a stag movie must show sexual activity, it certainly was. But still, you got what you paid for.

Even supposedly reputable sources — newsstand magazine reviews of specific movies, for example — could not be trusted. When *Time* magazine described the 1965 Japanese sci-fi/crime flick *The Love Robots* as "a feature length [actually, a shade over one hour], slightly bowdlerized stag film," the minds that isolated that quote within the film's publicity material were clearly hoping that potential American viewers would be unaware of precisely what nineteenth-century English editor Thomas Bowdler gave to the language.

In 1965, however, a new magazine appeared that promised to take all the guesswork out of buying films. It was called *Banned* because, it insisted, the films it presented were so explicit they were considered unreleasable *anywhere*. Anybody seeking the latest information on the hottest new stag movies would inevitably have made a beeline for a copy. They would not have been disappointed by either the reviews or the accompanying illustrations. Where they may have run into difficulties, however, is in attempting to actually procure the movies that *Banned* bandied about with such enthusiasm. For not only were the films under discussion (and so lavishly illustrated) unlikely to be released, many were unlikely to even be made. Dian Hanson wrote, "There's a slight possibility *Banned* did have access to forbidden film stills, but more likely the editors were just making their movies up, printing strange, often hippie-oriented photos left over from [the publisher's] girlie titles."[4]

Fiction-driven or not, *Banned* was an immediate success, and other publications soon flourished in its wake. *Wildest Films* launched later in 1965; *Torrid Film Reviews, Daring Films & Books, Cine Femmes* and *Fiery Films* followed in 1966; *Cinema Scorchers* debuted in 1967; and *Cinema Close-Up, Wild Screen Reviews* and *The Erotic Cinema* arrived during 1968.

It would be grossly unfair to tar all of these publications with the same brush; several of them were, indeed, conscientious enough to ensure that the movies they discussed actually existed. Neither were they all driven by the stag industry. The mid- to late-1960s were the age of David Friedman and Russ Meyer, directors who all but blue-printed the so-called sexploitation movie blockbuster, and whose names alongside the title were frequently all the recommendation a new film required. Their work, and that of their manifold imitators, constituted a large proportion of the movies under discussion in this new breed of movie magazine.

Other favorite arenas, however, were less clear-cut. For this was also the era of the hippie, a social and cultural revolution that, once one bypasses the stereotypical imagery with which the term is now saddled, represented one of the most important artistic flowerings of the twentieth century. Music is the discipline most readily associated with the movement; at the time, however, it was considered just one facet of an all-encompassing multimedia experience, that incorporated dancing, painting, sculpture and film.

It was also dedicated to breaking down barriers within each of those disciplines.

It was New York artist Andy Warhol who first popularized the notion of projecting movies onto a performing band, screening his own films onto a backdrop while the Velvet Underground played onstage during 1965–66. Other groups were experimenting in the same area, however, with the then-blossoming hippie stronghold of San Francisco leading the way.

Possibly apocryphal are the tales that once circulated through a disapproving mainstream media of bands who would perform alongside screenings of hardcore erotic movies — performances that would end with a full-scale orgy taking place on the dance floor. Had such entertainments taken place, however, San Francisco is undoubtedly the place where they would have happened, for developing alongside and within the hippie culture was a vibrant filmmaking community that would, almost single-handedly, change the face of the erotic-movie business forever.

Man Meets Machine

Undertaker's Dream

As the boundaries surrounding acceptable sexual behavior receded through the 1950s and early 1960s, technological innovation advanced. Color stag films were becoming increasingly common, as costs continued to decline and equipment continued to improve. "Studios are elaborate," an unnamed vice inspector told journalist Otto Ward. "The era when filthy pictures were taken by 16mm home-movie equipment is gone."[1]

A handful of stag-makers even began experimenting with sound, although most quickly learned it was not worth the effort. "Terry," a student at the same University of Pennsylvania where, seventy years before, Eadweard Muybridge was making his stop-start films of naked weightlifters, tried shooting a "talkie" stag in 1961 with two girlfriends. He remembers spending so long "getting the levels set that all spontaneity was gone by the time we were ready to actually start filming. I wound up with about three minutes of desultory lesbian action, before the girls announced they were too cold to continue and stormed off, calling me every name under the sun."[2]

More experienced filmmakers enjoyed greater success. Dating from as early as the late 1940s, *Shipwreck Kelly* accompanies its action with a salty voice-over, straight out of a period pulp magazine. Others eschewed speech for an accompanying menagerie of grunts, groans and gasps, likewise dubbed in during post-production. The early-1970s gangster porn classic *Blue Heat* lightheartedly illustrates this process with a scene in which the young woman recruited to add her moaning to a movie discovers she works best if the technician duplicates the onscreen action with her.

Other movies, however, had less inclination for realism. More than one film from the era includes the sound of a woman screaming in orgasm at the same time as a penis disappears down her throat, or some similarly implausible (not to mention physically impossible) scenario.

Some filmmakers even layered on the sexual sound effects, regardless of whether the onscreen action demanded it. There is a priceless moment in one (apparently untitled) example from the late 1960s, where the squelching sounds begin before the woman has even entered the room, but pause, hilariously, just as the man picks up the telephone. In an age before Ringtones, one can only imagine what a road-show audience would have made of that, or if it even noticed. Indeed, in a room full of caterwauling onlookers, where it was hard enough to hear yourself think let alone comprehend what was being said by the flickering figures projected onto the wall, most viewers simply didn't care whether or not a stag had sound. They'd been supplying their own soundtracks for the past sixty years. Why stop now?

Deep into the 1960s, then, the majority of stag-makers continued employing that 1920s-style standby printed caption, a device that lends an endearingly old-time aspect to even the most up-to-date production. Others challenged the audience to figure out for itself what was being said, continuing a lip-reading tradition that dated back to the early-1930s opus *Miss Park Avenue*, and one of the most intriguing sequences to be found in a stag movie. The maid, having fellated her lover beyond orgasm, licks her lips and then speaks directly into the camera. "Guess what she is saying?" teases the accompanying caption.

Sound was an important innovation, however — not in the road shows, but elsewhere, in the burgeoning market for home viewing, and in the arcades, where coin-operated peep-show machines were making an unexpected comeback.

The direct descendants of the first Nickelodeons and Mutoscopes, these machines had never completely fallen from fashion. Director Alex de Renzy's *A History of the Blue Movie* includes one delightful sequence in which literal flashes of flesh are linked by a series of captions requesting more money from the hapless viewer:

Part one has ended, but don't feel blue
Just one more coin to see part two
Part three is next, now hold your hat
Drop one more coin and you're up to bat.

The fact that, as late as 1960, these so-called midget movies still cost a nickel should not, however, be taken as a recommendation. To watch even a full-length ten-minute film would cost the patient viewer upward of a couple of dollars and, for that, he would be unlikely to see any more flesh than the average nudie cutie dispensed for a fraction of the price. Strippers and burlesque-style dancers were as risqué as the average midget movie dared go.

Many of the arcades that specialized in midget movies did so in the full glare of the public. New York's Time Square was, predictably, the haunt of a great many, with the machines simply arrayed across the storefront floor, offering no more privacy than could be afforded by the viewer's own clothing. Long raincoats became a popular mode of dress among habitués of such establishments.

The machines began moving behind their own individual sets of curtains during the mid-1960s, with the majority now being established in stores that already catered to the erotic trade in some fashion — generally, the archetypal "dirty bookshop," whose retail stock outwardly voyaged no further than the law would allow, but whose cupboards and drawers were crammed with more "specialized" merchandise. Already an illegal operation for both the owner of the premises and his customers, the addition of the viewing booths simply opened up another avenue of profit, without materially compounding the crime.

"Tony," a self-described grandfatherly Midwesterner who ran a small store in Des Moines, Iowa, during this period, explains, "If the cops decided to bust you, it didn't matter whether you had one photograph or a hundred, you were still busted. And they told me that themselves. So it just made sense to have a hundred."[3]

The movies that flickered across these particular screens were not, strictly speaking, stag films. Not for these films a life spent traveling from hall to hall, to be fumbled in and out of creaking old projectors while the audience howled and catcalled. These new films were loops, so-named because they were designed to be looped through the mechanism of a viewing machine, with each section screened in timed increments, according to how many quarters a punter dropped into the slot.

It is a crucial difference, albeit a largely aesthetic one. James "Dale" Chastain, whose Blue Vanities company has been marketing video (and, more recently, DVD) compilations of stag movies since 1987, explains, "I think it's very important to separate the stags from the seventies and eighties porno loops. It's an age thing. Most of my customers that buy the stags are over fifty, and the loop buyers are fifty and under.

"I tell my new buyers, when asked, that stag films were produced prior to 1970, were sold underground, were predominantly black and white, and many were made by amateurs. The interesting thing is that many of the Web site customers in their thirties and forties really do not understand the difference between stag film and a porno loop, so when they tell me that they have stag films, they really don't."[4]

A Michigan adult-store owner, "Tom," recalls, "We had forty-eight of the old film projectors in the twenty-five-cent booths, and we changed the loops every other Wednesday. The company sent guys to collect and split the money every other week, and leave us new movies to change on the off week."[5]

"Rich from Oakland" describes his own experiences in such an establishment: "The first machines were flat on top, and you looked down into them. They had 400-foot reels on the projectors, and it took five or six quarters to go through the entire movie. The timers weren't very accurate so the time varied. When you put in a quarter, it started and ran for a while and, when it stopped, it didn't go back to the beginning, it just stopped where it was. The next quarter started it up and continued from where it was until the timer ran out again. If you wanted to see the entire film, you had to keep putting in quarters.

"The action started fairly soon after the movie started, so you really didn't waste much money. The hook was if you wanted to see what happened next, well, put in another quarter. Sometimes I would see a good show from the middle, and I wanted to see the beginning to see how they got to that point, so, more quarters. But as time went on, they kept changing the viewing time, making it shorter and shorter for your quarter. As the technology got better, the time shortened even more. The last time I saw any it was down to about sixty seconds."[6]

The booths, usually separated by cloth drapes, quickly developed a reputation for a certain kind of behavior. "Rich from Oakland" continues, "Sometimes if I was looking at a show, someone next to me would put his hand over and start massaging my cock through my pants." Other users would leave the curtain pulled back slightly, "so anyone walking by could see them playing with their exposed cocks while watching the flicks. If someone lingered in the hallway, watching, he might pull the curtain back more and jack off for the viewer."

While men were the target audience for the peep shows, an early-1960s stag, *Rent-a-Film*, suggests they were not exclusively a male preserve, as a woman enters the establishment and settles down to view a reel, masturbating right up until the desk clerk joins her in the cubicle.

The sleazy aspect of these peep shows never went away. If anything, it only worsened, once store owners realized their customers' need for more privacy than could be afforded by a sheet of cloth and started installing solid walls and doors. "In the early days," Rich concluded, "I even had men offer to suck me off right there in the porn shop."

Author Steven Ziplow found the residue of such encounters when he "took a stroll around the area of 42nd Street and 8th Avenue in New York City" in 1977. "If you have only one quarter and don't know which show to take a peek at, I advise you to look on the floor. The booth with the messiest floor is usually the hottest show."[7]

The exhibitors' pitches for such shows rarely changed. Ziplow continued, "Outside or beside each booth is usually displayed a hastily written description of each show. 'New from Sweden — One young 13-year-old girl fucking sucking her way through four men of different colors' or 'Just in — Young starlet takes on two 15-inchers and a Great Dane.' [But] it is not unusual to see a sign advertising a stag film made by some great star in her leaner years. In one week alone I saw promotions for loops supposedly starring such names as Barbra Streisand and a collector's item, an early Jayne Mansfield."

By the late 1960s, the popularity of the peep-show machines had exploded, and the sheer quantity of stags and loops being churned out reached epidemic proportions.

Unfortunately, although the decade saw more films made (and survive) than at any time in the past, and more extreme scenarios play out on a regular basis, the loops also took on a grinding predictability.

There were, quite simply, too many amateurs with too many cameras and too little imagination. Far from relieving the genre of its reputation for being poorly made and formulaic, color filming only exacerbated it, as moviemakers dropped any pretence at "plot," "situation" or even basic premise and, in the name of giving the viewer the most action for his quarter, cut straight to the action. In fact the only true "improvement" one could realistically identify was that the actors tended to be a lot younger and better-looking than they used to be.

The hippie movement, with its loudly spoken credo of free love, offered an unexpected boon to the sex industry — not so much in terms of plotlines and scenarios, but in the appearance, availability and, above all, adventurousness of the very actors and actresses employed in the films.

It would, to reiterate a now familiar point, be a grotesquely sweeping generalization to say that the majority of performers seen in early stag movies were less than attractive, although many passing mentions of the subject do note the ugliness of some of the stars. Rather, the filmmakers worked with the materials they had at hand — the workmate who thought it'd be good for a laugh, the would-be actress who'd been would-be for too long, the neighbor's bored wife, whoever. Beggars, as they say, could not be choosers and, if a film-maker was stuck with a forty-year old man with a paunch and a bald spot, and a heavyweight woman with more cellulite than teeth, then that is who he filmed.

Now, however, society was suddenly infused with an entire generation of women in their teens and early twenties who — perhaps for the same reasons so many 1920s flappers made a similar journey — were only too willing to prove the sincerity of their hippie credentials by bearing it all for the cameras. More than that, many were equally willing to step far beyond the sexual boundaries that had constricted the past sixty years' worth of American stags and embrace sexual practices that had rarely, if ever, been depicted onscreen.

The stags did not have a good track record when it came to capturing the latest nuance of teenage fashion. A decade earlier, a number of movies attempted to portray what they imagined to be the everyday life of the beatniks, those dreadfully serious young people who dressed in black, took a lot of drugs and then quoted dreary poetry at one another.

But *The Beatniks* emerged little more than an oddly costumed, strangely unenthusiastic group sex scene, a failing only exaggerated when what might have been the same quartet reconvened for *The Junkies — Hophead, Weedie and Cokie and the Nightmare* (a.k.a. *Opium Den*) and donned such ridiculous disguises that the movie is akin to an orgy wherein every participant is Groucho Marx. Many viewers, incidentally, have described the movie's lone female character as the ugliest woman ever seen in a stag, the titular nightmare indeed. This may or may not be accurate, but she is certainly responsible for some of the most unerotic oral sex ever filmed.

The problem with the beatnik movies appears to have been that nobody involved with the production seemed to know where to find a real beatnik, or at least how to approach one. A similar difficulty arose around attempts to shoot an erotic rejoinder to *The Wild Ones*, or any other manifestation of the biker cult. Simply lining up a row of impressive-looking Harley motorcycles and staging an orgy on and around them (as in *Hot Pips and Pipes*) was not sufficient.

Hippies, on the other hand, were everywhere, as H.C. Shelby pointed out in *Stag Movie Review*: "Hippie and co-ed themes are dominant in . . . stags presently. There are the off-beat films which include a variety of fetishes and perversions. Women and big dog relationships are increasing in popularity."[8]

In the past, such visualizations might well have dismayed, or even disgusted, the typical stag audience. If it was bad enough to watch a girl your daughter's age having sex with a boyfriend, how much ghastlier would it be to see her doing it with three men and a dog?

By the late 1960s, however, the girls in the film no longer resembled your daughter, and the audiences were no longer comprised wholly of their dads. Now the kids were hippies — a breed apart in the eyes of middle America, a filthy, degenerate race from whom you would expect nothing better.

For the traditional stag audience — a gathering of Elks, for example — this new breed of movie bypassed the normal sexual receptors, feeding instead into a deeply rooted set of preconditioned beliefs, those that allowed the viewer to distance himself and, therefore, his family from the characters on the screen, because the actors were hairy . . . probably smelly . . . most likely Communists . . . free-lovers . . . HIPPIES! (Arguably, a similar response might well have been employed by viewers of the imported bondage and bestiality films of an earlier era — "Of course it's disgusting, they're foreigners.")

The hippies themselves viewed these films with an enthusiasm that bordered on pride, as Dian Hanson explains when she recalls her first sighting of a magazine similarly devoted to the movement and likewise shameless in its depiction of sex and nudity: "I bought a few . . . and shared them with my friends, all of whom thought it was so groovy that we were winning the sexual revolution. We had absolutely no doubt that hippy porn was made by and for hippie, and we gobbled it up."[9]

Later in life, a more cynical approach crept into her outlook. Such magazines as *Sundisk*, *Sexual Freedom Now*, *Ankh Life Symbol* and, with a weary inevitability, *Hippies* were produced by precisely the same companies that had been cranking out similar publications all decade long. And it is more than certain that a good proportion of the stag films now being produced were likewise the work of film-makers who didn't care a fig for love and peace, but who knew a good thing when they saw it.

Others, however, were shot by genuine hippies — or, at least, people who were absolutely in tune with the moods and desires of the time and who viewed erotic art with the same antiauthoritarian sentiments as the libertines and subversives of centuries past. They were returning that much-abused word "pornography" to its true antiestablishmentarian standing.

The era's fascination with art and beauty did allow for some remarkably luxurious photography. Some genuinely creative notions, too, emerged from this period. Not every movie simply filled a room with long-hairs and left them to their own devices, or sat a guru cross-legged on a rug, while his concubines cavorted before him (although an awful lot of them did).

One late-1960s effort, for instance, lined up the denizens of a little girl's toybox — G.I. Joe, Raggedy Ann, Barbie and so on — then imagined what they might get up to once their owner was asleep. Another, *Donnie and Clyde* zeroed in on the hyper-repressed sexuality that overhung the Hollywood blockbuster *Bonnie and Clyde* by visualizing what might have transpired had Warren Beatty not rebuffed Faye Dunaway's advances in favor of reading his newspaper.

Others toyed with such hitherto taboo concepts as transgenderism — a rutting couple, both luxuriously long-haired so that it is impossible to determine who is doing what to whom. Another,

The Telephone Call, featured a woman seemingly engrossed in a phone conversation, no matter what her man was doing at the time. It's only as the movie progresses that it becomes apparent that who-ever's on the other end of the line is well aware of precisely what's taking place and wants a closer listen to the action.

One especially watchable stag, *The Undertaker's Dream*, even toyed with the concept of necrophilia, although the viewer must wonder, is it still necrophilia if the corpses awaken?

And others still seemed dedicated to breaking down the naive notion that the viewer was still witnessing "real" people having sex, by encouraging their (primarily female) stars toward greater feats of exhibitionism, while inadvertently blueprinting a notion that the modern viewer simply takes for granted — the posing starlet strip-ping away any sense of innocence and realism from the action by purposefully preening throughout the performance, playing as much for the camera as for her partner.

The veneer of voyeurism that is the secret of all great (and ghastly) cinema is broken there, and, with it, a little enjoyment is sapped, to be replaced by a new fission of excitement, but also by a cynical sigh. For sixty or more years, the most enjoyable hardcore featured a cast that either appear unaware of the cameras or, if they're not, they respond with becoming shyness. Rampant sluttish-ness was a new development altogether.

It is not always easy to distinguish between the films made with true "hippie values" and those that merely chased the fast buck. But many of the era's most prolific filmmakers would go on to carve out considerable careers in the erotic film industry; and, as if to prove just how much things had changed as the sixties swung on, their very names became as well-known in contemporary circles as their predecessors' were closely guarded secrets.

New Yorker Alex de Renzy was a former survival instructor in the United States Army Air Forces, and his closest friends during his service years included one "Doc" Kaminski, a student who owned a small filmmaking studio specializing in whatever work came to his door — commercials, industrial and educational movies, documen-taries, anything.

De Renzy was fascinated by the entire process; Kaminski was an excellent teacher and, by the time de Renzy left the service and moved to San Francisco in the early 1960s, he was determined to follow Kaminski into film.

Shooting documentaries for Gordon News Films, de Renzy fell in with another aspiring young filmmaker, singularly known as Don. The movies this new acquaintance was making, however, were a long way from those that either Kaminski or Gordon News had specialized in. Don made stag films to distribute around the local adult arcades.

Again, de Renzy was fascinated, and was soon shooting his own stags. But, unwilling to confine his movies (and the attendant profits) to so many outside entities, he instead broke with tradition and, in 1967, opened his own adult theater, the Screening Room, at 220 Jones Street. There, seven performances a day alternated between live sex shows and vignettes, and the 16mm stag movies de Renzy was now making. And it was his movies that attracted the most attention, not only for their sexuality, but also for the sheer passion of de Renzy's direction.

The Masseuse, in which a young man attempts to seduce an inexperienced masseuse, has been described as "a true masterpiece of eroticism"[10] and, via both a slow tease and the players' own mounting excitement, it certainly rose above the bulk of the increasingly mass-produced-flavored stags of the period — and that despite not actually depicting any sex whatsoever. The movie was softcore at best, yet its scenario, its dialogue (from the outset, de Renzy employed both sound and color) and even its acting were superb.

The massage parlor was a fairly standard setup in late-1960s stags — as, indeed, it had been since the mid-1930s, when *Swedish Massage* first suggested that country might have more to offer the American male than meatballs. (It was only a suggestion, however. Though the movie's title might indicate that it predates Sweden's arrival on the world erotica scene by a full thirty years, the Swedish massage itself is merely a full-body palpitation. The real meat lies in the French massage.)

Interviewed by *Man's World* in 1970, JB Sales Co. publicist Sandy

Brody describes a similar movie as her own first experience as a stag actress. "'Okay,' the director said, 'Here's the plot. You're a masseuse, Sandy, and you're working in your bra and panties. He gets turned on and reaches for you. You shake him off and he offers to change places and give you an oil rub. Then you drop the bra and panties. . . .'"[11]

De Renzy's actress lost her bra and panties, too, but it was the loss of her inhibitions as her client turned the table on her that gave the movie its impact and the camera its determination to remain on her face, even as her voice ("I don't think you should be doing that, sir") demanded it focus elsewhere. De Renzy subsequently included *The Masseuse* in his 1970 documentary *A History of the Blue Movie*, and it did not seem at all out of place.

De Renzy set the standard for moviemaking, just as he did for presentation. The industry had no alternative but to follow where he led. Just a few years before, a stag could be made with nothing more than a well-lit motel room, a camera and a cast, and then launched onto either the road show or the arcade circuit. Now, even shoe-string operations were working with banks of lights and a scampering crew, and renting the results out to bona fide movie houses — or, at least, the so-called "pocket theaters" that were now springing up all over town.

In the spirit of the sixty-year-old Nickelodeons, the majority of pocket theaters were short-term leases on empty storefronts, carefully designed to avoid the attentions of both fire marshals (by limiting the number of seats) and other city officials (by falling within zoning requirements). The only other costs would be a 16mm projector, a suitably inclined floor and some kind of elemental sound system — a record player would do.

Sharon, a California grandmother whose life as a teenage stag actress bookended the mid-1960s, recalls, "I did a couple of films around 1964 with my boyfriend and, if we closed our eyes, we could pretend there was nobody else in the room. Then, after I graduated, I needed some money, so I got back into it and suddenly there were two cameramen, a couple of sound guys, someone running around taking stills, a makeup girl — I was like, 'Are we gonna fuck or remake *Gone with the Wind?'* All that, and it was still only ten minutes long. But it was still a thrill to walk down Mission one afternoon and see my ass staring back at me from a flyposter on the wall."[12]

It was at the Screening Room that de Renzy first came into contact with Art and Jim Mitchell, brothers who were likewise destined to become giants of the American sex-film scene of the 1970s and 1980s.

The first stag film that Antioch war babies Jim and Artie Mitchell ever saw was *The Nun's Story, or Something Old, Something New*, a local, Northern California production. It was also among the first stags that "Rich from Oakland" ever saw: "A nun, very attractive, came into a house and undressed, slowly, and sat on the bed and started feeling her tits, pinching her nipples, and her other hand went between her legs and she began to frig herself off. Her head went back in ecstasy, eyes closed, as she enjoyed herself. Next it showed a man looking in the window watching her. He quietly entered the room and pulled his hard cock out and when she saw him she was startled but when she saw his cock, she reached out and pulled it to her.

"After he was undressed, they started kissing and his cock was close to the entrance to her pussy. She backed away and pushed his head down . . . he got between her legs and started lapping away at her pussy (I had never seen anything like that before), and when he put his cock in there, it slipped right in. The film was extremely hot and I came in my pants without even touching myself."[13]

The Nun's Story is numbered among the most controversial American stags of all time. Regardless of their religious persuasion, audiences were so discomforted by the appearance of a Holy Sister in such a film that the distributors trimmed both the beginning and end (where the nun redresses), and reissued it under the innocuous (if misleading) title *College Co-Eds*.

Jim and Artie Mitchell were not among those viewers who complained about *The Nun's Story's* desecration of the Holy genitalia; they loved every minute of the movie, although the common mythology that they decided there and then that their futures lay in sex moviemaking is not as firm as its supporters might like it to be.

Both brothers enlisted in the U.S. Army, Jim in 1961, Artie in 1963 (he only narrowly missed out on being posted to Vietnam), and, upon their return to Antioch, they might have simply faded into the white-collar background had Jim not decided to use his VA entitlement to further his education.

He majored in English at Diablo College and then moved on to San Francisco State to minor in film and photography. His future had not taken shape and would not do so until the end of his first semester, when every student in the class was instructed to shoot a short film of their own devising. Jim hightailed down to the San Francisco waterfront and persuaded a girl to let him film her removing her top.

Soon Jim was making a tidy living selling seminude photos to vendors around Market Street, graduating to full nudes once he found the market for them and moving on to pictures once he'd been introduced to that field. Artie was his inevitable partner.

Placing casting calls in the free press, weeding out anybody who even looked like a hooker or a "professional," the Mitchells required only two qualities in their actors: good looks and a lot of enthusiasm.

Shot on standard 16mm film, the Mitchells' earliest productions were so-called beaver films, near-anatomical studies of the female sex organs that their owner would manipulate for the camera lens. *Sacramento Salami*, in which a woman masturbated with a sausage, was about the closest these films came to actual penetration.

Such movies had been around since at least the 1940s, but while "beaver" has circulated as gynecological slang since the 1920s, the term "beaver films" appears not to have been coined until the 1960s. No sooner had it arrived, however, than there was a sudden flood of them, from the Mitchells' studio and many others.

Reflecting upon the coarse humor that was once among the stags' most treasured provinces, some of these efforts were titled with groan-making puns, often rooted in the renown of other, more conventional movies: *Beaver Madness, I Am Curious… Beaver, The Manchurian Beaver* and, inevitably, *Leave It to Beaver* all played on 1960s screens.

Other beavers, however, were more inventive and, for anybody who believed that a movie's title must surely have some link to its content, extraordinarily intriguing. Who, after all, could resist checking out *Swedish Hang-gliding Beavers*?

The earliest beaver films were fairly straightforward, a (usually) slow striptease ending with the girl falling onto her back and parting her legs, and then manipulating her flesh in close-up. And the more flesh she manipulated, the more the audiences loved it. Soon, moviegoers were being tempted with both beaver films and *split* beaver films. Other variations followed. The immortally titled *Ruthless Shaved Beavers* succinctly summarizes one; *Frisco Beaver Action* implies another; and, though its title is linguistically incorrect (the collective noun for beavers, sadly, is the non-alliterative "colony"), the lesbian party *A Barrel of Beavers* wraps up a third.

The Mitchells ruled the world of beavers and, before long, they were feeding a stream of 16mm films into San Francisco's Tenderloin district. Neither was it the pocket theaters alone that picked up the beavers, especially once the sheer profitability of the genre became clear. According to advertisements placed in the *San Francisco Chronicle* in 1967, both the Roxie, on 16th Street and Valencia, and the Peerless, at 3rd and Mission, long-established "traditional" movie houses now fallen on hard times, offered such treats as *Naughty Nymphs and Eager Beavers at Their Busy Best, Beaver Picnic, Beaver Protest, Beavers at Sea* and *Beavers in Bloom*, with the Roxie openly proclaiming itself the "Home of the Eager Beaver Films" and offering a solid two hours' worth of beavers for your buck.

It would be 1971, a few years more, before the *New York Times Sunday Magazine* christened San Francisco "the Porn Capital of America," but already the city's reputation was set.

The 1970 Commission on Obscenity and Pornography left nobody in doubt as to the profit that a well-run 16mm theater could rake in, "primarily because of the typical $5-$15 admission charge, and because the theaters are usually open for at least 12 to 14 hours per day."[13] The report noted flourishing 16mm cinemas as far afield as Seattle, Dallas, Detroit and New York City, mostly "converted storefronts . . . located in decaying downtown areas." But it was San

Francisco that most caught its attention. "Local sources . . . estimated that the gross box-office receipts for an average 16mm theater in that city are approximately $3,000-$4,000 per week, and a few very successful theaters gross as much as $8,000 weekly."[15]

Now the *New York Times* chimed in: "What distinguishes San Francisco from any place else, [however,] is the style with which porn is marketed, its practitioners' attitude toward it and the tolerance most square citizens display concerning the whole question. The flourishing underground press in San Francisco all share the idea that porn, even at its sleaziest and most bizarre, is an important and healthily revolutionary ingredient of the new culture."[16]

Beavers were not the only beasts abroad, after all, just as the 16mm theatrical presentations were not the stag's sole manifestation. The 8mm trade continued to flourish, too, primarily selling through mail-order ads to home-movie enthusiasts. Elmer Batters, the one-time publisher who single-handedly transformed women's feet into a fetish (and was hit with an obscenity charge for his pains) produced several 8mm films built exclusively around the stockinged legs and feet of his photographic models. He made these available through advertisements in such self-published magazines as *Succulent Toes* and *Leg Art*.

The world of the transvestite also flickered onto the screen. B-movie legend Ed Wood, famed as the cross-dressing director of *Plan 9 from Outer Space* and immortalized in Tim Burton's 1994 biopic, spent the last years of his life in the adult trade, as editor of such magazines as *Swap*, *One Plus One* and *Unreleased Blazing Films*, as author of a string of transvestism-themed pulp novels and, fittingly, the maker of a number of 8mm stag films that may or may not have been shot for the so-called Scarface of Porn, Greek-born publisher and gangster Michael Thevis.

Sadly for posterity, no record or cataloging of these productions is known to exist. But it would be lovely to discover that Wood was responsible for *The Shrew*, a genuinely gender-bending shocker that has been dated to the late 1960s — around the same time Wood made his own entrance into the world of underground erotica.

In this film, middle-aged and none-too-attractive woman is

reclining on a couch when she is disturbed by the entrance of a nubile young visitor. They embrace, and slowly the girl is undressed, to be caressed and kissed by her lesbian lover. But then the older woman undresses and suddenly reveals that she isn't really a woman after all. But that's okay, because after a moment's stunned hesitation, her partner reveals that she's not really a lesbian.

What an older generation might now call "women's lib" moved in — or, at least, an acknowledgment that men did not always have things their own way. An English offering, *Escort Agency*, utterly eschews the traditional setup by placing the man beneath the microscope, to be checked out by a clipboard-wielding woman who steadfastly refuses to allow him to leave the room until she's filled in every detail on her questionnaire.

Gay stags began to proliferate, often rubbing shoulders (and more) with conventional heterosexual movies, as if to evidence the open-mindedness of the prevalent culture. And, after decades in the shadows, fetishism and bondage at last arose as dominant themes in the American stag — and, if many of the resultant films (or, at least, the costumes worn therein) now resemble little more than sexually active episodes of *The Avengers* TV series, that might be because Emma Peel's black leather catsuit was the brainchild of British fashion designer John Sutcliffe, mastermind behind the models featured monthly in the *über*-bondage magazine *Atomage*.

Sutcliffe personally never ventured into filmmaking; his fantasies were being played out every week on prime-time television, after all, but one would be foolish to doubt the erotic power exerted by Ms. Peel's exotic leatherwear. Fellow enthusiasts on both sides of the Atlantic were soon more than happy to walk where the master balked, and at the same time that San Francisco commenced her rise to the apex of American sex-film production, so London — after a painfully slow start — found herself undertaking a similar journey.

The English Disease

Satan's Children

Great Britain's stag industry can be dated
back at least to the 1910s, although her output
certainly enjoyed (or, perhaps, endured) a
most peculiar reputation, at least if historian
Curt Moreck is to be believed: "England,
which manufactures such films in the main
for South Africa, [favors] flagellation, and the
sadistic abuse of Negroes. Sexual cruelty also
plays an important role in its erotic literature and graphics."[1]

The Baking Fish is the earliest British stag for which we have any
written documentation, although no copy of the movie is known to
have survived. In fact, with the exception of a handful of dubiously
attributed movies from the 1920s and 1930s, it was not until the
immediate post–World War II period that the industry commenced
its slow struggle into life.

London vice developed hand-in-hand with the gradual transformation of a once-prospering west-end neighborhood known as
Soho. "A rabbit warren of narrow streets, passageways and alleys,"
according to writer Gilbert Kelland, it had once been home to a
variety of cafés and craftsmen. But "as the leases of the premises

housing the small business expired, they were acquired by shady entrepreneurs who let and sublet them at high rentals that could only be met by the burgeoning vice industry."[2]

London was not the only British city to host such a neighborhood — Birmingham, Manchester, Leeds and many others had their own notorious red-light districts. Soho, however, became the model to which they all aspired, if only by force of reputation.

It was during the war years, with London invaded by an army of (comparatively) wealthy American G.I.'s, that Soho first adopted its off-color camouflage, as strangely shabby little men began popping out of doorways to tempt passing uniforms with "dirty pictures." The Americans bought them, but so did Englishmen, surreptitiously visiting Soho from the better-heeled corners of town to buy real photographs of activities that they'd previously only read about on the letters pages of *London Life* — a prewar pinup magazine whose illustrations were curiously neutered, but whose mailbag abounded with that same peculiarly English brand of kinkiness that Moreck contemplated.

Hot water bottles, rubber mackintoshes, stiletto heels, corsets, caning, schoolgirl uniforms, amputees — if something could be sexually objectified, it would be, and the weirder it sounded, the better. As late as the 1970s, business cards affixed to the country's public telephone boxes still offered disciplinary services by a plethora of exotically named madames, each equipped with her own supply of unlikely fetishes. Gasmasks were an especially popular inclusion, presumably reawakening adolescent experiences from the early years of World War II, not to mention one of *London Life*'s most memorable covers, a May 1941 depiction of three Windmill Theatre showgirls clad in skimpy undies and hulking gasmasks.

Prostitution and gaming were the initial bane of the policemen patrolling the Soho streets. Slowly, however, more overt operations began to creep in — peep shows, bookstores and naked dancing, all so careful to appear just within the boundaries of the law that it was painfully (but unprovably) obvious that their true business lay far beyond it.

Officially, it was assumed that the vast majority of stag films circulating in the U.K. during the late 1940s and early 1950s were foreign in origin, smuggled in from other countries to wreak their evil influence upon otherwise chaste Britons. French bondage movies were especially (and predictably) popular, as Ado Kyrou confirmed when he recalled, in 1957, "France is the greatest exporter of pornographic film, and whenever a city is set to host a large gathering of visitors, a significant number of films clandestinely crosses the frontier. Thus, during the coronation of the Queen of England, Elizabeth II, in 1953, the English police force seized hundreds of films shipped into the country from France."[3]

The perfidious European was not, however, the sole source of the stag movies that circulated around the London sex underground. In fact, many were shot in London itself, as can be seen from the occasional glimpses through windows and doors, and were then given French-sounding titles to keep the law off the trail. The mid-1960s lesbian stag *Deux Femmes par Auto à Sappho*, in which a pair of girls excite themselves by poring over a collection of erotic photographs, is a typical example of this subterfuge. Its cover, however, is blown by a brief opening sequence in which the traffic is clearly driving on the right. French traffic, like American, drives on the left.

Of course, some themes were so quintessentially English that no amount of cunning linguistics could disguise their origins — those that played, for example, on the English girl's traditional love of horses, or anything that involved schoolgirls and hockey sticks.

Nevertheless, the various deceptions worked. "We must face it," insisted the Lord Chancellor, the fiercely Conservative Viscount Kilmuir, during the second reading of Britain's Obscene Publications Bill in 1959. "Grossly obscene films in houses or the rooms of clubs are one of the evils of life. I think they ought to be struck at."[4] And so they were, with the institution of a package of antiobscenity laws that remained essentially unchanged for the rest of the century.

It was a difficult regime to enforce, relying as often on luck as anything approaching good old-fashioned police work. Public displays of mucky movies were, nevertheless, broken up with considerable regularity, and in some often surprising locations. According to *Villain's Paradise* author Donald Thomas, a summer 1966 raid on the

Fisher & Ludlow car plant in Castle Bromwich was apparently only minutes shy of catching the night shift watching a blue film show; two years later, a 3 a.m. visit to a radio factory in Prittlewell, Essex, caught another group of workers red-handed.

Soho however, was even harder to police, particularly during the 1950s, when genuine hardcore productions vied for shelf space alongside the infinitely less explicit (and quite legal) nudist and stripper films produced by other individuals.

Included among this latter number was a company with the defiantly alluring name of Stag Films, the astonishingly prolific mid-1950s brainchild of producer Stanley Long and director Arnold Louis Miller. The pair are estimated to have produced well over 100 8mm shorts, all extolling the joys of the nudist life, before turning their attention to the big screen with 1961's *Nudist Memories* featurette. (Fans of British TV comedy might well be shocked to learn that the movie's lead, Anne, is played by actress Anna Karen, the decidedly unglamorous Olive in the long-running *On the Buses*.)

The cast members of Miller and Long's productions were drawn from the ranks of the capital's strippers and dancers. Other filmmakers, however, cast their nets far and wide to gather in a cast that ran the gamut from "Soho prostitutes and their clients"[5] to runaways and street kids, and on to the archetypal bored housewives. There is an exquisite scene in the 1971 movie *Not Tonight, Darling!* when a bored and boring solicitor stops off in a Soho club for a drink and catches sight of the wife he's ignored for years co-starring in an orgy-themed stag film.

But it was not all fun and games. In 1969, the *News of the World* newspaper transfixed its readers with the cautionary tale of a pair of teenagers who fled their home in rural England for the bright lights of London, only to wind up making a living on the streets, their dreams shattered and their savings exhausted. Desperate to keep body and mind together, the girl turned to prostitution for a time. Another encounter saw the pair accept an offer of £60 each to star together in a blue movie shot in a squalid apartment in the wilds of south London, while an elderly man — the movie's financier — sat beside the bed watching.

Finally the pair fled back home, but made the mistake of discussing what had happened to them during their absence. Incredibly, the boy was promptly arrested and sentenced to two years in juvenile detention for living off immoral earnings, a fate that caused considerable outrage at the time and prompted director Pete Walker to film their story as *Cool It Carol!* (released in the United States as *The Dirtiest Girl I Ever Met*).

As *Cool It Carol!* pointed out, filmmakers operated across the city, some in the center of things — Soho and the West End — others further out from those gaudily spotlit streets. Michael W., a London cab driver during the mid-1950s, not only remembers buying 8mm films from an otherwise respectable-looking junk store in north London's Tottenham High Road, he also remembers his shock the day he saw one of the movies' stars leaving the shop as he was entering it: "I started paying more attention to what was going on elsewhere in the films, and realized that the view out of one of the windows was the same as you'd get if you went upstairs at the shop. The bloke who ran the shop was filming them himself, and then selling them in the shop!"[6]

Such a trade was, of course, illegal. Although British law did permit the private filming of consenting adults, the sale and distribution of the resultant films was ferociously forbidden. But there was room to maneuver even there.

With no long tradition of road showing, as in the United States, and no network of well-appointed brothels like pre–De Gaulle France, the British erotic-film industry operated either on a retail basis or through membership in the select band of private clubs that began springing up through the 1960s. Gaudily lit and seedily furnished, venues with such alluring names as the Exxon, the Albatross, Swedish Paradise and Cin Cinema sprang up, all taking advantage of the legal loophole that permitted the owners to show whatever movies they wanted, so long as the only customers were fully paid-up members.

The conditions of membership were scarcely designed to ensure exclusivity (both "trial" and "guest" options were available to all), but still such cinemas so successfully exploited this ruling that the only charge many proprietors ever faced arose from circumstances that were literally out of their hands: masturbating moviegoers, who opened the clubs up to the charge of "running a disorderly house," rowdy patrons causing a disturbance on the street outside and so forth.

There would develop, too, a small coterie of distribution companies whose advertisements became as obliquely ubiquitous in the U.K. girlie mags as those of their counterparts across the Atlantic, and whose prices ranged from between £5 and £25, depending on the individual film. Older black-and-white efforts lay at the cheaper end; films shot in color and sound, or featuring certain specialized subjects, were costlier.

Ingenious, too, was the manner in which films were actually produced. No less than their American cousins, some hardy souls learned how to process and duplicate their movies themselves, or knew a friendly lab worker who would do it for them. But, as Gilbert Kelland explains, Britain's proximity to the continent encouraged others to send their movies to Germany and Scandinavia for processing and duplication, and then smuggle them back into the country, packed "into boxes similar to those used for other products that were being imported in container lorries and mix them with the genuine cargo. Although the Customs authorities sometimes made seizures — usually when they acted on information — it was quite impossible for them to open and examine every container lorry arriving at English ports."[7]

Other moviemakers preferred to trust the personal touch when it came to ferrying material back and forth across the English Channel. A legend in that particular line of work, Charlie Brown was a diminutive Pole (born Walter Bartkoski) working as a steward on the cross-Channel ferries. Mike Freeman, one of London's leading film distributors, recalled, "He used to phone me from Germany and, if there was a good-selling line, he used to order them in batches. They were twenty-minute 8mm prints in proper boxes with photographs on the outside. He used to get the stuff through Calais, somehow."[8]

Against this hive of ingenuity were ranged the powers of the Obscene Publications Squad, better known to the public as the Porn

Squad and headed up for most of the 1960s by the legendary Detective Chief Superintendent Bill Moody — a man who later earned infamy of his own when it was revealed that, at the same time as he led one of the biggest-ever investigations into police corruption, he was collecting enormous bribes from a variety of Soho booksellers and theaters. (It has even been suggested that the investigating officer who is so easily seduced in the 1967 English stag *Vice Probe* was based on Moody.)

Long before any such transgressions came to light, however, Moody was a well-known figure around the Soho streets, and their moviemakers were well-known to him.

In terms of media recognition, the leader of the Soho vice pack was undoubtedly Evan "Big Jeff" Phillips, a man widely touted as the first Briton ever to become a millionaire from erotic entertainment.

The truth behind this assertion is difficult to confirm. Phillips' moviemaking career lasted a mere eight years, beginning with his first crude black-and-white 8mm films in 1965, and continuing on until 1973, when he was arrested on a charge of possessing obscene material and jailed for eighteen months. Shortly after his release, he committed suicide over an unrequited love affair.

He was certainly prolific, however. At the same time as he was shooting his first films, Phillips was also importing movies from Scandinavia, where directors Curt Nilsson and Lasse Braun (in reality, an Italian named Albert Ferro) were quietly revolutionizing the European stag trade, selling their high-quality color Super-8 films for less than their competitors — Phillips among them — demanded for their fuzzy black-and-white shots.

Sensing that the future of film could not help but follow the Scandinavians' lead, Phillips switched to color, slashed his prices, and the profits from his endeavors were sufficient for him to own, at one point during his meteoric career, a luxury yacht (it was subsequently sold to the Sultan of Oman and can be glimpsed in the movie *Ashanti*), a Rolls Royce and two luxury homes, an apartment in west London's trendy Sloane Square and a manor house in Berkshire.

Mike Freeman and Ivor Cooke were Phillips' greatest competitors. Freeman had been active in the Soho industry from the early 1960s and was among the pioneers of color 16mm stags, around 1965. He employed only professional models for his shoots and took special care when overdubbing sound in postproduction, and his empire supplied films throughout Soho and London's West End for much of the 1960s.

Cooke, meanwhile, was the brilliant eye whose "Climax Films Present" trademark precedes some of the most exquisitely realized British stags ever made.

The teacher-pupil partnership of *End of Term*, the faintly incestuous *Equal to Mummy*, and *Pussy Galore* (no relation to the David Friedman film of the same name), in which a uniformed lass abandons the chores her mother left her with and invites her boyfriend around instead, set the stage for many of these high-quality films (particularly once the latter's loving couple are interrupted by a second female participant).

Climax Films was also responsible, however, for *First Audition*, in which a woman performs an extraordinarily effective striptease for a prospective employer, and the film that H.C. Shelby described as the stags' first-ever double-penetration epic, *One Hundred Per-Cent Lust* — and that is only one reason for the movie's subsequent notoriety. There was also a persuasive rumor going around that its dark-haired heroine was Christine Keeler, the London call girl at the center of the 1961 Profumo scandal. (Keeler has denied this, and close examination of the footage agrees with her.)

Other Climax classics included *The Hell Fire Club*, a lavishly costumed effort named for Sir Francis Dashwood's legendary eighteenth-century gentleman's club, and, best of all, *Satan's Children*, a contrarily uncostumed drama built around the regular reports of sinister black-magic rituals being played out in the pages of Britain's Sunday tabloid press throughout much of the late 1960s.

Satan himself is clearly a skinny guy with what looks like a burlap bag draped over his head and a taste for waving his riding crop around; his children are the three women who, in drawing such surprisingly copious amounts of communion "wine" from his erect penis, were essentially test-piloting the first genuine "special effect" in adult-cinema history — a thin tube, inserted into the mouth alongside the erect penis, through which a suitably colored liquid (probably milk) was pumped at the moment of "climax." Unconvincing though they may be, the resultant cascades ensure that *Satan's Children* features some of the most electrifyingly messy fellatio scenes in stag history.

Furthermore, the scenario is played out with such obvious enjoyment that any technical shortcomings are readily subsumed by the realization that films such as this were physically rewriting the laws of the erotic short, abandoning the hitherto unbreachable notion that it was variety, not versatility, that kept the punters coming back.

The frantic pace of earlier stags was supplanted by seductively lingering material: nipples being sucked for long minutes, full-blooded caresses replacing the swift swipes of the past, entire films devoted to long, slow close-ups of an act pursued to its climax.

Abandoning the stereotypical British obsession with rubber and other fetishwear, fetishism was now confined to the ubiquitous schoolgirls (with occasional deviations toward stewardesses, nurses, secretaries and au-pair girls). Likewise, bondage was abandoned, and the most protracted sexual sequences now tended to be oral, imbibed with a naturality and lingering enjoyment that many American filmmakers now seemed convinced could be captured only via the most gratuitous grandstanding.

The Brits, however, demonstrated that a woman did not need to bare her teeth, loll her tongue and generally behave as though she'd just passed a kidney stone in order to convince the audience that she was enjoying either her own, or her partner's part, in the action. Closed eyes and a lemur-like smile were just as effective, and probably a lot more enjoyable for viewer and participant alike.

With the change in pacing of these movies, fellatio-inspired orgasms were now regarded as simply one event within the unfolding action, as opposed to the literal climax of the movie — *Satan's Children*, for example, features no fewer than *four* "money shots" and, although another Climax offering, *Free For All*, does rely on a pair of voluminous male orgasms for its closing sequence, few foursomes have ever choreographed that moment to such striking simultaneity.

Movies such as these represented the hierarchy of London film-makers: other operators worked lower down the pecking order. Anthony Frewin's masterful novel *London Blues* depicts the life and times of one such, in a saga that is alive with period color (and also taps into the enduring mystique surrounding Christine Keeler). But these people, too, were responsible for some fascinating movies. *Part-Time Job*, with its mid-1960s London street scenes and a newspaper headline that mourns "London Fares Up — Official," recalls the days when an increase in the cost of public transport really was a headline event (as opposed to a regular occurrence) and it was perfectly natural for a middle-aged bachelor to employ a fresh-out-of-school girl to perform tasks around the house.

Schoolgirl Lust and *Young Lust* highlight a clutch of well-performed stags credited to the wonderfully named Pornographer Goes to the Pictures; these films not only featured the same set, they even utilized the same kitchen table. *Back Door Coach* is, of course, titled for an (oddly inept) anal sequence, but is actually most notable for a slapstick routine involving a penis sandwich — and that's a real sandwich, complete with bread and butter. And *Tonight at 8* (no relation to the American stag of the same name) offers such an evocative tour of London's West End in the winter of 1967–68, that it could have doubled as an X-rated outtake from Antonioni's *Blow-Up* — albeit one saddled with an almost embarrassingly inexperienced cast.

Into this maelstrom marched John Lindsay. Willowy, trendily bespectacled, his gaunt face topped by a mass of unruly blonde hair, the Glasgow-born John Jesnor Lindsay began his career as a photojournalist for the Scottish *Daily Herald*, where his daily grind comprised pets shows, weddings, baby contests or anything else that would fill some space on the page.

He was good, though, and when he relocated to London to work for the *Daily Express*, he also came to the attention of *Vogue*. Deeper ambitions, meanwhile, encouraged Lindsay to take a series of topless photographs of a girlfriend and submit them to a men's magazine; asked for more, and impressing all who saw his work, Lindsay soon found himself conducting regular shoots for the British monthlies *Mayfair* and *Penthouse*, the cream of the post-*Playboy* line of "respected" British girlie magazines.

He eventually moved further afield, freelancing in the underworld of hardcore European publications, and it was through these connections that Lindsay took his first steps into motion pictures.

Lindsay made his first 16mm stag in 1966, after one of his neighbors (himself an established moviemaker) introduced him to the vast amounts of money the field had to offer. Little, if any, of Lindsay's early work is recognizable today — like so many of his contemporaries, he was working so far underground and on such minuscule budgets that none of his later flair for direction and texture was even dreamed of, let alone called for.

He was a fast learner, however, and in 1969, Dutch publisher Joop Wilhelmus, an entrepreneur whose *Chick* (the self-styled "sex magazine for the worker") was one of Lindsay's regular photographic outlets, offered him the role of cameraman on a stag he was about to shoot in Germany with director John Darby.

Ever cautious, Lindsay contacted Scotland Yard's vice squad before accepting the offer, inquiring about the precise legality of the new opportunities. Then, having ascertained that his new career would not overstep the legal boundaries (at least at that point — he would subsequently branch out), he accepted the job and, days later, he traveled to Germany to start work.

He was joined on the trip over by the young woman he had already handpicked for the starring role. Her name was Mary Maxted; Lindsay's friends and associates called her Mary-from-Dorking (her home town). The public would eventually come to know her as Mary Millington.

Lindsay first met Maxted sipping coffee in a Kensington café, and initially approached her to pose for some straightforward glamour photographs, a line he frequently used on beautiful young women. Wholesome girl next door Maxted, however, was very different from the shrinking violets and bashful beauties with whom he normally ended up. Arriving at Lindsay's studios at 37b Berwick

Street, in the heart of Soho, she threw herself into the photographer's every suggestion, so much so that it took him just two days to sell the pictures taken during that initial fifteen-minute session.

Maxted was soon appearing in ever more provocative and revealing poses for Lindsay's lens and, when he asked whether she would be interested in appearing in what the British euphemistically called "Swedish movies," she readily agreed.

Her first film, and Lindsay's first for Wilhelmus, was *Miss Bohrloch* (the German title translates as "bore-hole"), a fourteen-minute color and sound opus in which Maxted plays a Deep Southern prostitute who entertains a pair of men who discovered her details on the wall of a phone booth. Maxted's stunning beauty aside, however, the film is best remembered for a sequence that takes place before the two men have even arrived (aboard a chauffeur-driven bicycle) at Miss Bohrloch's apartment.

Naked, she is talking on the telephone, giving them directions, when suddenly, with neither warning nor explanation (or consequence), a ping-pong ball eases itself out of her vagina, falls to the floor and bounces out of sight. Long after the movie's actual title and plot had been forgotten, a generation of British moviegoers could still effortlessly and delightedly recall "the one with the ping-pong ball."

Miss Bohrloch is scarcely a directorial triumph on par with so many of Lindsay's later shoots. The filming is straightforward at best, amateurish in places, and the movie is certainly scarred by the obvious uncertainty of its cast, with even Maxted little more than workmanlike. Nevertheless, Lindsay was thrilled to have discovered a girl with so few inhibitions and a sexual repertoire that even astonished one of her co-stars ("I've never had that done before," he sighs, as Maxted's tongue begins working on his anus); and, while the actress's subsequent fame would account for much of the film's future success (that and the ping-pong ball), *Miss Bohrloch* readily scooped the Golden Phallus Award at the annual Wet Dreams ceremony in Amsterdam, confirming Lindsay's change in career direction.

Learning on the job, editing as he shot and dubbing dialogue as he wrote it, Lindsay's Taboo Films company was soon producing thirty-plus movies a year, filming in London, Frankfurt and the Netherlands. Wilhelmus was still financing many of Lindsay's productions, but the arrangement was becoming increasingly fraught. The Netherlands, Lindsay liked to say, was a land where "almost anything is permissible." One thing that wasn't, however, was pedophilia — and that was one of the main things Wilhelmus required from the films he paid for. He wanted schoolgirl sex, and lots of it.

He got it, too, although it is unclear whether he ever discovered that Lindsay never once filmed a bona fide schoolgirl. Rather, he worked with a strictly handpicked cast of overage erotic actresses, suitably costumed and unmadeup, and laden with the fetishist paraphernalia of school uniforms and hockey sticks. Neither does Wilhelmus (or any other fetishist) seem to have cottoned on to the deception — today, such productions as *Juvenile Sex*, *Girl Guide Rape*, *Sex Kittens* and *Boarding School* remain among the best, and certainly the most archetypal, "schoolgirl" movies ever made, while 1971's *Jolly Hockeysticks* single-handedly made an icon of Hungarian actress Ava Cadell.

Lindsay and Wilhelmus parted company in January 1971; that month, the Dutchman was arrested and jailed over the contents of his flagship publication, the child-centric magazine *Lolita*. Lindsay, however, was swift to move on. He was coproducer (with Laurence Barnett) of the feature-length sex comedy *The Love Pill*; but he was the co*star* of Stanley Long's *Naughty*, a documentary discussion of British sexual mores hampered only by the law's refusal to allow the sex itself to be screened.

In its stead, audiences had to rest content with footage of naked hippies misbehaving at the 1970 Wet Dream awards, an interview with Al Goldstein, editor of the American magazine *Screw*, and a handful of dramatizations that veer between the painfully sad (the henpecked husband whose wife has a lifelong headache) to the mother advising her daughter on what to expect on her wedding night — "Hold tight, and remember it happened to the Queen."

Lindsay's role in all of this was to be caught amid the behind-the-scenes footage from another of his schoolgirl romps, *Sex After*

School, and despite the anodyne nature of the scenes in question, still it was a crucial inclusion. In the same year that the Michael Caine gangster thriller *Get Carter* flashed a few frames of a British blue film onto the mainstream cinema screen (the sequence was shot as part of the movie itself, as opposed to being lifted from an extant stag), Lindsay was seen directing the real thing, and uttering the remark that would, over the next three years, become a virtual mantra at his productions: "I want 100 percent action. I want everything. Sucking, licking, fucking, screwing, you name it, I want it and I want it good."

Usually, he got it, as well.

For the general viewer, the most familiar of all Lindsay's stags is *Wet Dream* — not for its content, but for its inclusion as the centerpiece in one of the finest documentary-style studies of the stag industry ever shot, 1973's *The Pornbrokers*.

Produced in response to the 1972 publication of antismut crusader Lord Longford's report *Pornography in the U.K.,* and co-directed by Laurence Barnett, *The Pornbrokers* was intended as an appraisal of the erotic movie as a force for . . . if not good, at least harmless diversion, and a considerably healthier pursuit than many of those indulged in by the very authorities that were now condemning it.

Heavy-handedly, perhaps, but certainly effectively, *The Pornbrokers* opened with scenes from "real life," including napalm-drenched Vietnamese children and Middle Eastern public executions, and so forth. From there, the movie turned to look at the people who were behind the European industry: the magazine publishers, fellow filmmakers and so on who elaborate eloquently on the valuable social services enacted by their chosen trade, while dismissing accusations of exploitation, brutality and worse. The cornerstone of the film, however, rests upon a dramatization of Lindsay's own working methods, cut with behind-the-scenes footage from the *Wet Dream* shoot.

As he proved with his discovery and introduction of Mary Maxted, Lindsay preferred working with unknowns, recruiting them initially as fashion models and then talking them around to the more lucrative glamour work. He did not push, he did not cajole. The decision of whether or not to step out of her clothing was the girl's alone, as was the supposedly inevitable next step, from still photography to moving pictures. As he exclaimed in *Naughty*, "The girls I use in my films are nice girls. Because they screw and have it up here and up there and in their mouths and that, this doesn't mean to say they're not nice girls."

The Pornbrokers follows seventeen-year-old Maureen O'Malley (destined to follow Millington's post-Lindsay footsteps into publisher David Sullivan's erotic empire) from her introductory interview at the Berwick Street studio, through the "color test" at which Lindsay would assess her potential as a nude ("Just get the clitoris up if you can, darling") and on to an almost grandfatherly verbal initiation into the world of blue movies.

It is a landscape, Lindsay explains, populated by "handsome young guys" who would probably "come all over your titties." But in return she would receive a standard £15 per scene — a month's rent for a single girl in London at the time, while inhibitions would be eased, perhaps paradoxically, by the sheer absence of intimacy from any of the shots.

Maureen is one of some half a dozen actors and actresses — all of whom will be performing for Lindsay's cameras over the course of the day — who gather outside Baker Street underground station to await the non-descript Transit van that will take them to the shoot. Even before the movie narration makes the same point, the viewer is struck by the absolute absence of anything even remotely approaching sexiness that permeates the footage.

Devoid of mood-establishing soundtracking, moving awkwardly around a set that is purposefully littered with the filmmakers' equipment, the young would-be thespians yawn, grimace and hesitate their way through their scenes. It is all a far cry from the polished effect of *Wet Dream* itself, a hard dose of realism exploding out of a world that many regarded as one nonstop sexual fantasy.

But realism was a cornerstone of the trade few of its adherents were ever likely to forget. Within a decade, Lindsay would be in prison, jailed on charges that even his most outspoken opponents acknowledged were probably a setup — he was released in 1985 and left the erotic business altogether.

Joop Wilhelmus, too, spent much of the 1970s and 1980s behind bars, before the Netherlands' best-known pedophile was murdered on the Rotterdam docks in 1994, just days after completing his latest prison sentence.

And Mary Millington, after spending close to a decade fighting for an overhaul of Britain's prehistoric obscenity laws, was hounded to suicide by an establishment that realized it was the only way she could ever be silenced. Viewed from little more than a quarter of a century later, Millington's final words, in a letter to publisher David Sullivan, read like a relic from another age entirely:

> *The police have framed me yet again. They frighten me so much. I can't face the thought of prison. . . . I do so hope that porn is legal one day, they called me obscene names for being in possession of it, and I can't go through much more. The Nazi tax man has finished me as well. Please print in your magazine how much I wanted porn legalized. But the police have beaten me.*[9]

I Am Curious — Red, White and Blue

The Nun

While Britain seethed (and continued to seethe for another three decades) beneath some of the most repressive obscenity laws in the Western world, across the North Sea in Scandinavia, the locals had flung all such concerns aside. Sweden was first to dismantle the bars against free sexual expression in 1967; Denmark quickly followed.

Now both countries were reaping the rewards of their permissiveness — a litany of triumphs that ranged from a massive decline in sex crimes to a major increase in tourism, and an unshakable reputation as the proud sponsor of the hottest sex films ever made.

Perhaps that is why people who have never even seen it can still get hot and bothered over *I Am Curious — Yellow*. It's Swedish. Therefore it has to be very rude. The country's reputation as the nexus of all European sexuality began there.

Released in Sweden in October 1967, *I Am Curious — Yellow (Jag är Nyfiken — Gul)* was the first of two movies by director Vilgot Sjöman designed to investigate the various currents of social and political thought then swirling through his homeland. Both it and

233

the following year's *I Am Curious — Blue (Jag är Nyfiken — Blå)* took their titles from the colors of the Swedish flag, and together they offered a disjointed but curiously compelling depiction of Swedish society, as seen through the turbulence of the late 1960s.

A masterpiece of political subversion, *I Am Curious — Yellow* caused both controversy and acclaim in Sweden. When the local movie industry gathered for the annual Guldbagge Awards ceremony, *I Am Curious — Yellow* streaked away with the Best Movie gong; its star, actress Lena Nymen, took Best Actress.

The movie's intended impact diminished the further from its targets it traveled — a biting dismantling of Sweden's pacifism, for example, was scarcely going to raise hackles in the U.K., and *I Am Curious — Yellow* was passed for British distribution with just a handful (eleven minutes) of excisions, all based around the movie's sexual content.

The U.S., however, was a very different proposition, which was why Barney Rosset, owner of the publishing house Grove Press, chose to import it in the first place. Rosset had spent a large part of his career fighting America's censorship laws and generally winning (it was Rosset who successfully defended your right to read Henry Miller's *Tropic of Cancer* and D.H. Lawrence's *Lady Chatterley's Lover*). But he also knew that anybody watching *I Am Curious — Yellow* without an intimate understanding of the film's intended meaning would be struck by another text altogether.

Lena spends a large part of the movie wandering around stark naked, at a time when pubic hair was prohibited from public display in the United States. She also has sex on a number of occasions . . . nothing too explicit, and there was no penetration, but it was definitely more realistic than you tended to see in American cinema. Oh, and in one memorable scene, she plants an affectionate kiss on her lover's flaccid penis.

Under cover of the 1930 Tariff Act, U.S. Customs seized the movie the moment it landed on American soil in late 1967, holding it until a federal court could decide whether or not the movie was obscene. Perhaps unsurprisingly, a jury trial sided with Customs — filmed nudity and genital kisses often had that effect on people in those days. Rosset, however, appealed the decision to the U.S. Court of Appeals for the Second Circuit, where it was reversed under the same established standard that freed up the publication of *Fanny Hill* two years earlier.

Of course, being permitted to enter the United States did not mean that *I Am Curious — Yellow* would find any theater owners willing (or able) to screen it. "Community standards," after all, are set by individual communities and, while no fewer than 125 theaters around the country did eventually exhibit the movie, many were permitted to do so only after legal battles of their own, and several cities (including Boston, Baltimore, Kansas City and Spokane) succeeded in banning it altogether.

Nevertheless, the court ruling opened up for the movies the same freedom American publishing had recently been enjoying: the knowledge that absolutely any form of artistic expression was now permissable, so long as someone, somewhere, could isolate something, no matter how insignificant it might be, that could be construed as informative or educational.

The law was not the only edifice shifting to accommodate the most liberal arts, however. Change was afoot, too, in the movie industry.

The Hays Code, for all the abuse that has been hurled at it in the decades since it was introduced, was not necessarily a bad thing. Certainly its most frequently condemned purpose — preventing the American public from witnessing scenes on film that the individual alone should be charged with discriminating against — was censorious at best and utterly prudish at worst. Joe Breen, who headed the Hays Office between 1934 and 1954, once defended the code by insisting that, without it, "they'd put fucking in Macy's window, and they'd argue till they were blue in the face that it was art."[1] The code's staunchest critics were the people who believed that it could, indeed, be art.

But the code also protected film*makers* from the kinds of complaints, lawsuits and worse that today bedevil the creators of almost every film and television program, from the miscreants who blame their crimes on something they saw at the theater, to the parental lobbies who complain that television is turning their children into obese, foul-mouthed couch-bound psychopaths. Geoffrey Shurlock, Breen's chief assistant (and later successor), recalled the day when anthropologist Hortense Powdermaker was granted permission to inspect the office files and discovered paperwork pertaining to the decision to excise a close-up of an elephant's genitalia from one particular movie.

Railing against the absurdity of such a demand, she delivered a damning indictment on everything the code and its upholders stood for. A furious Shurlock, however, refused to accept her condemnation. "If Miss Powdermaker," he wrote, "should ever see the sex organs of an elephant projected on a 65-foot outdoor drive-in screen before a typical mixed American audience, she would understand why the request [to delete the scene] was made and acceded to."[2] Viewed in that context, it is difficult not to share Shurlock's view.

With the dissolution of the code, such censorship was no longer an issue. In late 1968, just months after the Supreme Court rendered its decision on *I Am Curious — Yellow*, the Production Code was abandoned, to be replaced by a new classification series rating movies according to the lower limits of the age group they were appropriate for: "G" for general, or family audiences; "M" and "R" for different teenage groups; and "X" for adults only.

(There was no further qualification, incidentally, no "double-X" and beyond. Those designations were dreamed up by quick-thinking filmmakers who, already celebrating the fact that they could now push any film they desired into mainstream theaters, wanted to let the world know just how extreme that film might be. Within months, David Friedman's "exposé" of the movie industry, *Starlet*, became the first movie to be proclaimed xxx — because, the advertising poster insisted, it was "so adult one X isn't enough!")

For an entire generation of makers of erotic movies, the challenge was simple: to produce a film that, having passed muster under the law of the land, would then prove attractive enough for national distributors to want to take it on board.

Suddenly erotic filmmakers no longer believed they had to hide away in lofts and garages, shooting their dirty little films on the cheapest gear they could lay their hands on. There was a whole world out there that wanted to see more, and was willing to pay for the privilege of doing so.

They organized. In November 1968, Sam Chernoff of the sexploitation-hungry Astro-Jemco Film Co. in Dallas, convened a meeting of 110 producers, distributors and exhibitors in Kansas City, with the object of forming what became the Adult Film Association of America, a body designed to mediate between the filmmakers and the authorities in every arena, but most particularly to safeguard them from prosecution. Chernoff was elected the AFAA's first president; he was succeeded in 1971 by David Friedman.

The movies' stars, too, were at last emerging from beneath the anonymity that had hitherto cloaked them: the husband-and-wife team of Tina and Jason Russell, who had shot some eighty stags together by 1972; Harry Reems and Jamie Gillis, who between them appeared in virtually every early- to mid-1970s erotic feature of note; John Holmes, who proudly proclaimed in a 1974 interview that he had already made 2,706 movies ("'I keep track,' he says with an offhanded exactitude"[3]); and many, many more.

Not all of them sought instant recognition. Author Anthony Crowell spoke to several aspiring starlets "who will work in TV or movies during the daytime, and work the stag films too. Many of these girls are adept at changing their facial appearance. They spend great sums of money on wigs and contact lenses of different hues. Thus a girl who is naturally a red head with blue eyes will show up on the set of a stag film as a glowing blonde with hazel eyes. A bit of nose putty and their own mothers wouldn't recognize them."[4] But, in many cases, the disguise was not donned in order to mask their identity. It was to allow them to take an even larger number of parts, without the audience tiring of the same old faces. (Presumably, the same old tits were less of an encumbrance.)

For each of these stars and starlets, their induction into stag movies followed the same tried and trusted route that had lured so many others into camera shot. Harry Reems recalled, "A fellow actor said, 'I know where you can pick up an extra hundred bucks for an hour's work.' I was scared, I had to take three subways and thought

I was being followed. That's how paranoid I was. But I did it, I walked into this room and the next thing I know, I'm in bed with these two beautiful girls — and it was nirvana. I had no problem creating the fourth wall — it was like, 'Go ahead and film, I'm focusing on what I get to look at.'"[5]

This new openness did not suit everybody, including those liberated souls whom one might have expected to welcome such a development. Cult-movie director John Waters famously described watching hardcore as akin to witnessing "open-heart surgery," and other directors similarly went out of their way to distance themselves from the ultrapermissive portal that had suddenly opened up.

Even David Friedman, whose sexploitation flicks had titillated an entire generation of drive-in veterans, furiously decried the changes. Sex, he insisted, belonged in the stags, not on the big screen: "Everybody in the world who can fire a camera and find a broad that will fuck, will make [a movie]," he proclaimed, "and every guy who can find a thirty-foot storefront will open a theater."[6]

Friedman's dire prediction rapidly proved correct. By early 1969, San Francisco hosted an estimated twenty-five cinemas dedicated to hardcore erotic films, with more appearing every month; by the following year, no less an authority than the *New York Times Sunday Magazine* would credit the city by the bay with a staggering 150 adult theaters.

So far, the San Francisco police had left the industry alone, and it flourished. Domestic productions abounded; European material was flooding in through as many loopholes as its importers could find. Quality, too, became a concern, especially after one exhibitor screened the German stag, *Cara Nanie*, a movie that was rightly praised not so much for its content, but for the sheer inventiveness of its scenario.

A supernatural thriller, it begins with a worried young man summoning a nurse to administer to his sick wife. The nurse, however, has other plans, mesmerizing the patient and sending her to sit on a chair, and then taking over the bed to seduce the stunned husband. Some basic, but very effective, camera trickery allows the nurse to execute bewildering disappearing acts, while the movie's finale of death, decay and madness — is genuinely surprising. In later years, with the likes of the Mitchells and others turning out full-length erotic feature films, the brief span, but long-lasting premise, of *Cara Nanie* would prove a lingering influence.

There was, however, a moment when it looked as though nobody would ever get to make another erotic movie again. In the spring of 1969, word spread that a film showing a man having sex with a pig was going the Tenderloin rounds, a sequence that fell far beyond even the most liberal interpretation of the obscenity laws. The district attorney pounced.

Soon busts were routine, operators were going out of business. No matter that the majority of them were operating within the letter of the law, the police needed only suspect (or say they suspected) that more extreme material was on display to be granted the necessary warrants. They would then impound all the films and materials they discovered on the premises, holding them until a court determined it should be returned. Many operators, however, could not afford to take matters that far, and those that could would soon be beaten down, simply by busting them again . . . and again . . . and again. As fast as they had opened, the cinemas now began closing down.

Jim and Art Mitchell were among the police department's earliest victims. The brothers opened their own theater, the O'Farrell, on July 4, 1969, taking over a once-crumbling downtown corner building at Polk and O'Farrell, and thoroughly refurbishing it. Three weeks later, they were busted for the first time.

A couple of weeks later, the cops were back again. But where other theater owners crumbled beneath such constant intrusions, the Mitchells did not. Rather, they hired the radical young attorney Michael Kennedy, who'd worked with William Kunstler (the flamboyant lead defense attorney in the trial of the Chicago Seven) and fought back, via both the courts and, increasingly, in the media.

Portraying themselves as defenders of free speech, the Mitchells set about cultivating every journalist they met, offering free showings, free drink, free dope, whatever it took. *San Francisco Chronicle* journalist Sandy Zane later laughed, "The Mitchell brothers corrupted a generation of reporters."[7]

They were also smart enough to realize that freebies were not the only way to a movie critic's heart. In August 1969, hitting back at reviews that dismissed their work as mere "dirty movies," the Mitchells unveiled *Requiem*, a fifteen-minute opus in which a redhead is followed from the graveside of her recently deceased husband to her home, where she masturbates to the sound of Gregorian chants.

The movie's first audience was as assemblage of local journalists. All professed themselves thoroughly impressed. Later, film historian John Hubner went so far as to describe *Requiem* as "a significant departure in the dreary annals of American sex films. The lizards in sharkskin suits in New York who were making beavers that featured lifeless, tattooed hookers would never have used a Gregorian choir in a film. The smooth operators in L.A. who cranked out loop after loop that were as devoid of feeling as an industrial film that follows a can of soup from the vat to the shipping crate, would never have come up with a storyline that involved a grieving widow."[8]

Alex de Renzy, too, was becoming increasingly well-versed in the niceties of the obscenities law. Soon, the Screening Room was maintaining bail bondsmen and lawyers on weekly retainers, in readiness for the next inevitable bust. The theater changed its program every week, and every week the police would descend upon the premises in the hope that this time they would finally be able to bust de Renzy for exhibiting "obscene material."

De Renzy tolerated the law's attentions at first, partly because he was careful to ensure that he always operated within the realms of the law, but also because the publicity surrounding the busts was incredibly good for business. But finally he had enough, the week the Screening Room received its fifty-second visit from the cops. This wasn't law enforcement, he declared, it was harassment, and when he took the matter to court, the justices agreed with him. De Renzy was granted a restraining order against the city of San Francisco. And with the law at last at bay, he could return his attentions to what he did best — making movies.

I Am Curious — Yellow opened in the United States in 1969, followed with inevitable immediacy by the first homegrown responses to the new climate. Released in rapid-fire succession over the next year or so, *The Marriage Manual*, *Sexual Education in Scandinavia*, *101 Acts of Love*, *Man and Wife* and *He and She* (the latter pair produced by Matt Cimber, Jayne Mansfield's husband at the time of her death) were feature-length documentaries marketed and, indeed, presented as the visual accompaniment to the marriage manuals that had always sold so well.

Each was constructed around some learned dissertations on how to perform various sexual acts, narrated by a scholarly looking medical professional clad in a regulation white coat (hence the quickly assumed generic nickname "white coaters") and acted out by "real life" patients.

It goes without saying that the larger proportion of their audience comprised people who knew perfectly well how to do such things and just wanted to watch other people doing them too; it was also glaringly obvious that those selfsame "informative" couplings were no different in either content nor execution to those that had flickered across the stag screen for the past sixty-plus years. But, like the nudes in *National Geographic*, or the unexpurgated dictionaries of the English language with schoolboy thumbprints on the pages where the rude words lurk, the films could no longer be blamed for how their audiences perceived them.

Not every movie that took this route did so with tongue wholly distant from cheek. With a total running time that certainly placed it within the realm of the traditional stag movie, *Preliminary Overtures* opens with a pretty brunette writhing by the fireside with a paramour who appears to have mistaken her clitoris for a flea bite. An extraordinarily tender (and, based on the man's earlier behavior, thoroughly undeserved) blow job follows, before the couple launch into an increasingly surreal sex-education course, demonstrating first the correct method of donning a condom, and then a series of "variations on intercourse positions," starting with the breasts, but then progressing to the armpit, the elbow and, finally, the crook of the knee. Perhaps there are some people who really do enjoy these positions. But there were an awful lot more who found the idea of trying quite hilarious.

Alex de Renzy tested the educational waters with a short untitled stag movie in which a naked young woman sits and discusses, in very matter-of-fact language, precisely what turns her on, evidencing her own excitement by gently masturbating while she speaks. Reminiscent of French director Bernard Nathan's 1920s masterpiece *Je Verbalise*, the movie represented a major departure from the traditional stag milieu, but de Renzy was only warming up.

He was still recuperating from a near fatal and seriously disfiguring motorcycle accident when, in November 1969, he travelled to Denmark to film that year's Copenhagen Sex Fair, the first industry-wide celebration of the Danish authorities' decision to legalize all forms of adult sexuality in 1967.

The fair met de Renzy's every expectation. Vendors sold everything from sex toys to sex itself, and the American's cameras devoured it all. On the streets, he filmed anything and everything that epitomized the Danes' sexual enlightenment, from the stores that openly displayed dildos and vibrators, to the movie houses draped in advertising for the latest hardcore cinematic sensation from the undisputed masters of the genre — Curt Nilsson, Lasse Braun, Ole Ege and the Theander brothers. But where other countries would have relegated their wares to the shoebox cinemas in the local tenderloin, Denmark rejoiced in their absorption into the mainstream.

So did de Renzy. A full-length documentary presentation, *Pornography in Denmark: A New Approach,* opened at the Screening Room in early 1970 and grossed $25,000 in one week. It was also bust-proof, all the more so after de Renzy changed its title to *Censorship in Denmark* and began advertising in the mainstream press.

So far as American audiences were concerned, *Censorship in Denmark* displayed some of the most explicit sex ever screened outside of a stag showing, including a live lesbian sex act, some "behind the scenes" style footage of a Danish sex film and an extraordinary interview with an actress named Toni, who sits quietly naked, talking about the pleasures (carnal and otherwise) she gets from her work, intercut with scenes from a stag that she, her boyfriend and a second woman had recently made.

Those sequences are now rightly lionized as the first genuine stag footage ever to be shown in "mainstream" American cinema and, according to the letter of the law, the whole thing was legal. De Renzy had not, though his detractors howled otherwise, made a sex movie. He had made a movie *about* sex movies.

Censorship in Denmark wound up playing cinemas across the country, even attracting the attentions of *New York Times* reviewer Vincent Canby, who praised it as "an impolite film that makes very little pretense of being anything else," while observing that, while "some of the sequences . . . are erotic . . . it is a fleeting, certainly harmless kind of eroticism that depends largely on shock and curiosity, which turn into an almost scholarly interest and then dwindle into a sort of arrogant boredom."[9] Indeed, of all the criticisms that can and have been laid at the door of the full-length erotic feature, that is possibly the most lingering. You can get way too much of a good thing.

De Renzy's documentary was followed into the theaters by the first full-length effort by a Brooklyn newcomer, hairdresser-turned-director Gerard Damiano. *Sex U.S.A.* sought to contrast Scandinavian attitudes toward sexuality with those prevalent in turn-of-the-decade America. With the pairing of the then unknown (but soon to be legendary) Linda Boreman —soon to be Lovelace — and Harry Reems very visible in the cast, a roomful of "young people" discussed and demonstrated their own sexual preferences, while a round-table discussion on the nature of so-called pornography introduced a sociological angle to the proceedings.

It was a dry and often boring production, its antiseptic opinions and actions so ultimately dull that even the hardcore content could not rescue it. But both critical and public response saw *Sex U.S.A.* echo the success of *Censorship in Denmark* and, while Damiano returned to shooting stag movies as he planned his next full-length effort, de Renzy turned his attention to immortalizing them.

The History of the Blue Movie, essentially a visual companion to the books that were already flooding out, was a compilation of stags (many of which, though it was not stated, were his own productions) run together with a narrative based around *Playboy's* November 1967 history of the stag film.

Opening, inevitably, with *A Free Ride*, *The History of the Blue Movie* traveled on through *On the Beach*, the *Buried Treasure* cartoon, *Keyhole Portraits*, *The Nun's Story*, Candy Barr's *Smart Aleck!* and de Renzy's own *The Masseuse*, a selection that even today, with so many more stags having been rediscovered and reissued to the public, is difficult to argue with. Certainly no history of the genre could be without them. The entire experience wrapped up with another de Renzy production, a mini-documentary that follows a young couple through the filming of a stag movie at the Screening Room itself.

The success of *A History of the Blue Movie* inevitably spun off a wealth of follow-ups, all likewise mining the stag archive for the majority of their length, but shot through with either documentary or interview material: Bill Osco's *Hollywood Blue*, J. Nehemiah's seldom-seen *Making the Blue Movie* and others. Later still, in 1974, British directors Peter Neal and Anthony Stern's eighty-five-minute collage of generally Edwardian-plus film footage, *Ain't Misbehavin'*, incorporated stags alongside vaudeville dance routines and minstrel shows, family vacations and primitive newsreels in an exhilarating helter-skelter of flickering imagery. There was no actual sex depicted in the film (Britain's ferocious obscenity laws saw to that), but still there was sufficient suggestion to ensure that the entire movie house would be staring intently at the screen, scanning for the remote possibility that the editor's scissors had missed a crucial frame.

But historical documentaries were not the only long-form films now taking wing. Ten minutes across town from the Screening Room, the Presidio on Chestnut Street was also enjoying a boom, courtesy of director Allan Silliphant's *The Stewardesses*.

Pieced together from a series of soft-core stags that Silliphant had shot in 3-D sometime before, *The Stewardesses* documented the adventures of an airline flight crew during the eighteen-hour break between landing in L.A. and departing for Honolulu the following day. Fifty-six different girls and a bewildering welter of storylines then filled in the gaps.

The Stewardesses was not a hardcore film. Rather, it was more akin to the bawdy sex comedies the British film industry was then just beginning to produce, films with titles like *The Nine Ages of Nakedness* and *Some Like It Sexy*. It did feature a lot of nudity, though. The plot essentially lurched from one sexual situation to another and, at a time when air hostesses were up there with nurses and schoolgirls among the most sexually desirable of all feminine stereotypes, it featured a lot of uniformed lovelies as well. Plus, it was filmed in 3-D, a device that played havoc with the rampant libidos that sat in the stalls waiting for the first monster breast to swing out of the cockpit.

Three weeks after opening, *The Stewardesses* had grossed $18,000, outstripping every other movie in town, including *Love Story, Ryan's Daughter* and *Gimme Shelter*. By May 1971, on the eve of the Cannes Film Festival, *The Stewardesses'* earnings topped $5 million. And that total was derived from a mere seventy theaters nationwide.

The movie gathered further plaudits when it was revealed that it was actually being reedited, even while it played in the theater. Almost from the moment *The Stewardesses* started its run, and certainly once the money began rolling in, Silliphant reshot scenes, recut footage and sharpened the dialogue, and then ensured that the prints in the projection booth were altered on a weekly basis. Fans began returning to the theater every week, just to see how the movie had changed.

Watching industry analysts were quick to point out that it was the movie's novelties, as opposed to the acting, that lit such a fire beneath *The Stewardesses'* reputation. But its success nevertheless opened a door through which American cinema would never pass back.

Sherpix, the movie's production company, followed *The Stewardesses* with Bill Osco's *Mona: The Virgin Nymph*. Originally screened only at Osco's own cinema, the Eros in Hollywood, the story possessed little more substance than you'd expect to find in the tale of a prenuptial nymphomaniac celebrating her last days of freedom by fellating every man she can lay her hands on. However, Osco at least offered audiences something new to chew on, both by exploring the reasons behind his heroine's oral fixation and by introducing a genuine element of suspense to the proceedings. Despite her nymphomania, Mona was still a virgin. The question was, would she remain one by the time the film was over?

In a corner of the industry where *The Stewardesses'* $5 million gross was considered miraculous, *Mona* performed at least as well. It even prompted at least one *Village Voice* critic to describe director Osco as the closest thing the erotic-movie industry had to its own Fellini. The *New York Times Sunday Magazine* responded by dubbing de Renzy the industry's Jean-Luc Godard. Now all it needed was a Busby Berkeley, a visionary who could choreograph the genre's elevation out of the art house and into the cinematic mainstream.

This vacancy would not remain unchallenged for long. Leasing an old warehouse on San Francisco's Potrero Hill, the Mitchell Brothers set about erecting what would become the largest soundstage in the city. There, at the rate of one a month, they pumped out a series of plot-based erotic films that reached first for the thirty-minute mark, and then sixty.

Such films — "action beavers," as they were initially termed; swiftly followed by "talking beavers," as sound crept in — were a development the Mitchells neither encouraged nor even appreciated. They made the movies because the marketplace demanded them. It was a purely financial arrangement.

"The purest form of titillation is the single girl auto-masturbation film," Jim Mitchell explained. "And the beaver film was a truer form for getting off on some autoerotic fantasy. When it opened up and you added fucking, you had to show the man and you covered up the girl. It disrupted the autoerotic trend of sex films. It was boring, because all anyone wanted to see was the close-up penetration shots." And, as for the growing insistence among other filmmakers that what they were doing was in some way artistic, he snapped, "The only Art in this business is my brother."[10]

Nevertheless, where the Mitchells led, soon, every aspiring filmmaker in San Francisco . . . California . . . the western states . . . the entire country . . . was following, until New York's *Village Voice* was moved to look back on the controversies that surrounded *I Am Curious — Yellow* and declare, in 1970, "There's no longer any need to be curious, yellow or blue. Gaping cunts and hardened cocks can be seen cavorting in the bloody warm flesh-tones of color film, all in gigantic close-up, on select screens throughout our fair city." That same city's police department sounded almost resigned when it confessed, again in 1970, that the Big Apple now hosted "about 125 establishments catering to the debased fancies of the public through an assortment of sub-moral titillations."

Not all of these establishments left their clientele feeling satisfied. The *Village Voice* reported on a visit to the Mine Cine, a picture house that lured in the unwary with the promise of "watching an actual pornographic film being made. But my appreciation is cut short when the 'director' appears from behind the curtain with a camera that resembles a 1910 Brownie pinhole . . . [and] directs [a] couple into a variety of sexual poses and manipulations, all about as thrilling as a pair of coital chipmunks."[11]

There would be plenty of that over the next few years — just as there had been for the past six decades. The quest to create erotic film's first true blockbuster, meanwhile, continued. And when it was achieved, it was an outsider who pulled it off, a Florida-based hustler whose girlfriend seemed to possess a never-ending supply of startling sexual party tricks, and wasn't ashamed to demonstrate them.

TV Casting Director

Deep Thoughts

Chuck Traynor had been involved in stag movies, he claimed, since the early 1950s. Born in 1937, he was just sixteen or seventeen when he took a part in "a nudist camp movie. On my first shoot, they wasted a whole roll of film because, when I squatted down with my back to the camera, my balls were showing."[1]

It was an inauspicious start, but a few years later, around 1960, Traynor landed another part, following a chance meeting with photographer Bunny Yeager. He was driving dump trucks for Miami's Kendall Canal project at the time and had discovered that pinup girl Maria Stinger, "Miami's Marilyn Monroe," lived nearby. He began haunting the neighborhood, hoping to catch a glimpse of Stinger, but never did. He did, however, pluck up the courage to stop in front of her house one day and watch while another woman unloaded some film equipment on the lawn.

They fell into conversation. Traynor introduced himself as a devout fan of Ms. Stinger; the woman, who turned out to be Yeager, asked if he wanted to make a movie with her. Traynor did not need to be asked twice.

Already regarded as among America's top glamour photographers, Yeager's move into motion pictures was inspired wholly by the success of Russ Meyer's *The Immoral Mr. Teas*. If he could do it, she declared, so could she, even if it did require Yeager and her husband sinking $10,000 — their entire life savings — into the project.

Room Eleven was a voyeuristic study of all the things that happened in one room in a hotel over the course of a succession of guests. Like *The Immoral Mr. Teas*, it was suggestion, not sight, that powered the film's erotic content. "There was no dirty language, no complete nudity and only simulated sex scenes,"[2] Yeager recalled. Traynor, however, was not complaining. Not only did he wind up in bed with Stinger, he also got to "play with her tits,"[3] as he put it.

Yeager made only a handful of movies before the demand that she "make them sexier" saw her lose interest. Traynor, however, could not get enough of the action. In 1968, he bought out an old biker bar on North Miami Beach, rechristened it the Las Vegas Inn and, when it became apparent the clientele was certainly game for something more exciting than the topless dancers that usually entertained the room, Traynor started locking the outside doors and staging nude dancing instead. Soon after, he met Linda Boreman.

In later years, the relationship that was ignited that day would become a veritable battleground between the exponents and the opponents of "pornography," as Boreman's accusations of frightening abuse and violence were countered by equally ferocious denials not only from Traynor, but also from the many people who encountered the couple over the next five years. Wherever the truth may lie, however, one fact is indisputable. Together, Boreman and Traynor were responsible for some of the most extreme American stag films of the era.

Their first efforts, including such titles as *The Foot* and *The Fist*, were shot soon after they met, in Florida. Boreman appeared on camera, while Traynor operated behind the scenes. But it was following their move north to New York, in 1969, that things really started moving.

Sharing an apartment with a hooker named Brandy, who had traveled up from Florida with them, the pair fell in with a local loop producer, the late Ted Snyder (he was shot to death on his Miami front lawn in 1991), and soon the two women were shooting 8mm lesbian loops together, at Snyder's loft on 42nd Street.

Actress Carol Connors, a former regular on television's *The Gong Show*, was another friend. She recalled, "When Chuck was into filmmaking, we got together one night, we all got high and we were feeling very good, and we put together a movie . . . . Linda and I seduced a young girl, and we used a little bit of bondage. I think it turned out quite well."[4]

However, Boreman's New York career continued low-key until Snyder paired her with Rob Everett, a struggling actor who made contact through one of the directors' "Talent Wanted" ads in the back of *Screw* magazine. Later to become considerably better known as Eric Edwards, Everett would be Boreman's partner across some two dozen stags and, when questioned about Traynor's alleged abuse of the girl, he insisted that the only iniquity he ever witnessed was the fact that his costar was paid $10 more than him — he would take home $40 per film, while she received $50.

"Linda was nice," Everett recalled. "She enjoyed working with me. She loved sex. She and Chuck Traynor seemed like normal folks, laid-back. They looked happy together. I never saw Linda with bruises or black eyes. No guns were held to her head to make her perform. She loved what she did."[5]

Soon Everett's wife Cathy was also taking part in his shoots with Boreman, and the team branched out to work with other local directors. Bob Wolf shot their most notorious threesome, the everything-goes *Piss Movie* — which ends with Boreman and Everett urinating over Cathy. It was Wolf, too, who shot the notorious stag in which Boreman, still unsatisfied following a bout of anal sex with Everett, looks around and espies a watching German shepherd.

"I was floored," Everett recalled. "After I finished doing Linda, I just sat back and watched. She was really into it. I was in awe. I had never seen a woman with a dog before, but it became the thing to do. It was a strange period. There were no real laws then. The business was going any which way it could. There were stud dogs and there were losers. We'd have a strange dog come onto the set to do actress A and he wouldn't like her and he wouldn't get into it. So the actress would try placing a hot dog in her pussy and covering it with mayonnaise. But this dog was a stud. He knew what to do."[6]

As to the nature of her relationship with Traynor, the claims and counterclaims that surround this film — Boreman's insistence that she was forced at gunpoint to perform; the independent testimony of everybody else in the room that there was no coercion — will never be satisfactorily resolved. Boreman certainly gained a reputation for her enthusiasm for dogs, however, even reportedly staging special bestiality shows at the Playboy Mansion in West Los Angeles.

The movie itself, however, was never as popular as its notoriety might suggest. As an unnamed producer told author Anthony Crowell, "We got one little girl who loves to blow a dog, but nobody uses her much. That's going a bit too far out. Lots of folk get a little charge out of watching a pretty girl jerk a dog off, but that's about it."[7] (For much the same reason, the Danish actress Bodil Jørgensen gained little more than a cult following in the U.S., despite her ravenous enthusiasm for pigs.)

Nevertheless, Boreman's name quickly reached the ears of one Louis "Butchie" Peraino, a partner in Gerard Damiano's eponymous Film Productions Inc., and, in 1970, the pair recruited her for what would become her big-screen debut, the full-length documentary Sex U.S.A.

It was there that she first encountered actor Harry Reems and, once the movie shoot was over, he joined Boreman in the FPI stable, shooting a clutch of further stags while the director contemplated his next cinematic move. It was Traynor who brought it to him.

The first time Traynor watched Boreman swallow a penis . . . literally take the whole thing into her mouth and down her throat . . . he was astonished. No matter that the act itself was already familiar from the gay movie scene, nor that countless women in heterosexual stags had likewise affected it (the act had been caught on film as far back as the early 1920s' Strictly Union). Boreman brought a whole new dimension to the act — one that, depending upon one's point of view, brought eroticism to an unprecedented level.

Not everybody was impressed. Erotic author Chrissie Bentley

spoke for many when she said, "The problem . . . was, no matter how into it [Boreman] seems to be, the fact is, she really doesn't look good while she's doing it. Her face is all screwed up, there's veins and tendons sticking out. She's not sucking the cock in, she's vomiting it out. It's just not attractive, and any guy on the receiving end of that is going to be thinking, 'Well, it feels great, but does she have to pull those faces?'

"There's a visual aesthetic to blow jobs that goes beyond the actual act, and most guys will tell you, a girl who relaxes into the experience, and looks like she's having the time of her life, is a lot more exciting than one who's straining and spluttering, and looks like she's coughing up a hairball."[8]

Traynor was one of those guys who would argue the contrary. He was also convinced that if something had so profound an effect on him, it was going to floor everybody else. Linda Boreman did not invent the "deep throat" technique of oral lovemaking. But from the moment Traynor coined the term, an awful lot of people would believe that she had.

The movie Damiano shot around Boreman's ability, *Deep Throat*, is little more than sixty minutes long — that is, the length of half a dozen stag movies, and, pound for pound, it comprises considerably less hardcore action than they would. Indeed, the movie shamelessly recycled at least one of the stags Boreman and Harry Reems had already shot for Damiano (fittingly, it featured Boreman in a nurse's uniform), while several of its other sequences might easily have been borrowed from an old road-shower's library.

Its star's name certainly was. It was Damiano who coined the name "Linda Lovelace" for both the movie's lead character and the actress who played her; he told Boreman that he based it on the same alliterative appeal that made goddesses of Brigitte Bardot and Marilyn Monroe. More prosaically, however, the same surname is heard in a stag movie shot almost two decades before.

Prescription for Love, a very rare example of a well-dubbed sound film, opens with a young married woman visiting her doctor. She enters the examination room while her husband waits outside. Both are promptly seduced, the husband by the receptionist (whom

Donald Gilmore identifies as a cocktail waitress from Chicago), and the wife by the physician, who proceeds to school her in the art of oral sex.

Then, as the couple leaves, he addresses her by name . . . Mrs. Lovelace.

Linda, of course, became *Miss* Lovelace and, for the next three decades, until her death following an auto accident in April 2002, she remained *the* face of American adult film, even during those years when she contrarily established herself as its most vociferous foe.

Likewise, from the moment it was released in 1972, *Deep Throat* established itself as, unquestionably, the best-known, the most-discussed and the most overanalyzed erotic movie in history. Every second of the movie's preproduction, filming and promotion has been laid bare in forums whose participants range from prurient thrill-seekers to po-faced academics, while its impact on American cinema, both as the first hardcore movie ever to meet a mainstream audience, and as grandfather-midwife–Fairy Godmother to the entire modern adult industry, will never be repeated.

It was hip as hell. One sequence took on the latest Coca-Cola commercial; another visited Paul McCartney's latest album (1971's *Wildlife*) and dug out the original version of "Love Is Strange" — what else?

Political figureheads, showbiz icons, chat-show hosts — they not only went to see the film, they talked about it as well, not always approvingly, and certainly not in a manner that could be deemed "irresponsible." But, a quarter of a century before the Bill Clinton–Monica Lewinsky scandal shoved oral sex down the throat of Middle America, *Deep Throat* showed that same community what it was in the first place — and maybe taught them some new tricks as well.

Courting couples comprised a major part of the movie's audience, and contemporary accounts of *Deep Throat*'s dramatic impact invariably include at least one testimonial (fictional or actual, it can be difficult to differentiate) in which the awestricken youngsters drive straight to Lover's Lane to try some deep throat of their own.

But old ladies were spotted in the audience as well, and everybody in between.

Even today, it remains the most successful adult movie ever made, and certainly the most profitable. Filmed in Miami for $24,000, its theatrical gross exceeded $25 million, from just seventy-three cities nationwide. Indeed, more than thirty years after it opened, *Deep Throat* remains a watershed moment in American movie history, the moment in which an entire society discovered that dirty movies didn't appeal only to dirty old men.

But it was also the moment when the stag movie left the building.

A Jazz Jag

The noble stag did not die immediately. For a start, there were markets where the prevalent legal situation continued to mitigate against full-length movie production — in the U.K., for example, John Lindsay continued producing stag-length movies up until the time of his final arrest in 1983, and he was not alone in his endeavors. But even there, longer features were finding ways around the law, and it was not long before domestic producers began to follow suit.

Similarly, the ten-to-fifteen-minute time span was too useful to be discarded altogether, although increasingly the demand for such shorts (within the home viewing-market, where 8mm and 16mm projectors continued predominant, and continuing with the home VCR market and the DVD) was met by slicing individual scenes from longer movies.

But it would be several decades more before the true spirit — not to mention the content and attitude — of the original stag movie reasserted itself on the erotic entertainment scene, and it is ironic that technology needed to move on to another level entirely before anything approaching that traditional sensibility could return.

The vehicle that returned the stag to prominence was the Internet, intertwined with the late-1990s boom in readily accessible of digital video recording units. Together, this coupling conspired to unleash an entire new generation of do-it-yourself filmmakers onto the Web sites of the world.

Swiftly absorbed into the now flourishing adult entertainment mainstream, such efforts are not at all disparagingly dubbed "Amateur," and have developed such a vast following that many major DVD manufacturers now actively solicit home movies from their regular viewers. This is a tacit acknowledgment that, no matter how skillfully modern surgical technology can render the "perfect" female and male forms, and no matter how many new positions, variations and even orifices the modern adult movie can discover, there is still a vast audience for nothing more complicated than an ordinary couple having sex in their kitchen.

Moffit Timlake, CEO of the genre's most prolific DVD producer, Homegrown Video, explained, "A lot of [mainstream] porn is just overdirected, and the girls make the same noises in every scene, no matter who they're with, and it's like the stripper mentality. You can tell when they're doing it for the money, and we try to avoid that. People are tired of fully shaven girls with perfectly tan bodies and tits, and they want to come back to reality."[1]

San Diego-based Homegrown started operations in 1982, in the earliest days of the adult industry's VCR-sponsored boom; indeed, before Timlake and brother Farrell took the company over in 1996, Farrell and his wife-to-be were numbered among the amateur film-makers who provided the company with footage.

Since that time, the Timlakes have transformed Homegrown into what *Adult Video News* described as "a profit machine," pumping out what *Newsweek* once called "the longest-running series in the history of porn." August 2006 saw the release, incredibly, of the 685th volume in the company's flagship *Homegrown Video* library, an achievement that proclaims both the phenomenal popularity of the so-called amateur movie and the vast cross-section of people who are interested in making such movies — from, according to the *Adult Video News,* "affluent swingers, to people that literally are living in a trailer home. People shooting in mansions, people that live in a vw bus, and they shoot in the mountains. People having sex in the snow."

As Timlake discusses this, however, one cannot shake the impression that he is describing not only those modern-day enthusiasts who submit their sex lives to the scrutiny of Homegrown's viewership, but also everybody who, over the past hundred years or more, has bared all and more for cameras that care nothing for "personality," "fame" or awards — people who simply enjoy what they do and don't care who's watching.

Blue Vanities' James "Dale" Chastain agreed: "It's only my opinion, of course, but I feel that the producers today have never heard of the words 'tease' or 'erotic.' The videos today are being made for the younger buyer, and us older guys with all the money have been forgotten about. The girls today all look alike, blonde, fake boobs, ugly tattoos, shaved with body piercing. I can still remember when women wore earrings in their *ears.*"[2]

"We look for . . . people who like having real sex," Timlake concluded. "For us, it's all about the heat in the scene, and they have to be happy and smiling and enthusiastic."[3]

Heat and happiness — there are precious few other words in the English language that can more succinctly sum up the stag movie at its best.

Not all of the films that fall into the milieu are great works of art; not all explode with enthusiasm and exuberance. Some are, indeed, as workmanlike as the most gratuitously protracted modern adult mundanity.

But when the cast is in form and the camera's working correctly, when the flesh is willing and the Melty Man's away someplace else, a great stag movie isn't merely the closest thing to sexual perfection it's possible to witness without resorting to private fantasy. Sometimes it can be even better than that.

Acknowledgments

My thanks to everybody who contributed to this book, most of all to Chrissie Bentley, for her invaluable assistance in tracking down both films and filmmakers, and for introducing me to many of the individuals whose words and memories appear in this book.

Chrissie, in turn, would like to acknowledge the website www.eroticstories.com and the overwhelming response she received from its membership when requesting personal memories and recollections of the stag era. For reasons of their own, the majority of these sources either requested total anonymity or suggested an alias I could use — these are noted in the text within quotation marks ("Jimmy," "Rich from Oakland," "Tom from Michigan," etc).

I would also single out "Joan," who could be credited with inspiring this book in the first place; and Jimmy "Dale" Chastain, of Blue Vanities, without whose generosity and knowledge, this book might never have been completed. Also David Hanson, for answering those tricky technical questions, and Carl Bennett (www.silentera.com) for sundry dates and data.

Other invaluable comments and commentaries are acknowledged in the text and the bibliographic notes. However, thanks as always are due to Amy Hanson; to all at ECW Press; and to everybody else who helped bring the beast to life: Anchorite Man; Bateerz and family; Blind Pew; Mrs B East; Bob and Jane, whose entire life has been described as a stag film (scratchy, old and largely incomprehensible); Chris T; Gef the Talking Mongoose; the Gremlins who live in the heat pump; Jo-Ann Greene and K-Mart (not the store!); Karin, Bob and Elsa; Geoff Monmouth; Mrs Nose; Naughty Miranda; Nutkin; Oliver, Trevor and Captain Tobias Wilcox; Sandy, Tony and Macey, Sonny; a lot of Thompsons; and Neville Viking.

Endnotes

CHAPTER ONE

1. David T. Beito, *From Mutual Aid to the Welfare State Fraternal Societies and Social Services, 1890–1967* (University of North Carolina Press, 2000).
2. H.C. Shelby, *Stag Movie Review* (Viceroy Books, 1970).
3. Dwight Swanson, "Home Viewing: Pornography and Amateur Film Collections, A Case Study," *The Moving Image* 2:2, 2005.
4. Hollis Alpert and Arthur Knight, "The History of Sex in Cinema, Part 17," *Playboy,* November 1967.
5. Eric Schaefer, "Dirty Little Secrets: Scholars, Archivists, and Dirty Movies," *The Moving Image* 2:2, 2005.
6. Lo Duc, *L'Érotisme au Cinéma* (JJ Pauvert, 1957).
7. Ado Kyrou, *Amour-Érotisme et Cinéma* (Le Terrain Vague, Paris, 1957).
8. Kenneth Turan and Stephen F. Zito, *Sinema: American Pornographic Films and the People Who Make Them* (Praeger Publishers, 1974).
9. Martin A. Grove and William S. Ruben, *The Celluloid Love Feast: The Story of Erotic Movies* (Lancer Books, 1971).

CHAPTER TWO

1. Charles Musser, interview in *Edison: The Invention of the Movies 1891–1918* (DVD).
2. Quoted by Ray Phillips, *Edison's Kinetoscope and Its Films: A History to 1896* (Greenwood Press, 1997).
3. C.W. Kellogg, "The Great Fair," *Savannah Times*, August 10, 1893.
4. Charles Musser, *Edison Motion Pictures, 1890–1900: An Annotated Filmography* (Smithsonian Institute Press, 1997).
5. Herbert Stone, *The Chap Book* (Chicago, 1896).

CHAPTER THREE

1. Carl Bennett, correspondence with author, April 2006 (www.silentera.com).
2. Anonymous, e-mail interview with author, March 2006.
3. Curt Moreck, *Sittengeschichte des Kinos*, Dresden, 1926 (author's translation).
4. Ibid.
5. Ibid.
6. Kurt Tucholski, *Die Schaubühne*, September 1913 (author's translation).
7. Moreck, op. cit.
8. Eugene O'Neill, quoted in Al Di Lauro, Gerald Rabkin, *Dirty Movies: An Illustrated History of the Stag Film 1915–1970* (Chelsea House, New York, 1976).
9. "Police to Run Down All Illegal Films," *New York Times*, January 12, 1912.

CHAPTER FOUR

1. Kevin Brownlow, *Behind the Mask of Innocence: Sex, Violence, Prudence, Crime: Films of Social Conscience in the Silent Era* (University of California Press, 1990).
2. Professor Frank A. Hoffman (Buffalo State University), "Prolegomena to a Study of Traditional Elements in the Erotic Film," *Journal of American Folklore*, April–June 1965.
3. Paul Keegan, "Prime-Time Porn Borrowing Tactics from the Old Hollywood Studios," *Business 2.0*, June 2003.

CHAPTER FIVE

1. Moreck, op. cit.
2. Gerald R. Scott, "Some Nudity Becomes Art to the 20 Year Vice Foe," New York *Sunday Mirror Magazine* Section, February 3, 1935.
3. Donald H. Gilmore, PhD, *Sex & Censorship in the Visual Arts, Volume II* (Greenleaf Classic, 1969).

CHAPTER SIX

1. Quoted in Moreck, op. cit.
2. Peter Jelavich, *Berlin Cabaret* (Harvard University Press, 1993).
3. Quoted in Jelavich, op. cit.
4. Moreck, op. cit.
5. Alexandre Dupouy, *Collection Privée de Monsieur X* (Editions Astarte, Paris 1996).
6. Private notebook, Paris, December 6, 1931, quoted in Dupouy, op. cit.

CHAPTER SEVEN

1. *Stag*, October 1952.
2. *Man's Exploits*, August 1957.
3. *The Report of the Commission on Obscenity and Pornography* (Random House, 1970).
4. Ibid.
5. Ex-Flapper, "Flapping Not Repented Of," *New York Times,* July 16, 1922.
6. Eleanor Rowland Wembridge, "Petting and the Campus," *Survey,* July 1925.
7. Kyrou, op. cit.
8. Joan Crawford, quoted by Shaun Considine, *Bette & Joan: The Divided Feud* (E.P. Dutton, 1989).

CHAPTER EIGHT

1. Quoted in Nathan W. Pearson, *Goin' to Kansas City* (University of Illinois Press, 1987).
2. Ibid.

3. Gilmore, op. cit.

4. "Joan," interview with author, summer, 1995.

CHAPTER NINE

1. Theodore van de Velde, *Ideal Marriage: Its Physiology and Technique* (Random House, 1931).

2. Candy Barr interview, "Burlesque queen, ex-con, Jack Ruby's pal, porno's first (reluctant) star and a real lady," *Oui*, June 1976.

3. Joseph Slade, *Journal of Film and Video*, 45.2-3.

4. Jenna Jameson with Neil Strauss, *How to Make Love Like a Porn Star: A Cautionary Tale* (Regan Books, 2004).

5. Alpert and Knight, op. cit.

CHAPTER TEN

1. Quoted by Josh Lewin, "She Handles Public Relations for California's Biggest Porno Factory," *Man's World*, Vol. 16, No. 5, October 1970.

2. Jameson and Strauss, op. cit.

3. Quoted by David Kerekes, *Jolly Hockey Sticks! Fleshpot: Cinema's Sexual Myth Makers & Taboo Breakers,* ed. Jack Stevenson (Headpress/Critical Vision, 2000).

4. Quoted by Turan and Zito, op. cit.

5. "Rich from Oakland," email interview with author, March 2006.

CHAPTER ELEVEN

1. Dian Hanson, *History of Men's Magazines* (Taschen, 2004–2006).

2. Quoted in John Nichol and Tony Rennell, *Tail-End Charlies: The Last Battles of the Bomber War 1944–45* (Thomas Dunne Books, 2006).

3. Di Lauro and Rabkin, op. cit.

4. Kyrou, op. cit.

CHAPTER TWELVE

1. Quoted by Jimmy McDonough, *Big Bosoms and Square Jaws* (Crown Publishers, 2005).

2. Testimony to the U.S. Senate Judiciary Committee, Subcommittee to Investigate Juvenile Delinquency (hereafter SIJD).

3. Dwight Swanson, "Home Viewing: Pornography and Amateur Film Collections: A Case Study," *The Moving Image,* 2:2, 2005.

4. "George," e-mail interview with author, March 2006.

5. Quoted in *Man's Exploits,* op. cit.

CHAPTER THIRTEEN

1. *The Report of the Commission on Obscenity and Pornography,* op. cit.

2. Ibid.

3. Alpert and Knight, op. cit.

4. James H. Jones, *Alfred C. Kinsey* (WW Norton & Co., 1997).

5. Anonymous, e-mail interview, March 2006.

6. "Rich from Oakland," op. cit.

7. "George," op. cit.

8. DiLauro and Rabkin, op. cit.

9. Alpert and Knight, op. cit.

10. SIJD, op. cit.

11. *Man's Exploits,* op. cit.

12. SIJD, op. cit.

13. *Man's Exploits,* op. cit.

14. Shelby, op. cit.

15. Gilmore, op. cit.

16. Anonymous, e-mail interview, June 2006.

CHAPTER FOURTEEN

1. Anonymous, e-mail interview, March 2006.

2. Quoted by Ted Jordan, *Norma Jean: My Secret Life with Marilyn Monroe* (William Morrow & Co., 1989).

3. Ibid.

4. Marilyn Monroe, *My Story* (Stein & Day, 1974).

5. David Thomson, "Joan Dearest" (salon.com, November 2001).

6. *Man's Exploits,* op. cit.

7. Barbra Streisand, "Playboy Interview," by Lawrence Grobel, *Playboy,* October 1977.

8. Phil Hall, "Smart Alex," *Film Threat,* February 2006.
9. Candy Barr interview, op. cit.
10. De Lauro and Rabkin, op. cit.

CHAPTER FIFTEEN
1. Horace McCoy, *I Should Have Stayed at Home* (Alfred E Knopf, 1938).
2. William Francis, *Rough on Rats* (William Morrow & Co., 1942).
3. Quoted by Simon Sheridan, *Keeping the British End Up: Four Decades of Saucy Cinema* (Reynolds and Hearn, 2001).
4. Quoted in Knight and Alpert, op. cit.
5. Paul V. Russo, *Stag Starlet* (Midwood, 1961).
6. Adam Coulter, *Sin-ema Queen* (Epic Books, 1961).

CHAPTER SIXTEEN
1. Anthony Crowell, *Stag Films '69* (Barclay House, 1969).
2. Shelby, op. cit.
3. Quoted by Crowell, op. cit.
4. Hanson, op. cit.

CHAPTER SEVENTEEN
1. *Man's Exploits,* op. cit.
2. "Terry," interview with author, January 2006.
3. "Tony," e-mail interview with the author, February 2006.
4. Dale Chastain, interview with the author, June 2006.
5. "Tom from Michigan," e-mail interview with the author, March 2006.
6. "Rich from Oakland," op. cit.
7. Steven Ziplow, *The Film Maker's Guide to Pornography* (Drake Publishers, 1977).
8. Shelby, op. cit.
9. Hanson, op. cit.
10. Grove and Ruben, op. cit.
11. Lewin, op. cit.
12. Sharon, e-mail interview with the author, April 2006.
13. "Rich from Oakland," op. cit.

14. *The Report of the Commission on Obscenity and Pornography*, op. cit.
15. Ibid.
16. "The porn capital of America," *New York Times Sunday Magazine*, January 1971.

CHAPTER EIGHTEEN

1. Moreck, op. cit.
2. Gilbert Kelland, *Crime in London* (Grafton Books, 1989).
3. Kyrou, op. cit.
4. Quoted by Anthony Frewin, *London Blues* (No Exit Press, 1997).
5. Simon Sheridan, *Keeping the British End Up* (Reynolds & Hearn, 2001).
6. Michael W., e-mail interview with the author, February 2006.
7. Kelland, op. cit.
8. Quoted by David Hebditch and Nick Anning, *Porn Gold: Inside the Pornography Business* (Faber & Faber, 1988).
9. Mary's suicide note, quoted in *Come Play With Me: The Life and Films of Mary Millington* (Fab Press, 1999).

CHAPTER NINETEEN

1. Quoted by Jack Vizzard, *See No Evil — Life Inside a Hollywood Censor* (Simon & Schuster, 1970).
2. Ibid.
3. Turan and Zito, op. cit.
4. Crowell, op. cit.
5. Harry Reems interview, "Porn Again Christian," *The Observer*, by David A. Keeps, May 22, 2005.
6. Quoted in Turan and Zito, op. cit.
7. Quoted by John Hubner, *Bottom Feeders: From Free Love to Hard Core: The Rise and Fall of Counterculture Heroes Jim and Artie Mitchell* (Doubleday 2001).
8. Ibid.
9. Vincent Canby, *New York Times*, June 1970.
10. *Village Voice*, 1970.
11. Ibid.

CHAPTER TWENTY

1. Quoted by Les McNeil and Jennifer Osborne, *The Other Hollywood: The Uncensored Oral History of the Porn Film Industry* (Regan Books, 2005).
2. Ibid.
3. Ibid.
4. Carol Connors, interview, *Midnight Blue,* April 1975.
5. Quoted by McNeil and Osborne, op. cit.
6. Ibid.
7. Quoted by Crowell, op. cit.
8. Bentley, interview with author, March 2006.

EPILOGUE

1. Moffit Timlake, interview, "Homegrown Video: The Ultimate Amateur Evergreen," *Adult Video News,* April 2006.
2. Chastain, op. cit.
3. Timlake, op. cit.

OTHER SOURCES

A Man's Guide to the Sexual Scene (International Publications, 1963).

Adult Video News (various issues).

Bookleggers and Smuthounds: The Trade in Erotica 1920–1940 (University of Pennsylvania Press, 1999).

The Celluloid Love Feast: The Story of Erotic Movies by Martin A. Grove and William S. Ruben (Lancer Books, 1971).

Censored: The Story of Film Censorship in Britain by Tom Dewe Matthews (Chatto & Windus, 1994).

Cinema au Naturel: A History of the Nudist Film by Mark Storey (Naturist Education Foundation Inc., 2003).

Doing Rude Things: The History of the British Sex Film 1957–1981 by David McGillivray (Sun Tavern Fields, 1992).

Fleshpot: Cinema's Sexual Myth Makers and Taboo Breakers, ed. Jack Stevenson (Critical Vision, 2000).

Forbidden Films: Censorship Histories of 125 Motion Pictures by Dawn B. Soca (Checkmark Books, 2001).

Girls Who Do Stag Movies: Intimate Interviews with Female Sex Stars

(Melrose Square Publishing Company, 1973).

Grindhouse: The Forbidden World of "Adults Only" Cinema by Eddie Muller and Daniel Faris (St. Martin's Griffin, 1996).

Historical Dictionary of American Slang by Jonathan E Lighter (Random House, 1994).

Hollywood v Hard Core: How the Struggle over Censorship Saved the Modern Film Industry by Jon Lewis (New York University Press, 2002).

International Exposure: Perspectives on Modern European Pornography 1800-2000, ed. Lisa Z. Sigel (Rutgers University Press, 2005).

It's a Man's World: Men's Adventure Magazines, the Postwar Pulps by Adam Parfrey (Feral House, 2003).

The Lover's Tongue: A Merry Romp through the Language of Love and Sex by Mark Morton (Insomniac Press, 2003).

Men's Adventure Magazines: The Rich Oberg Collection (Taschen Books, 2004).

Porno Copia: Porn, Sex, Technology and Desire by Laurence O'Toole (Serpents' Tail, 1998).

Sex and the Teenage Girl by Denham S. Farnsworth (Council Publishing Corp., 1965).

The Sex Industry by George Csicsery (Signet, 1973).

Sin-a-Rama: Sleaze Sex Paperbacks of the Sixties, ed. Brittany A Daley (Feral House, 2005).

Sleazoid Express by Bill Landis and Michelle Clifford (Fireside Books, 2002).

The Stag Film Report by Larry Harris (Socio Library, 1971).

Striptease: The Untold History of the Girlie Show by Rachel Shteir (Oxford University Press, 2004).

Tijuana Bibles: Art and Wit in America's Forbidden Funnies 1930s–1950s by Bob Adelman (Simon & Schuster, 1997).

The X Factory: Inside the American Hardcore Film Industry by Anthony Petkovich (Critical Vision, 1997).

United States of America vs Sex: How the Meese Corporation Lied About Pornography by Philip Noble and Eric Nadler (Minotaur Press, 1986)

Filmography

Smart Aleck!

It is impossible to compile an accurate record of every stag film made, or even those known to have survived.

The following catalogs those that are currently available to the North American market, together with the title of the DVD collection on which it can most conveniently be found.

For American, Latin and many European stags, the most comprehensive collection is that released across ninety-three separate volumes by Blue Vanities, since 1987 the world's premier producer of DVD and VHS stag compilations. Blue Vanities' *Classic Stags* collections are of value not only for the quality of the prints employed, but also for the detailed information provided for each individual stag — services that most of the rival manufacturers do not offer. Blue Vanities is also the only major manufacturer to differentiate between stags and later peep-show and European loops. (These are available as a separate series within the Blue Vanities catalog.)

For French stags, collectors are directed toward Cult Epics' Vintage Erotica series, itself a DVD reissue of the earlier *Les Archives d'Eros* VHS series.

Please note: dates and attributions are approximate.

U.S. PRODUCTIONS

Adios, 1965–66 *(Classic Stags: Volume 266)*

Adventure *(Classic Stags: Volume 60)*

Adventures of Christine, The, 1926 *(Classic Stags: Volume 118)*

Affairs of Jane Winslow, 1935–40 *(Classic Stags: Volume 6)*

Agents Office, 1960s *(Classic Stags: Volume 127)*

All Day Sucker, 1960s *(Classic Stags: Volume 7)*

All Hands on Dick, 1960s *(Classic Stags: Volume 138)*

All Six, 1960s *(Classic Stags: Volume 411)*

Amateur Nudes, 1960s *(Classic Stags: Volume 235)*

Amateur, 1950s *(Classic Stags: Volume 287)*

Anita and Dildo, 1960s *(Classic Stags: Volume 24)*

Anniversary Party, 1949–52 *(Classic Stags: Volume 335)*

Announcer, The, 1960s *(Classic Stags: Volume 219)*

Anxious Maiden Gets Relief, An, 1948–52 *(Classic Stags: Volume 182)*

Anyone Can Play *(Vintage Porn from the Past)*

Anytime, Anywhere, Anyplace, 1960s *(Classic Stags: Volume 288)*

Apartment, The, 1960s *(Classic Stags: Volume 336)*

Apple, the Knockers and the Coke, The, no date *(Classic Stags: Volume 8)*

Artist and I, The, 1967 *(Classic Stags: Volume 310)*

Artist and Models, 1958–63 *(Classic Stags: Volume 163)*

Artist Model, 1946–50 *(Classic Stags: Volume 136)*

Artist, The, 1950s *(Classic Stags: Volume 154)*

Ass, 1960s *(Classic Stags: Volume 288)*

Atomic Jazzer, 1951–54 *(Classic Stags: Volume 260)*

Author's True Story, 1932–36 *(Classic Stags: Volume 182)*

Auto-Sex, 1968 *(Classic Stags: Volume 181)*

Aviator, The 1930s *(Classic Stags: Volume 26)*

Baby Sitter, 1947–49 *(Classic Stags: Volume 101)*

Bachelors Dream, 1952–54 *(Classic Stags: Volume 265)*

Bachelor's Dream, 1960s *(Classic Stags: Volume 60)*

Back Door Burglar, 1960s *(Classic Stags: Volume 127)*

Ballin' Baby, 1968 *(Classic Stags: Volume 210)*

Ballin' the Jack, 1960s *(Classic Stags: Volume 138)*
Ballin', early 1960s *(Classic Stags: Volume 22)*
Balling, 1960s *(Classic Stags: Volume 288)*
Ball'n Babes, 1960s *(Classic Stags: Volume 96)*
Banana Split, 1960s *(Classic Stags: Volume 60)*
Bang-Bang, 1960s *(Classic Stags: Volume 96)*
Bar Room Pickup, 1950s *(Classic Stags: Volume 109)*
Barbara and Steve, 1960s, *(Classic Stags: Volume 410)*
Bare Interlude, late 1950s *(Classic Stags: Volume 96)*
Bareback Rider, 1957–64 *(Classic Stags: Volume 210)*
Barker, The, 1948–52 *(Classic Stags: Volume 235)*
Bashful Bo, The, 1948–52 *(Classic Stags: Volume 264)*
Bashful Fish, The, 1950–1957 *(Classic Stags: Volume 410)*
Bashful Fisherman (See *Fisher Woman*)
Bathroom Frolics, 1949–52 *(Classic Stags: Volume 26)*
Bathroom Whims, 1958–62 *(Classic Stags: Volume 214)*
Beach Bums I, 1960s *(Classic Stags: Volume 219)*
Beach Bums II, 1960s *(Classic Stags: Volume 219)*
Beachcombers, late 1940s *(Classic Stags: Volume 139)*
Beat Me Daddy, 1930s *(Classic Stags: Volume 213)*
Bed Party, 1967 *(Classic Stags: Volume 96)*
Bed Session, 1960s *(Classic Stags: Volume 96)*
Bed Time, 1960s *(Classic Stags: Volume 183)*
Bedroom Frolics, 1940s *(Classic Stags: Volume 111)*
Bedtime, 1965–66 *(Classic Stags: Volume 312)*
Bellhop, The (*aka* The Intruder), 1930–35 *(Classic Stags: Volume 264)*
Big Blow, 1950s *(Classic Stags: Volume 237)*
Big Boy, 1967–68 *(Classic Stags: Volume 214)*
Big Tit Tease, 1961–65 *(Classic Stags: Volume 235)*
Bill Collector, The, 1947–51 *(Classic Stags: Volume 26)*
Black and White, 1940s *(Classic Stags: Volume 285)*
Black and White, 1967 *(Classic Stags: Volume 177)*
Black Impulse, 1960s *(Classic Stags: Volume 336)*
Black Market Potato Hosen, 1948–52 *(Classic Stags: Volume 111)*
Black Stinger, 1950s *(Classic Stags: Volume 180)*
Blackballed, 1940s *(Classic Stags: Volume 237)*

Blanco y Negro, 1930s *(Classic Stags: Volume 26)*

Blends, 1930s *(Classic Stags: Volume 335)*

Blonde Hitchhiker, The, 1955–56 *(Classic Stags: Volume 158)*

Blondie and Friend, 1960s *(Classic Stags: Volume 186)*

Blondie Blondell (See *Matinee Idol*)

Blow Job, The, 1940s *(Classic Stags: Volume 20)*

Blow Me Down, 1965–67 *(Classic Stags: Volume 215)*

Blowin' With Blondie, 1940s *(Classic Stags: Volume 134)*

Blue Belle (Pts. 1 and 2), 1950s *(Classic Stags: Volume 158)*

Blue Denim, 1960–65 *(Classic Stags: Volume 137)*

Blue Plate Special (Pt. 1), 1940s *(Classic Stags: Volume 213)*

Bob and Carol, 1960s *(Classic Stags: Volume 288)*

Bookie, The, 1958–63 *(Classic Stags: Volume 102)*

Bottoms Up, 1960s, *(Classic Stags: Volume 7)*

Boy Friend, The, 1958–63 *(Classic Stags: Volume 363)*

Boy Next Door, 1960s *(Classic Stags: Volume 311)*

Boy Wanted, 1966 *(Classic Stags: Volume 22)*

Boys Will Be Boys, 1960s *(Classic Stags: Volume 187)*

Breakfast, 1950s *(Classic Stags: Volume 187)*

Breakfast, The, 1958–63 *(Classic Stags: Volume 361)*

Buns Hai, 1960s *(Classic Stags: Volume 188)*

Burglar, The (*aka* Share and Share Alike), 1930s *(Classic Stags: Volume 158)*

Burglar Makes a Deal, The, 1945–50 *(Classic Stags: Volume 262)*

Burglar, The, 1950s *(Classic Stags: Volume 185)*

Busty, 1949–52 *(Classic Stags: Volume 213)*

Busty and Lusty, 1960s *(Classic Stags: Volume 287)*

Busty Babe, 1960s *(Classic Stags: Volume 288)*

Busty Model, 1960s *(Classic Stags: Volume 312)*

Busy Club, 1930s *(Classic Stags: Volume 260)*

Busy Girl, 1939–44 *(Classic Stags: Volume 262)*

Butcher Boy, 1950–55 *(Classic Stags: Volume 135)*

Butt Humper, 1960s *(Classic Stags: Volume 363)*

Call for Dr. Handsome (see *Roaring Twenties*)

Call Girl, The, 1948–52 *(Classic Stags: Volume 235)*

Call WA9-XXXX, 1960s *(Classic Stags: Volume 311)*

Camera Bug (*aka* Susie the Model), 1960–62 *(Classic Stags: Volume 133)*

Camera Man, The 1958–62 *(Classic Stags: Volume 102)*

Camera Shy, 1950s *(Classic Stags: Volume 216)*

Candy, 1960s *(Classic Stags: Volume 155)*

Card Game, 1950s *(Classic Stags: Volume 60)*

Carry On, 1960s *(Classic Stags: Volume 238)*

Cast Call, 1960s *(Classic Stags: Volume 219)*

Casting Couch, The, 1924 *(Classic Stags: Volume 264)*

Caught in the Act, 1964–66 *(Classic Stags: Volume 155)*

Caught With The Girlfriend, 1960s *(Classic Stags: Volume 361)*

Census Taker, 1946–50 *(Classic Stags: Volume 265)*

Change Partners, 1965–66 *(Classic Stags: Volume 123)*

Changing Partners, early 1950s *(Classic Stags: Volume 9)*

Cherry's Galore, 1960s *(Classic Stags: Volume 218)*

China Girl, 1950s *(Classic Stags: Volume 188)*

Chubby, 1960s *(Classic Stags: Volume 236)*

Clean and Horny, 1960s *(Classic Stags: Volume 363)*

Clean Floors, 1950s *(Classic Stags: Volume 10)*

Close Ups, 1960s *(Classic Stags: Volume 24)*

Clown, The, 1940–50 *(Classic Stags: Volume 235)*

Club, The, 1930s *(Classic Stags: Volume 118)*

Cocktails, 1960s *(Classic Stags: Volume 124)*

Coffee Break, 1950s *(Classic Stags: Volume 216)*

Coffee Break, 1960s *(Classic Stags: Volume 60)*

Coffee, Tea or Cum, 1930s *(Classic Stags: Volume 159)*

Come and Get It, 1960s *(Classic Stags: Volume 127)*

Come on Over, 1940s *(Classic Stags: Volume 184)*

Come Up For Air, 1960s *(Classic Stags: Volume 138)*

Coming Out (*aka* Dice Game), 1940s *(Classic Stags: Volume 119)*

Company Coming, 1950s *(Classic Stags: Volume 185)*

Cookie & the Nightmare in Positions, 1948 *(Classic Stags: Volume 262)*

Count Me In, 1960s *(Classic Stags: Volume 236)*

Country Cousin, 1967 *(Classic Stags: Volume 189)*

Cover Girl, 1948–55 *(Classic Stags: Volume 136)*

Cramming Students, 1950s *(Classic Stags: Volume 236)*
Crazy Cat House, 1930s *(Classic Stags: Volume 118)*
Crib Time, 1965–66 *(Classic Stags: Volume 312)*
Cuntinuity, 1930s *(Classic Stags: Volume 136)*
Custom Fit, 1960s *(Classic Stags: Volume 237)*
Daily Duty *(Reel Old Timers Volume Eight)*
Dance Fever, 1960s *(Classic Stags: Volume 219)*
Dancing Party, 1966 *(Classic Stags: Volume 181)*
Dancing Teacher, 1935 *(Classic Stags: Volume 260)*
Dancing Teacher, 1968 *(Classic Stags: Volume 27)*
Dead-Pan, 1940s *(Classic Stags: Volume 156)*
Debbie's Doctor (See *Nympho, The*)
Den Party, 1960s *(Classic Stags: Volume 156)*
Dentist, The, 1947 *(Classic Stags: Volume 6)*
Desk, The, 1948–52 *(Classic Stags: Volume 102)*
Detective One Hung Low (See *Hot Hotel*)
Dice Diddlers, The *(Vintage Erotica from the 40s Volume Three)*
Dice Game (See *Coming Out*)
Dice Game, The, 1950s *(Classic Stags: Volume 137)*
Dick and Jane, 1960s *(Classic Stags: Volume 288)*
Dick and Peggy, Early 1930s *(Classic Stags: Volume 138)*
Ding-a-Ling, 1950s *(Classic Stags: Volume 7)*
Dinner Time, 1966 *(Classic Stags: Volume 215)*
Director, The, 1940s *(Classic Stags: Volume 178)*
Dirty Pictures, 1960s *(Classic Stags: Volume 187)*
Do It, 1960s *(Classic Stags: Volume 287)*
Do Me Again, 1966 *(Classic Stags: Volume 189)*
Doc and Cher, 1968 *(Classic Stags: Volume 188)*
Doctor Fix-Em, 1958–62 *(Classic Stags: Volume 10)*
Doctor in Bed, 1960s *(Classic Stags: Volume 155)*
Doctor, The, 1934 *(Classic Stags: Volume 6)*
Doctor's Office, 1940s *(Classic Stags: Volume 124)*
Doing Their Thing, 1960s *(Classic Stags: Volume 218)*
Donnie and Clyde, 1960s *(Classic Stags: Volume 285)*
Don't Forget to Slide, early 1940s *(Classic Stags: Volume 25)*
Dopping, 1950s *(Classic Stags: Volume 25)*

Double Date *(Reel Old Timers Volume Two)*
Double Dildo, 1960s *(Classic Stags: Volume 310)*
Double Play, 1950s *(Classic Stags: Volume 154)*
Double Trouble, 1960s *(Classic Stags: Volume 237)*
Down the Hatch, 1960s *(Classic Stags: Volume 238)*
Dr. Hardon's Injections, 1931–36 *(Classic Stags: Volume 111)*
Dr. Longpeter, 1940s *(Classic Stags: Volume 119)*
Dream Job, 1950s *(Classic Stags: Volume 335)*
Dream On, 1960s *(Classic Stags: Volume 212)*
Dreamer, The *(Black & White Oldies Uncovered)*
Drunkards Paradise, 1948–52 *(Classic Stags: Volume 137)*
Egyptian Adventure, An, late 1920s *(Classic Stags: Volume 159)*
Electrician, The, 1961–62 *(Classic Stags: Volume 10)*
Enter the Wife, 1960s *(Classic Stags: Volume 336)*
Errand Boy, 1964–66 *(Classic Stags: Volume 210)*
Excuse Us, 1960s *(Classic Stags: Volume 266)*
Exercising, 1950s *(Classic Stags: Volume 10)*
Exotic Harem, 1960s *(Classic Stags: Volume 411)*
Experienced Honeymooners, 1936–38 *(Classic Stags: Volume 118)*
Family, The, 1960s *(Classic Stags: Volume 22)*
Fancy Meeting You Here, 1950s *(Classic Stags: Volume 22)*
Fanny Hill, 1963–66 *(Classic Stags: Volume 177)*
Fanny, late 1960s *(Classic Stags: Volume 22)*
Farmer's Daughter, 1930s *(Classic Stags: Volume 134)*
Fast Action (See *Fruit Salad*)
Fast and Furious, 1960s *(Classic Stags: Volume 188)*
Fat Man, 1965 *(Classic Stags: Volume 163)*
Father and the Nun, 1960s *(Classic Stags: Volume 163)*
Fatso, 1940s *(Classic Stags: Volume 136)*
Favorite Pastime, 1947–48 *(Classic Stags: Volume 265)*
Feel Those Jugs, 1960s *(Classic Stags: Volume 212)*
Fiesta, 1948–52 *(Classic Stags: Volume 261)*
Finger on the Problem, 1960s *(Classic Stags: Volume 187)*
Fireside Funnzies, Sex American Style #9, 1960s *(Classic Stags: Volume 8)*
Fireside Lights, 1958–62 *(Classic Stags: Volume 182)*

First Experience, 1950s *(Classic Stags: Volume 184)*

Fisher Woman (*aka* Bashful Fisherman), 1950–55 *(Classic Stags: Volume 135)*

Five Way Free for All, 1960s *(Classic Stags: Volume 286)*

Flat Tire, The, 1945–50 *(Classic Stags: Volume 265)*

Flower Girl, 1930s *(Classic Stags: Volume 178)*

For Bernie, 1958–62 *(Classic Stags: Volume 163)*

For Johnny, 1958–62 *(Classic Stags: Volume 184)*

Forced Entry, 1950s *(Classic Stags: Volume 10)*

Forced Entry, 1960s *(Classic Stags: Volume 310)*

Forest Friends, 1960s *(Classic Stags: Volume 27)*

Forget the Magazine, 1960s *(Classic Stags: Volume 237)*

Four for Fun, 1950s *(Classic Stags: Volume 217)*

Foxy Fireman, The, 1956–60 *(Classic Stags: Volume 135)*

Freakin' Off, 1960s *(Classic Stags: Volume 178)*

Free Groceries, 1960s *(Classic Stags: Volume 186)*

Free Lunch, 1956–62 *(Classic Stags: Volume 210)*

Free Ride, A (*aka* A Grass Sandwich), 1915 *(Classic Stags: Volume 111)*

French Striptease, mid-1940s *(Classic Stags: Volume 158)*

Friendly Relations, 1965 *(Classic Stags: Volume 109)*

Frigin' Fun, 1960s *(Classic Stags: Volume 213)*

Fruit Salad (*aka* Fast Action), 1948–52 *(Classic Stags: Volume 261)*

Fruit Salad, 1948–52 *(Classic Stags: Volume 101)*

Fuck My Ass, Climax #11, 1960s *(Classic Stags: Volume 8)*

Fuck You Tony, 1960s *(Classic Stags: Volume 217)*

Full Recovery, 1960s *(Classic Stags: Volume 124)*

Fun for Three, 1968–69 *(Classic Stags: Volume 177)*

Fun in the Sun, 1960s *(Classic Stags: Volume 184)*

Fun in the Tub, 1960s *(Classic Stags: Volume 187)*

Fun in the Woods, 1960s *(Classic Stags: Volume 238)*

G.I. Joe Returns Home, 1945–50 *(Classic Stags: Volume 135)*

G.I. Joe, 1950s *(Classic Stags: Volume 184)*

Gamblers, 1960s *(Classic Stags: Volume 361)*

Games You Love to Play *(Golden Age of Erotic Video Volume One)*

Gang's All Here, The, 1960s *(Classic Stags: Volume 7)*

Gay Count, The 1932 *(Classic Stags: Volume 182)*

Gay Girls, 1960s *(Classic Stags: Volume 24)*

Gay Times (Merry-Go-Round Pt. 2), 1947–50 *(Classic Stags: Volume 264)*

Gentlemen Prefer Blondes, 1930s *(Classic Stags: Volume 178)*

George and the Hillbilly, 1955–56 *(Classic Stags: Volume 157)*

Girl Farm, 1960s *(Classic Stags: Volume 183)*

Girl in Need, 1960s *(Classic Stags: Volume 311)*

Girl Named Beth, 1964–66 *(Classic Stags: Volume 96)*

Girl Next Door *(Vintage Porn from the Past)*

Girl of My Dreams, 1940s *(Classic Stags: Volume 133)*

Girls Best Friend, 1966–68 *(Classic Stags: Volume 335)*

Girls Eat Men, 1960s *(Classic Stags: Volume 311)*

Girls From Apartment 13 *(aka* Hot Party), 1926–28 *(Classic Stags: Volume 111)*

Girls Next Door, The 1967–68, *(Classic Stags: Volume 60)*

Glamour Girls, 1940s *(Classic Stags: Volume 136)*

Go Man Go (Pts. 1 and 2), 1960s *(Classic Stags: Volume 286)*

Go the Distance, 1960s *(Classic Stags: Volume 287)*

Going Down, 1930s *(Classic Stags: Volume 262)*

Goldilock and Bare, 1968 *(Classic Stags: Volume 361)*

Goldilocks Rapes The Wolf, 1964–66 *(Classic Stags: Volume 123)*

Good Deal, 1960s *(Classic Stags: Volume 156)*

Good Morning, 1960s *(Classic Stags: Volume 238)*

Good Time, 1960s *(Classic Stags: Volume 236)*

Good to the Last Drop, early 1930s *(Classic Stags: Volume 138)*

Goodyear, 1950s *(Classic Stags: Volume 163)*

Grass Sandwich, A (See *Free Ride, A)*

Great Fun, 1960s *(Classic Stags: Volume 237)*

Greek Way, The, 1960s *(Classic Stags: Volume 60)*

Greek, The, 1950s *(Classic Stags: Volume 285)*

Greek, The, 1960s *(Classic Stags: Volume 212)*

Gregory Pecker and Victor Manure, 1940s *(Classic Stags: Volume 118)*

Grocer Boy, The, 1965–66 *(Classic Stags: Volume 263)*

Grunt 'N Groan, 1968–69 *(Classic Stags: Volume 214)*

Guess What, 1960s *(Classic Stags: Volume 411)*

Gun for Hire, 1953 *(Classic Stags: Volume 260)*

Hairdresser, The, 1940s *(Classic Stags: Volume 135)*

Hairdresser, The, 1960s *(Classic Stags: Volume 127)*

Hammock Roll, 1960s *(Classic Stags: Volume 286)*

Handyman, The, 1950s *(Classic Stags: Volume 6)*

Handyman, The, 1930s *(Classic Stags: Volume 261)*

Happy Birthday, 1960s *(Classic Stags: Volume 138)*

Happy Feet, 1966 *(Classic Stags: Volume 312)*

Havin' Fun, 1960s *(Classic Stags: Volume 217)*

Heads and Tails, 1960s *(Classic Stags: Volume 288)*

Heat Wave, 1966–67 *(Classic Stags: Volume 155)*

Held's Angel, 1966 *(Classic Stags: Volume 215)*

Hell Fire Club, 1960s *(Classic Stags: Volume 310)*

Help Wanted, 1965–66 *(Classic Stags: Volume 180)*

Her Lady Love, 1927–32 *(Classic Stags: Volume 235)*

Here Pussy, 1950s *(Classic Stags: Volume 213)*

Hide and Go-Seek, 1930s *(Classic Stags: Volume 157)*

High Rise, 1960s *(Classic Stags: Volume 188)*

Highway Romance, A, 1930s *(Classic Stags: Volume 134)*

Hillbillies' Frolics, 1930s *(Classic Stags: Volume 134)*

Hippies Flower Party (Pt. 1), 1966–68 *(Classic Stags: Volume 60)*

Hippies, The, 1960s *(Classic Stags: Volume 238)*

Hippy Sex, 1960s *(Classic Stags: Volume 155)*

Hippy Sex, 1960s *(Classic Stags: Volume 27)*

Holly's Girl, 1960s *(Classic Stags: Volume 23)*

Home Cookin', 1966–67 *(Classic Stags: Volume 123)*

Home Movies, 1950–55 *(Classic Stags: Volume 185)*

Honeymoon Cottage, 1948–50 *(Classic Stags: Volume 101)*

Hooked on Women, 1960s *(Classic Stags: Volume 187)*

Horny Housewife, 1969 *(Classic Stags: Volume 188)*

Horny, 1960s *(Classic Stags: Volume 310)*

Hot and Bothered, 1960s *(Classic Stags: Volume 285)*

Hot Blonde, 1960s *(Classic Stags: Volume 238)*

Hot Delivery, 1960s *(Classic Stags: Volume 410)*

Hot Hotel (*aka* Det One Hung Low), 1948–52 *(Classic Stags: Volume 102)*

Hot in the Box, 1960s *(Classic Stags: Volume 179)*

Hot Lovers, 1960s *(Classic Stags: Volume 219)*
Hot Magazine, 1950s *(Classic Stags: Volume 183)*
Hot Panties, 1966–67 *(Classic Stags: Volume 184)*
Hot Party (see *Girls From Apartment 13*)
Hot Stuff, 1950s *(Classic Stags: Volume 262)*
House Calls, 1930s *(Classic Stags: Volume 178)*
How to be Pals, 1960s *(Classic Stags: Volume 155)*
Hunter, The, 1950s *(Classic Stags: Volume 157)*
Hycock's Dancing School, 1932–36 *(Classic Stags: Volume 119)*
Hypnosis, 1966–68 *(Classic Stags: Volume 214)*
Hypnotist, The, 1932–36 *(Classic Stags: Volume 159)*
In Crowd, The, 1960s *(Classic Stags: Volume 23)*
Indian Powwow, no date *(Classic Stags: Volume 8)*
Indifferent, 1948–52 *(Classic Stags: Volume 133)*
Inez, 1940s *(Classic Stags: Volume 262)*
Inspiration, 1940s *(Classic Stags: Volume 102)*
Interested, 1940s *(Classic Stags: Volume 155)*
Intermezzo, 1965–66 *(Classic Stags: Volume 217)*
Interview, The, 1927 *(Classic Stags: Volume 111)*
Intruder, The (See *Bellhop, The*)
Intruders, 1960s *(Classic Stags: Volume 237)*
Invitation Only, 1960s *(Classic Stags: Volume 179)*
Invite Me In, 1960s *(Classic Stags: Volume 189)*
Irene Gets Her Man, 1967 *(Classic Stags: Volume 362)*
Italian Radio Repairman, 1950s *(Classic Stags: Volume 101)*
It's Miller Time, 1950s *(Classic Stags: Volume 158)*
Jam Session, 1950s *(Classic Stags: Volume 101)*
Jamie and Phil, late 1960s *(Classic Stags: Volume 8)*
Jane and Sue, 1960s *(Classic Stags: Volume 101)*
Jazz Jag, A, 1920s *(Classic Stags: Volume 118)*
Johnny Twat Sucker, 1965–68 *(Classic Stags: Volume 109)*
Join the Fun, 1968 *(Classic Stags: Volume 214)*
Join the Party, late 1960s *(Classic Stags: Volume 8)*
Join Us, 1960s *(Classic Stags: Volume 156)*
Joy Plays, 1967–68 *(Classic Stags: Volume 215)*
Jumping Jennifer, 1950s *(Classic Stags: Volume 156)*

Junkies and The Nightmare (*aka* Opium Den), no date *(Classic Stags: Volume 118)*

Just Fishin', 1940s *(Classic Stags: Volume 133)*

Just Folks, 1950s *(Classic Stags: Volume 27)*

Just in Time, 1950s *(Classic Stags: Volume 164)*

Just Lovers, 1960s *(Classic Stags: Volume 266)*

Kensey Report, 1952–54 *(Classic Stags: Volume 154)*

Keyhole Portraits, 1920s *(Classic Stags: Volume 6)*

Kid Sister, The, 1946–52 *(Classic Stags: Volume 133)*

Kill the Giant *(Fucking in the Fifties)*

Killer Diller, 1950s *(Classic Stags: Volume 156)*

Killer-Diller, 1960s *(Classic Stags: Volume 27)*

Kim and Steve, late 1960s *(Classic Stags: Volume 8)*

Kiss My Cunt, 1965–66 *(Classic Stags: Volume 109)*

Knockers Up, 1960s *(Classic Stags: Volume 164)*

Kooky Party, 1960s *(Classic Stags: Volume 217)*

Lady Dreamer, 1951–54 *(Classic Stags: Volume 158)*

Lady Pays Her Bills (Pt. 1), 1940s *(Classic Stags: Volume 21)*

Lapping It Up, 1960–1964 *(Classic Stags: Volume 410)*

Las Dos Amantes (Pts. 1 and 2), 1950s *(Classic Stags: Volume 25)*

Late Date, A, 1949–52 *(Classic Stags: Volume 133)*

Late Supper, 1950s *(Classic Stags: Volume 180)*

Les Make Love, 1960s *(Classic Stags: Volume 410)*

Leslie and Liz, 1960s *(Classic Stags: Volume 187)*

Let Me Count The Ways, 1968 *(Classic Stags: Volume 189)*

Let Me Love You (See *Mary Ann*)

Let's Share, 1960s *(Classic Stags: Volume 218)*

Lez Tease, 1960s *(Classic Stags: Volume 188)*

Lick'in Good, late 1960s *(Classic Stags: Volume 43)*

Life on the Road, 1935–45 *(Classic Stags: Volume 135)*

Lilac Time, 1960s *(Classic Stags: Volume 287)*

Lip Service, 1960s *(Classic Stags: Volume 267)*

Live-In Lovers, 1960s *(Classic Stags: Volume 238)*

Lonesome Hearts, The, 1950s *(Classic Stags: Volume 265)*

Losing Game, The, 1955–56 *(Classic Stags: Volume 135)*

Lotus Blossom, 1960s *(Classic Stags: Volume 267)*

Love Burglar, The, 1947–52 *(Classic Stags: Volume 263)*
Love In, 1967–69 *(Classic Stags: Volume 215)*
Love Is A Ball, 1960s *(Classic Stags: Volume 266)*
Love Me Do, 1960s *(Classic Stags: Volume 216)*
Love Me Tender, 1950s *(Classic Stags: Volume 189)*
Love Nest, 1965–66 *(Classic Stags: Volume 21)*
Love Triangle, 1960s *(Classic Stags: Volume 361)*
Lover Come Back, 1960s *(Classic Stags: Volume 313)*
Lovers, 1958–62 *(Classic Stags: Volume 180)*
Lovers Frenzy, 1960s *(Classic Stags: Volume 362)*
Lovers, The, 1966–67 *(Classic Stags: Volume 185)*
Lucky Babysitter, 1969 *(Classic Stags: Volume 186)*
Lucky Bob, 1950s *(Classic Stags: Volume 183)*
Lucky Four, 1960s *(Classic Stags: Volume 179)*
Lust In The Afternoon, 1960s *(Classic Stags: Volume 216)*
Lust Lady, 1950s *(Classic Stags: Volume 135)*
Magic Made Easy, 1950s *(Classic Stags: Volume 187)*
Magic Room, 1950s *(Classic Stags: Volume 361)*
Magic Room, 1964–66 *(Classic Stags: Volume 235)*
Magician, The, 1960s *(Classic Stags: Volume 109)*
Maid Is Made, 1964–66 *(Classic Stags: Volume 123)*
Maid Service, 1958–63 *(Classic Stags: Volume 235)*
Making Up, 1950s *(Classic Stags: Volume 43)*
Male Hooker, 1960s *(Classic Stags: Volume 156)*
Male Prostitute, 1964–66 *(Classic Stags: Volume 312)*
Man Wanted, 1960s *(Classic Stags: Volume 311)*
Manpower, 1960–67 *(Classic Stags: Volume 20)*
Marilyn Gets Sucked, 1950s *(Classic Stags: Volume 236)*
Mary Ann (*aka* Let Me Love You), 1950–55 *(Classic Stags: Volume 133)*
Mary, Mary, Quite Contrary, 1960s *(Classic Stags: Volume 138)*
Marylyn Gets Sucked, 1950s *(Classic Stags: Volume 119)*
Masked Lovers, 1950s *(Classic Stags: Volume 180)*
Masked Raiders, 1960s *(Classic Stags: Volume 361)*
Masked Trio, 1950s *(Classic Stags: Volume 164)*
Masquerading Balls, 1947–50 *(Classic Stags: Volume 213)*

Matinee Idol (*aka* Blondie Blondell), 1930s *(Classic Stags: Volume 134)*

May–December Romance, 1950s *(Classic Stags: Volume 189)*

Member's only, 1960s *(Classic Stags: Volume 411)*

Men Are Everything, 1964–66 *(Classic Stags: Volume 411)*

Merry Four, 1960s *(Classic Stags: Volume 124)*

Merry Go Round, The (Pts. 1 and 2), 1947–51 *(Classic Stags: Volume 27)*

Merry Trio, 1950s *(Classic Stags: Volume 138)*

Mexican Lovers, 1950s *(Classic Stags: Volume 154)*

Michaelangelo, 1962–64 *(Classic Stags: Volume 182)*

Midnight 'Til Dawn, 1947–48 *(Classic Stags: Volume 135)*

Millie, 1950s *(Classic Stags: Volume 185)*

Mink, 1960s *(Classic Stags: Volume 179)*

Miss Horny, 1960s *(Classic Stags: Volume 212)*

Miss Park Avenue, 1937 *(Classic Stags: Volume 25)*

Mix and Snatch, 1962–66 *(Classic Stags: Volume 335)*

Mixed Relations, 1921 *(Classic Stags: Volume 111)*

Model, The, 1960–66 *(Classic Stags: Volume 156)*

Model's Interview, 1950s *(Classic Stags: Volume 136)*

Modern Gigolo, The, 1928 *(Classic Stags: Volume 111)*

Modern Magician, The, 1930s *(Classic Stags: Volume 111)*

Modern Pirates, The, 1930s *(Classic Stags: Volume 111)*

More Persuasion, 1950s *(Classic Stags: Volume 127)*

More Than Friends, 1960s *(Classic Stags: Volume 217)*

Mutt and Jeff, 1950s *(Classic Stags: Volume 179)*

My Girl, 1950s *(Classic Stags: Volume 260)*

Naughty But Nice, 1950s, Striptease *(Classic Stags: Volume 118)*

Naughty Girls, 1959–64 *(Classic Stags: Volume 210)*

Naughty Kitty (*aka* Ruthie), 1948–52 *(Classic Stags: Volume 180)*

Nautical Nudes, 1930s *(Classic Stags: Volume 159)*

New Frolic, A, 1965–1966 *(Classic Stags: Volume 410)*

New Ways (Merry-Go-Round Pt. 1), 1947–50 *(Classic Stags: Volume 264)*

New York Honeymoon, 1950 *(Classic Stags: Volume 111)*

News Reader, 1960s *(Classic Stags: Volume 216)*

Night School (Pts. 1 and 2), 1948–52 *(Classic Stags: Volume 136)*
Nina, 1945–50 *(Classic Stags: Volume 265)*
Nite Club, 1930–37 *(Classic Stags: Volume 260)*
Nite Club, 1960s *(Classic Stags: Volume 411)*
No Hang Ups, 1960s *(Classic Stags: Volume 267)*
Nooner, The, 1962–63 *(Classic Stags: Volume 214)*
Not Tonight Henry, 1960s *(Classic Stags: Volume 237)*
Nun, The, 1949 *(Classic Stags: Volume 27)*
Nuts To You, 1951–54 *(Classic Stags: Volume 264)*
Nylon Man, The (Pts. 1 and 2), 1940s *(Classic Stags: Volume 134)*
Nympho, The (*aka* Debbie's Doctor), 1961–62 *(Classic Stags: Volume 182)*
Oh, Doctor, 1930s *(Classic Stags: Volume 134)*
On My Tail, 1960s *(Classic Stags: Volume 60)*
On the Beach (*aka* The Goat), 1920–26 *(Classic Stags: Volume 6)*
On the Patio, 1960s *(Classic Stags: Volume 286)*
One Enchanted Evening, 1948–58 *(Classic Stags: Volume 134)*
One for the Road, 1960s *(Classic Stags: Volume 164)*
One Hot Night, 1940s *(Classic Stags: Volume 136)*
One-Eyed Queens, 1960s *(Classic Stags: Volume 313)*
Onesy, Twosy, Threese, 1968 *(Classic Stags: Volume 363)*
Open Your Mouth and Say Ooh!, 1960s *(Classic Stags: Volume 311)*
Opium Den (See *Junkies and The Nightmare*)
Orgy Time, 1960s *(Classic Stags: Volume 212)*
Orgy, 1968 *(Classic Stags: Volume 363)*
Oriental Hospitality, 1960s *(Classic Stags: Volume 138)*
Oriental's Dream, An, 1950–55 *(Classic Stags: Volume 133)*
Other Woman, The, 1940s *(Classic Stags: Volume 139)*
Our Toys, 1950s *(Classic Stags: Volume 127)*
Outnumbered, 1960s *(Classic Stags: Volume 267)*
Paid in Full (*aka* Two Unloaded Guns), 1930–36 *(Classic Stags: Volume 133)*
Pajama Game, 1965 *(Classic Stags: Volume 180)*
Panties for Sale, 1940s–1950s *(Classic Stags: Volume 185)*
Paradise, A, 1939–41 *(Classic Stags: Volume 159)*
Party Girl, 1940s *(Classic Stags: Volume 119)*

Party Time, 1965 *(Classic Stags: Volume 236)*
Patient in Room 13, 1940s *(Classic Stags: Volume 410)*
Patty Gets a Nooner, 1960s *(Classic Stags: Volume 21)*
Paying the Rent, 1958–63 *(Classic Stags: Volume 361)*
Pay-off, The, 1946 *(Classic Stags: Volume 9)*
Pee For Two (see *Free Ride, A*)
Peeping Tom, 1960s *(Classic Stags: Volume 157)*
Pem Girls, 1960s *(Classic Stags: Volume 186)*
Pepper Sucks, 1960s *(Classic Stags: Volume 163)*
Personal Touch, 1966–67 *(Classic Stags: Volume 7)*
Pet My Pussy, 1960s *(Classic Stags: Volume 213)*
Photographer, The, 1950s *(Classic Stags: Volume 264)*
Piccolo Pete, 1930s *(Classic Stags: Volume 177)*
Pick Up, The, 1923 *(Classic Stags: Volume 118)*
Pick-Up, The, 1950s *(Classic Stags: Volume 158)*
Picnic (Pt. 2), 1945–50 *(Classic Stags: Volume 182)*
Picture Hanger, 1960s *(Classic Stags: Volume 287)*
Pin-Ups *(Classic Stags: Volume 265)*
Pipe Cleaners, 1940s *(Classic Stags: Volume 135)*
Players, The, 1960s *(Classic Stags: Volume 127)*
Playing for Sex, 1960s *(Classic Stags: Volume 218)*
Playmates, 1960s *(Classic Stags: Volume 24)*
Playthings, 1960s *(Classic Stags: Volume 164)*
Playtime, 1960s *(Classic Stags: Volume 236)*
Plumber, The, 1960s *(Classic Stags: Volume 60)*
Plumber, The, 1940s *(Classic Stags: Volume 235)*
Plumber's Son, 1950s *(Classic Stags: Volume 261)*
Pom-Pom Girls, 1960s *(Classic Stags: Volume 187)*
Positions, 1960s *(Classic Stags: Volume 237)*
Preview, 1958–62 *(Classic Stags: Volume 363)*
Price of Love, 1949 *(Classic Stags: Volume 139)*
Private Nurses *(Retro Sex)*
Private Sexsational, 1960s *(Classic Stags: Volume 23)*
Private Show, 1960s *(Classic Stags: Volume 189)*
Pussy for Two, 1960s *(Classic Stags: Volume 411)*
Radio Man, The, 1931 *(Classic Stags: Volume 111)*

Radio Repairman, The, 1948–52 *(Classic Stags: Volume 264)*
Rainbow Express, 1960s *(Classic Stags: Volume 127)*
Read Me a Story, 1950s *(Classic Stags: Volume 183)*
Real Cool Man, 1950s *(Classic Stags: Volume 164)*
Reluctant Hobo, The, 1950s *(Classic Stags: Volume 179)*
Rent Collector, 1966–67 *(Classic Stags: Volume 185)*
Rent-a-Film, 1960s *(Classic Stags: Volume 96)*
Revels of 1940, 1940s *(Classic Stags: Volume 136)*
Revolving Bed, 1960s *(Classic Stags: Volume 164)*
Ring Around the Rosy, 1960s *(Classic Stags: Volume 22)*
Ring Me Up, 1960s *(Classic Stags: Volume 287)*
Roaring Twenties, The (see *Free Ride, A*)
Rob the Cookie Jar, 1960s *(Classic Stags: Volume 189)*
Robber, The, 1960s *(Classic Stags: Volume 155)*
Rock 'N Roll, 1960s *(Classic Stags: Volume 312)*
Roman Orgy, 1960s *(Classic Stags: Volume 23)*
Romeo and Juliet, 1960s *(Classic Stags: Volume 218)*
Room 69, 1960s *(Classic Stags: Volume 124)*
Root Injection, 1966–67 *(Classic Stags: Volume 185)*
Rover Boys (Pt. 2), 1962–66 *(Classic Stags: Volume 266)*
Ruthie (see *Naughty Kitty*)
Ruthie, 1950s *(Classic Stags: Volume 265)*
S, 1960s *(Classic Stags: Volume 102)*
Sad Husband (Grocer Boy Pt. 2), 1965–66 *(Classic Stags: Volume 263)*
Safe at Home, 1960s *(Classic Stags: Volume 23)*
Sailors Dream, 1950s *(Classic Stags: Volume 236)*
Saleswoman, The, 1960s *(Classic Stags: Volume 363)*
Salt and Pepper, 1950s *(Classic Stags: Volume 159)*
Sammy's Choice, 1960s *(Classic Stags: Volume 9)*
Satisfied, 1948–52 *(Classic Stags: Volume 263)*
Saturday Afternoon, 1950s *(Classic Stags: Volume 212)*
Scamp, 1964–66 *(Classic Stags: Volume 124)*
Scream, 1960s *(Classic Stags: Volume 186)*
Screw, 1960s *(Classic Stags: Volume 178)*
Screwdriver, 1960s *(Classic Stags: Volume 23)*
Service Man, The, 1960s *(Classic Stags: Volume 20)*

Sewing Room, Color, 1968 *(Classic Stags: Volume 96)*
Sex Addicts, 1960s *(Classic Stags: Volume 410)*
Sex and More to Come, 1965–66 *(Classic Stags: Volume 123)*
Sex Capade Through Comic Land *(What Got Grandpa Hard?)*
Sex Party, 1960s *(Classic Stags: Volume 219)*
Sex Treatment, 1960s *(Classic Stags: Volume 217)*
Sexy Honeymooners, The, 1960s *(Classic Stags: Volume 219)*
Share a Joint, 1960s *(Classic Stags: Volume 186)*
Share and Share Alike (see *Burglar, The*)
Share and Share Alike, 1930s *(Classic Stags: Volume 119)*
She Knows Her Onions *(Authentic Antique Volume One)*
She's a Peach, 1950s–1960s *(Classic Stags: Volume 266)*
Shiek, The, 1925 *(Classic Stags: Volume 137)*
Ship Wreck Kelly, 1940s *(Classic Stags: Volume 410)*
Shopping Run Dan, 1958–63 *(Classic Stags: Volume 210)*
Should a Gentleman Offer a Lady a Joint?, 1968 *(Classic Stags: Volume 184)*
Show Offs, 1940s *(Classic Stags: Volume 410)*
Shower Power, late 1960s *(Classic Stags: Volume 7)*
Shrew, The, 1962–64 *(Classic Stags: Volume 363)*
Shy Lovers, 1950s *(Classic Stags: Volume 238)*
Side by Side, 1960s *(Classic Stags: Volume 237)*
Sisters in Heat, 1950s *(Classic Stags: Volume 361)*
Sisters, 1960s *(Classic Stags: Volume 96)*
Six Cylinders, 1930s *(Classic Stags: Volume 263)*
69er's, The, 1960s *(Classic Stags: Volume 186)*
Skinny Minnie, 1950s *(Classic Stags: Volume 236)*
Sleeping Beauty, 1968 *(Classic Stags: Volume 215)*
Sleepwalker, The, 1948–52 *(Classic Stags: Volume 213)*
Sleepy, 1950s *(Classic Stags: Volume 285)*
Slip and Slide, late 1950s*(Classic Stags: Volume 22)*
Slippery Eel, The, 1945–49 *(Classic Stags: Volume 264)*
Smart Aleck!, 1951 (Candy Barr) *(Classic Stags: Volume 6)*
Smash-Up Romance, A, 1926 *(Classic Stags: Volume 363)*
Smoochers, 1960s *(Classic Stags: Volume 312)*
Social Call, 1950s *(Classic Stags: Volume 260)*

Sock It to Me, 1960s *(Classic Stags: Volume 238)*

Solitaire Miss, 1960s *(Classic Stags: Volume 310)*

Solitaire, 1960s *(Classic Stags: Volume 212)*

Something Always Happens at Harry's, 1960s *(Classic Stags: Volume 310)*

Soul Mates, 1960s *(Classic Stags: Volume 361)*

Spa Frolics, 1960s *(Classic Stags: Volume 156)*

Spanked, 1960s *(Classic Stags: Volume 237)*

Spring Cleaning, 1960s *(Classic Stags: Volume 218)*

Stacked Deck, A, 1960s *(Classic Stags: Volume 313)*

Stag Show, 1958–62 *(Classic Stags: Volume 235)*

Stiff Game, A, 1930s *(Classic Stags: Volume 261)*

Strange Love Impulse *(Vintage Erotica from the 40s Volume One)*

Strange Love, 1966–67 *(Classic Stags: Volume 177)*

Strangers, 1950s *(Classic Stags: Volume 20)*

Streets of New York, 1960s *(Classic Stags: Volume 215)*

Strictly Union, 1919 *(Classic Stags: Volume 154)*

Strip Chess, 1960s *(Classic Stags: Volume 219)*

Strip Poker, 1940s *(Classic Stags: Volume 163)*

Strip Poker, 1955–56 *(Classic Stags: Volume 134)*

Strip Poker, 1960s *(Classic Stags: Volume 127)*

Stud Service, 1940s *(Classic Stags: Volume 410)*

Stud Time, 1960s *(Classic Stags: Volume 212)*

Studio, The (Pts. 1 and 2), 1960s *(Classic Stags: Volume 179)*

Suck a Wot, 1960s *(Classic Stags: Volume 212)*

Suck It, 1960s *(Classic Stags: Volume 216)*

Suck My Cunt, late 1950s *(Classic Stags: Volume 24)*

Suck on This, Babe!, 1960s *(Classic Stags: Volume 286)*

Sucker, The, 1950s *(Classic Stags: Volume 218)*

Sudden Sex, 1960s *(Classic Stags: Volume 60)*

Suds and Sex, 1960s *(Classic Stags: Volume 187)*

Sultan Slaves, 1920s *(Classic Stags: Volume 154)*

Super Salesman, 1949–53 *(Classic Stags: Volume 102)*

Super Saleswoman, 1945–50 *(Classic Stags: Volume 263)*

Surprise Awakening, 1940s *(Classic Stags: Volume 262)*

Surprise Me, 1960s *(Classic Stags: Volume 219)*

Surprise!, 1960s *(Classic Stags: Volume 286)*
Susie the Model (See *Camera Bug*)
Swappers Circus, 1960s *(Classic Stags: Volume 183)*
Swedish Massage, 1932–36 *(Classic Stags: Volume 154)*
Sweet Pussy's, 1960s *(Classic Stags: Volume 22)*
Sweet Temptations, 1960s *(Classic Stags: Volume 362)*
Sweet Treat, 1960s *(Classic Stags: Volume 266)*
Swingers, The, 1964–67 *(Classic Stags: Volume 189)*
Swinging Deb's, 1950s *(Classic Stags: Volume 238)*
Take It All, 1960s *(Classic Stags: Volume 336)*
Tax Collector, The, 1940s *(Classic Stags: Volume 118)*
Tea Time, 1960s *(Classic Stags: Volume 96)*
Teacher, 1960s *(Classic Stags: Volume 96)*
Teasing Tillie (Pts. 1 and 2), 1950s *(Classic Stags: Volume 137)*
Teen Scene, The, 1966–67 *(Classic Stags: Volume 181)*
Telephone Call, 1960s *(Classic Stags: Volume 60)*
Television Repairman (Pts. 1 and 2), 1950s *(Classic Stags: Volume 133)*
Tennis, Anyone?, 1960s *(Classic Stags: Volume 210)*
Thai Dance, 1950s *(Classic Stags: Volume 159)*
That Tickles, 1960s *(Classic Stags: Volume 216)*
Thief Makes Out, The, 1967 *(Classic Stags: Volume 214)*
This Is the Life, 1948–52 *(Classic Stags: Volume 262)*
Three Against One, 1960s *(Classic Stags: Volume 288)*
Three Bares, 1960s *(Classic Stags: Volume 267)*
Three Bucks Worth, 1955–65 *(Classic Stags: Volume 102)*
Three Came to Conquer, 1960s *(Classic Stags: Volume 310)*
Three for All, 1960s *(Classic Stags: Volume 236)*
Three Graces, The, 1930s *(Classic Stags: Volume 159)*
Three Masketeers, The, 1930s *(Classic Stags: Volume 159)*
Three of a Kind, 1960s *(Classic Stags: Volume 7)*
Three Pals, 1930s *(Classic Stags: Volume 118)*
Three Roses, 1960s *(Classic Stags: Volume 23)*
Three Swing, 1960s *(Classic Stags: Volume 179)*
Three to Get Ready, 1965–66 *(Classic Stags: Volume 178)*
Three Way Lust *(Vintage Erotica from the 40s Volume Three)*
Time Out for Sex, 1960s *(Classic Stags: Volume 187)*

Tipsy Neighbor, The (Pts. 1 and 2), 1950s *(Classic Stags: Volume 336)*

Tit for Tat, 1950s *(Classic Stags: Volume 9)*

Together Again, 1960s *(Classic Stags: Volume 336)*

Tom and Jerry, 1966–67 *(Classic Stags: Volume 236)*

Tom Boy, 1960s *(Reel Old Timers Volume Two)*

Tongue Lashing, 1940s *(Classic Stags: Volume 154)*

Tonight at 8, 1950s *(Classic Stags: Volume 135)*

Too Hard to Handle *(Black & White Oldies Uncovered)*

Toots Surprise Party, 1966 *(Classic Stags: Volume 178)*

Topless Swimsuit, The, 1964 *(Classic Stags: Volume 158)*

Trial Marriage, The, 1947–51 *(Classic Stags: Volume 136)*

Trim My Horns, 1950s *(Classic Stags: Volume 22)*

Trio, 1940s *(Classic Stags: Volume 118)*

Trip to Pleasure Island, 1938 *(Classic Stags: Volume 181)*

Truck Driver, 1964–66 *(Classic Stags: Volume 362)*

Try Me, 1960s *(Classic Stags: Volume 183)*

Tunnel of Love, 1950s *(Classic Stags: Volume 24)*

TV Casting Director, 1964–66 *(Classic Stags: Volume 109)*

TV Man, 1962–63 *(Classic Stags: Volume 184)*

TV Repair, 1965–66 *(Classic Stags: Volume 213)*

Two Against One, 1960–66 *(Classic Stags: Volume 186)*

Two for the Show, 1960s *(Classic Stags: Volume 285)*

Two Hot Chicks, 1947–50 *(Classic Stags: Volume 111)*

Two Pair Wins, 1960s *(Classic Stags: Volume 218)*

Two Plus Two, 1960s *(Classic Stags: Volume 288)*

Two Sided Triangle, The *(Golden Age of Erotic Video Volume One)*

Two Timer, The, 1945–50 *(Classic Stags: Volume 262)*

Two to Groove, 1960s *(Classic Stags: Volume 311)*

Two Unloaded Guns (See *Paid in Full*)

Twosome, 1965–66 *(Classic Stags: Volume 21)*

Twosome, 1950s *(Classic Stags: Volume 285)*

Undertaker's Dream, The, 1966 *(Classic Stags: Volume 215)*

Unexpected Company, 1948–52 *(Classic Stags: Volume 135)*

Up, Up and Away, 1968 *(Classic Stags: Volume 99)*

VD Inspector, 1960s *(Classic Stags: Volume 362)*

Vibrations, 1950s *(Classic Stags: Volume 23)*
Vice Probe, 1967 *(Classic Stags: Volume 119)*
Village Ball, The, 1966 *(Classic Stags: Volume 96)*
Village People, 1950s *(Classic Stags: Volume 179)*
Virgin Bride, 1948–52 *(Classic Stags: Volume 185)*
Vision, The, 1966 *(Classic Stags: Volume 155)*
Vogue, 1960s *(Classic Stags: Volume 217)*
Waiter, The, 1967–68 *(Classic Stags: Volume 181)*
War and Piece, 1960s *(Classic Stags: Volume 218)*
Weedheads, The *(What Got Grandpa Hard?)*
Weekend Rendezvous, 1950s *(Classic Stags: Volume 264)*
Wet Dream Blow Job, 1950s *(Classic Stags: Volume 215)*
Wet Dream, 1935–45 *(Classic Stags: Volume 111)*
Wet Noodle, 1960s *(Classic Stags: Volume 23)*
Wham Bam, 1960s *(Classic Stags: Volume 286)*
What's New Pussycat?, 1968 *(Classic Stags: Volume 186)*
While the Cat's Away, 1950–55 *(Classic Stags: Volume 265)*
Whip Me, 1960s *(Classic Stags: Volume 183)*
Who Is Mary Poppin?, 1965–66 *(Classic Stags: Volume 163)*
Who's on First, 1950s *(Classic Stags: Volume 24)*
Wild Card, 1968 *(Classic Stags: Volume 215)*
Wild Night, 1965–66 *(Classic Stags: Volume 21)*
Wild Ones at Home, 1960s *(Classic Stags: Volume 186)*
Winds Up Winner, 1960s *(Classic Stags: Volume 186)*
Wine Girl, The, 1964–67 *(Classic Stags: Volume 137)*
Wolfman, 1950s *(Classic Stags: Volume 362)*
Wolfman, 1963–66 *(Classic Stags: Volume 21)*
Woman and the Barrel, 1930s *(Classic Stags: Volume 154)*
Wonders of the Unseen World, 1927 *(Classic Stags: Volume 139)*
Working Hard, 1950s *(Classic Stags: Volume 238)*
Yes I Do, 1960s *(Classic Stags: Volume 183)*
You and Me, late 1940s *(Classic Stags: Volume 9)*
Young and Tender, 1964, Canadian *(Classic Stags: Volume 134)*
Young at Heart, 1965–66 *(Classic Stags: Volume 123)*
Young Lovers, The, 1950s *(Classic Stags: Volume 20)*
Young Masturbator, The, 1940s *(Classic Stags: Volume 264)*

Your Place or Mine, 1960s *(Classic Stags: Volume 10)*
Yum Yum Girl, 1963–66 *(Classic Stags: Volume 177)*

LATIN AMERICAN PRODUCTIONS

Bride and Groom, 1940s *(Classic Stags: Volume 160)*
Busty, 1948–52 *(Classic Stags: Volume 20)*
Convicts, The, 1940s *(Classic Stags: Volume 118)*
Daily Duty, 1950–55 *(Classic Stags: Volume 260)*
Dos Amigos, 1950s *(Classic Stags: Volume 217)*
El Satario, 1920s *(Classic Stags: Volume 119)*
El Tio, 1950s *(Classic Stags: Volume 25)*
Free For All, 1950s *(Classic Stags: Volume 261)*
Gardener, The, 1930s *(Classic Stags: Volume 235)*
Holiday (Pts. 1 and 2), 1950s *(Classic Stags: Volume 26)*
Hot Rod, 1949 *(Classic Stags: Volume 9)*
Intimidad, 1940s *(Classic Stags: Volume 27)*
Jumping Beans, 1940s *(Classic Stags: Volume 134)*
Kutie Kut Ups, 1950s *(Classic Stags: Volume 261)*
La Senora Y La Criada, 1946–56 *(Classic Stags: Volume 154)*
Las Primas, 1950s *(Classic Stags: Volume 26)*
Masked Pussies, 1950s *(Classic Stags: Volume 261)*
Mexican Dreamer, 1950s *(Classic Stags: Volume 310)*
Novios Impacientes, 1950–52 *(Classic Stags: Volume 158)*
One Hung Low, late 1950s *(Classic Stags: Volume 285)*
Peeper, 1950s *(Classic Stags: Volume 287)*
Prowler, 1950s *(Classic Stags: Volume 123)*
Un Accidente Afortunado, 1949–52 *(Classic Stags: Volume 101)*
Un Ladron En La Alcobo, 1950s *(Classic Stags: Volume 25)*
Viase De Bodas, early 1920s *(Classic Stags: Volume 158)*

FRENCH PRODUCTIONS

A La Français, late 1940s *(Vintage Erotica Anno 1940)*
Amour Et Ballerine, 1930s *(Vintage Erotica Anno 1930)*
Apres La Confession, 1920s *(Vintage Erotica Anno 1920)*
Attachement, 1950s *(Vintage Erotica Anno 1950)*
Au Clair de la Lune, 1920s *(Vintage Erotica Anno 1920)*

Catch Cache, late 1940s (*Vintage Erotica Anno 1940*)
Cherry Pickers, 1930s *(Classic Stags: Volume 154)*
Danseuse aux Seins Nus, 1950s (*Vintage Erotica Anno 1950*)
Deux Petite Bonnes, 1930s (*Vintage Erotica Anno 1930*)
Dressage au Fouet, 1930s (*Vintage Erotica Anno 1930*)
En Vacances, 1930s (*Vintage Erotica Anno 1930*)
Ersats Seule, late 1940s (*Vintage Erotica Anno 1940*)
Esprit de Famille, late 1940s (*Vintage Erotica Anno 1940*)
Étape en Forêt, 1930s (*Vintage Erotica Anno 1930*)
Femmes Infidèles, 1950s (*Vintage Erotica Anno 1950*)
Femmes Seules, 1950s (*Vintage Erotica Anno 1950*)
Flagellation en Bord de la Marne, 1930s (*Vintage Erotica Anno
    1930*)
Gisele et le Groom, 1920s (*Vintage Erotica Anno 1920*)
Jeunes Filles sans Uniforme, 1930s (*Vintage Erotica Anno 1930*)
L'amour Chez Minouche, 1920s (*Vintage Erotica Anno 1920*)
La Clinique en Folie, late 1940s (*Vintage Erotica Anno 1940*)
La Coquette aux Bas Blancs, 1920s (*Vintage Erotica Anno 1920*)
La Femme au Portrait, 1952 *(Classic Stags: Volume 157)*
La Grand Bagarre, 1930s (*Vintage Erotica Anno 1930*)
La Grande Bagerre, 1930s *(Classic Stags: Volume 26)*
La Leçon du Piano, 1920s (*Vintage Erotica Anno 1920*)
La Nouvelle Secrétaire, 1930s (*Vintage Erotica Anno 1930*)
La Partie des Cartes, late 1940s (*Vintage Erotica Anno 1940*)
La Puce, late 1940s (*Vintage Erotica Anno 1940*)
La Representante, late 1940s (*Vintage Erotica Anno 1940*)
La Sauvageonne, 1930s (*Vintage Erotica Anno 1930*)
La Tournée des Grands Ducs, 1930s (*Vintage Erotica Anno 1930*)
La Vase Brisé, late 1940s (*Vintage Erotica Anno 1940*)
La Vie Parisienne, 1930s (*Vintage Erotica Anno 1930*)
Le Pedicure Enflammé, 1920s (*Vintage Erotica Anno 1920*)
Le Retour de l'Explorateur, 1920s (*Vintage Erotica Anno 1920*)
Le Satyr Casimir, 1920s (*Vintage Erotica Anno 1920*)
Le Songe de Butterfly, 1930s (*Vintage Erotica Anno 1930*)
Le Télégraphiste, 1920s (*Vintage Erotica Anno 1920*)
Le Vendeur des Journaux, 1950s *(Classic Stags: Volume 26)*

Le Verrou, 1930s (*Vintage Erotica Anno 1930*)
Le Voleur Entôlé, 1950s (*Vintage Erotica Anno 1950*)
Les Amies, 1950–54 *(Classic Stags: Volume 158)*
Les Aventures de Ben Ali, 1930s (*Vintage Erotica Anno 1930*)
Les Bas-Fonds Napolitains, 1920s (*Vintage Erotica Anno 1920*)
Les Deux Columbines, 1920s (*Vintage Erotica Anno 1920*)
Les Deux Roses, late 1940s (*Vintage Erotica Anno 1940*)
Les Mésaventures de Monsieur Gross Bitt, 1920s (*Vintage Erotica Anno 1920*)
Madame et sa Bonne, late 1940s (*Vintage Erotica Anno 1940*)
Mariage Ultra-Moderne, 1920s (*Vintage Erotica Anno 1920*)
Mektoud, Fantaisie Arabe, 1930s (*Vintage Erotica Anno 1930*)
Merry Widow, The, 1930s *(Classic Stags: Volume 136)*
Monsieur a Sonné, late 1940s (*Vintage Erotica Anno 1940*)
Mousquetaire au Restaurant, 1908 (*Vintage Erotica Anno 1930*)
New Secretary, The, 1934 *(Classic Stags: Volume 27)*
Nudist Bar, 1930s (*Vintage Erotica Anno 1930*)
Peeping Tom, 1950s (*Vintage Erotica Anno 1950*)
Petit Conte de Noël, late 1940s (*Vintage Erotica Anno 1940*)
Pic-Nic, 1950s *(Classic Stags: Volume 26)*
Pierette Allait à la Rivière, 1920s (*Vintage Erotica Anno 1920*)
Plaisirs Champêtres, 1950s (*Vintage Erotica Anno 1950*)
Reporter, 1930s *(Classic Stags: Volume 159)*
Scenes d'Extérieur de M. X, 1930s (*Vintage Erotica Anno 1930*)
Scenes d'Intérieur de M. X, 1930s (*Vintage Erotica Anno 1930*)
Séduction (Le Duc de Sommerange), 1920s (*Vintage Erotica Anno 1920*)
Service Après Vent, 1950s (*Vintage Erotica Anno 1950*)
Sous les Caresses du Martinet, 1930s (*Vintage Erotica Anno 1930*)
Strange Love, 1950s *(Classic Stags: Volume 24)*
Surpris par le Garde-Champêtre, 1930s (*Vintage Erotica Anno 1930*)
Trois Gouttes de Rosée, 1930s (*Vintage Erotica Anno 1930*)
Un Apres-Midi à la Fumerie, 1920s (*Vintage Erotica Anno 1920*)
Un Rasage en Douceur, 1950s (*Vintage Erotica Anno 1950*)
Zut! Zut! Ma Légitime, 1920s (*Vintage Erotica Anno 1920*)

BRITISH PRODUCTIONS

Artist, The, 1960s *(Classic Stags: Volume 164)*
Backdoor Coach, 1960s *(Classic Stags: Volume 312)*
Bed Set, 1965–66 *(Classic Stags: Volume 155)*
Bedtime, 1960s *(Classic Stags: Volume 213)*
Betrayed, 1960s (*Mary Millington Collection* — Pirate DVD)
Bi-Bye Guys, 1960s *(Classic Stags: Volume 100)*
Boy Oh Boy, 1960s *(Classic Stags: Volume 100)*
Bra and Panties, 1960s *(Classic Stags: Volume 100)*
Casting Couch, 1960s *(Classic Stags: Volume 100)*
Cat Burglar, 1964–66 *(Classic Stags: Volume 181)*
Champagne for Two, 1960s *(Classic Stags: Volume 9)*
Choice Stuff, 1960s *(Classic Stags: Volume 100)*
Comparing Couples, 1960s *(Classic Stags: Volume 100)*
Cum Clean, 1968 *(Classic Stags: Volume 160)*
Dancing Pal, 1967 *(Classic Stags: Volume 155)*
Desire, 1960s *(Classic Stags: Volume 336)*
Deux Femmes Par *(Black & White Oldies Uncovered)*
Do It Yourself, 1960s *(Classic Stags: Volume 219)*
Double Sex Party, 1960s *(Classic Stags: Volume 311)*
Eeny Meene, 1960s *(Classic Stags: Volume 164)*
End of Term, 1967–68 *(Classic Stags: Volume 160)*
Equal to Mummy, 1968 *(Classic Stags: Volume 6)*
Escort Agency, The, 1960s *(Black & White Oldies Uncovered)*
Evening at Home, 1960–66 *(Classic Stags: Volume 76)*
Exhibition, 1967–68 *(Classic Stags: Volume 184)*
False Pretenses, 1960s *(Classic Stags: Volume 212)*
Fanny, 1960s *(Classic Stags: Volume 362)*
Fat Girls, 1960s *(Classic Stags: Volume 288)*
Finger in the Dyke, 1950s *(Classic Stags: Volume 157)*
First Audition, 1966–67 *(Classic Stags: Volume 160)*
Flatmates, 1964–66 *(Classic Stags: Volume 124)*
Free for All, 1967 *(Classic Stags: Volume 21)*
Full Treatment, 1967 *(Classic Stags: Volume 211)*
Girlfriend, The, 1967 *(Classic Stags: Volume 124)*
Good Life, The, 1967 *(Classic Stags: Volume 211)*

Hot Rocks, 1960s *(Classic Stags: Volume 100)*
Hotel, 1966–67 *(Classic Stags: Volume 188)*
Humiliation, 1966–67 *(Classic Stags: Volume 362)*
Judo Lessons, 1960s *(Classic Stags: Volume 267)*
Kinky Lez, 1966–67 *(Classic Stags: Volume 177)*
Kinky Lovers, 1966–67 *(Classic Stags: Volume 266)*
Lady Lovers, 1960s *(Classic Stags: Volume 177)*
Late Date, 1960s *(Classic Stags: Volume 100)*
Little Girl Lost, 1966 *(Classic Stags: Volume 211)*
Living for Kick, 1965–67 *(Classic Stags: Volume 335)*
Love for Three, 1967–68, *Classic Stags: Volume 178)*
Love for Sale, 1967–68 *(Classic Stags: Volume 164)*
Lucky Girl, 1968 *(Classic Stags: Volume 211)*
Lusty au Pair, 1967–68 *(Classic Stags: Volume 210)*
Maid to Measure, 1968 *(Classic Stags: Volume 210)*
Man Crazy, 1967 *(Classic Stags: Volume 214)*
Message Treatment, 1960s *(Classic Stags: Volume 362)*
Miss Bohrloch, 1960s *(Mary Millington Collection* – Pirate DVD)
Miss-Conduct, 1968 *(Classic Stags: Volume 181)*
More Arts and Crafts, 1966–67 *(Classic Stags: Volume 217)*
More Beatnik Bedlam, 1968 *(Classic Stags: Volume 211)*
More Suds and Sex, 1968 *(Classic Stags: Volume 180)*
Music Masters, 1965–67 *(Classic Stags: Volume 178)*
Nightspot, 1960s *(Classic Stags: Volume 287)*
Nymphetts, The, 1966–67 *(Classic Stags: Volume 181)*
One Hundred Per-Cent Lust, 1965–66 *(Classic Stags: Volume 96)*
Opening Night, 1960s *(Classic Stags: Volume 183)*
Oral Connection, 1960s *(Mary Millington Collection* – Pirate
    DVD)
Orgy, 1967 *(Classic Stags: Volume 188)*
Out the Window, 1960s *(Classic Stags: Volume 287)*
Part-Time Job, 1964–66 *(Classic Stags: Volume 160)*
Personal Invitation, 1960s *(Classic Stags: Volume 335)*
Playboys, 1968 *(Classic Stags: Volume 211)*
Private Patient, 1967–68 *(Classic Stags: Volume 411)*
Pussy Club, The, 1966–67 *(Classic Stags: Volume 211)*

Pussy Galore, 1966–67 *(Classic Stags: Volume 20)*
Randy, 1964–66 *(Classic Stags: Volume 211)*
Rare Capture, 1960s *(Classic Stags: Volume 9)*
Rear Admiral, 1960s *(Classic Stags: Volume 138)*
Ring Up for Love, 1966–67 *(Classic Stags: Volume 123)*
Rub-a-Dub-Dub, 1960s *(Classic Stags: Volume 183)*
Satan's Children, 1960s *(Classic Stags: Volume 267)*
School Girls Dream, 1964–66 *(Classic Stags: Volume 311)*
School of Hard Cocks, 1960s *(Classic Stags: Volume 164)*
Schoolgirl Lust, 1966–67 *(Classic Stags: Volume 20)*
Secret Meeting, 1962–66 *(Classic Stags: Volume 160)*
Seduction, 1965–66 *(Classic Stags: Volume 310)*
Sex for Three, 1964–66 *(Classic Stags: Volume 311)*
Sex Gymnast, 1960s *(Classic Stags: Volume 100)*
Sex Orgy, 1966–67 *(Classic Stags: Volume 189)*
Sex Study, 1960s*(Classic Stags: Volume 124)*
Sex-Tet, 1960s *(Classic Stags: Volume 285)*
Sexy Secretaries, 1960s *(Classic Stags: Volume 267)*
Shower Nymph, 1968 *(Classic Stags: Volume 185)*
Six-Way Action, 1960s *(Classic Stags: Volume 123)*
Something Special, 1960s *(Classic Stags: Volume 123)*
Spanish Lust, 1968 *(Classic Stags: Volume 101)*
Spanked, 1966–69 *(Classic Stags: Volume 335)*
Staff Room, 1960s *(Classic Stags: Volume 156)*
Stallion, 1966–67 *(Classic Stags: Volume 266)*
Surprise Attack, 1960s *(Classic Stags: Volume 100)*
Thank You Girl, 1966–67 *(Classic Stags: Volume 213)*
Tonight at 8, 1966–67 *(Classic Stags: Volume 21)*
Triangle, 1966–67 *(Classic Stags: Volume 96)*
Twisted, 1967–68 *(Classic Stags: Volume 214)*
Two Can Play, 1960s *(Classic Stags: Volume 266)*
Two Times Two, 1960s *(Classic Stags: Volume 267)*
Two's Enough, 1960s *(Classic Stags: Volume 9)*
Unexpected Guests, 1962–63 *(Classic Stags: Volume 180)*
Welcome the Neighbors, 1960s *(Classic Stags: Volume 336)*
What the Butler Saw and Did, 1960s *(Classic Stags: Volume 286)*

Wild Night, 1960s *(Classic Stags: Volume 100)*
Young Lust, 1966–67 *(Classic Stags: Volume 20)*

SELECTED EUROPEAN PRODUCTIONS

Ad-Vice, 1960s, European *(Classic Stags: Volume 43)*
All Day Sucker, 1930s, German *(Classic Stags: Volume 157)*
Beat Me Daddy, 1960s, European *(Classic Stags: Volume 60)*
Cara Nanie, 1960s, German *(Classic Stags: Volume 157)*
Cock vs. Dildo, 1960s, German *(Classic Stags: Volume 163)*
Das Loch, 1960s, German *(Classic Stags: Volume 157)*
Deep Caresses, 1960s, European *(Classic Stags: Volume 7)*
Deer Garden, 1960s, Danish *(Classic Stags: Volume 160)*
Dessous, 1958, German *(Classic Stags: Volume 157)*
Die Hemmungslosen, 1960s, German *(Classic Stags: Volume 157)*
Even Thieves Do It, 1960s, Danish *(Classic Stags: Volume 160)*
Frühling's Serwachen, 1940s, German *(Classic Stags: Volume 157)*
Gli Sponsali de Cicillo, 1950s, Italian *(Classic Stags: Volume 25)*
Gross Plans, 1950s, German *(Classic Stags: Volume 160)*
Le Trou, 1920s, Italian *(Classic Stags: Volume 119)*
Love Happy, 1960s, European *(Classic Stags: Volume 22)*
Once Around for the Dealer, 1950s, German *(Classic Stags: Volume 157)*
Pick Up Artist, 1960s, German *(Classic Stags: Volume 137)*
Revue Pigalle, 1924, German *(Classic Stags: Volume 137)*
Sauerkraut, late 1940s, German *(Classic Stags: Volume 25)*
Suor Vaseline, 1913, Italian *(Classic Stags: Volume 119)*
Three for the Road, 1960s, German *(Classic Stags: Volume 137)*
Time for Love, 1960s, European *(Classic Stags: Volume 267)*
Weekend Rendezvous, 1950s, German *(Classic Stags: Volume 137)*
Zensuriert, 1950s, German *(Classic Stags: Volume 137)*